Official
Charts Company

THE
MILLION
SELLERS

CONTRIBUTORS

Tim Brock

Andy Gregory

Dan Lane

Justin Lewis

Mick Lynch

Dave McAleer

Martin Talbot

Matthew White

OMNIBUS PRESS

London / New York / Paris / Sydney / Copenhagen / Berlin / Madrid / Tokyo

Cover designed by Stuart Hammersley, Art Science.
Interiors designed by Fresh Lemon. Picture research by Jacqui Black.
Photographs courtesy Getty Images & Corbis Images.

ISBN: 978.1.78038.718.5
Order No: OP54956

Exclusive Distributors
Music Sales Limited,
14/15 Berners Street,
London, W1T 3LJ.

Music Sales Corporation,
257 Park Avenue South,
New York, NY 10010, USA.

Macmillan Distribution Services,
56 Parkwest Drive
Derrimut, Vic 3030,
Australia.

Every effort has been made to trace the copyright holders of the photographs in
this book but one or two were unreachable. We would be grateful if the
photographers concerned would contact us.

Printed in the EU.

A catalogue record for this book is available from the British Library.

Visit Omnibus Press on the web at www.omnibuspress.com

THE MILLION SELLERS
CONTENTS

THE MILLION SELLERS
AN EXPLANATION

The Million Sellers is the definitive guide to the UK's million-selling singles and is published to mark 60 years of the Official Singles Chart in 2012. It is based on a countdown of the all-time biggest-selling singles in the UK, which has been researched and collated by the Official Charts Company (the agency tasked by the UK music industry with overseeing the archive of charts and market data, from 1952 to date), with crucial assistance from Alan Jones, the UK's pre-eminent chart data researcher, who has been writing about the UK's sales charts for *Music Week* and *Record Mirror* for more than 30 years.

This list has been based on electronic records held by the Official Charts Company dating back to spring 1994, combined with researched data for the period prior to this – including contemporaneously published reports, official record label returns and a wide range of other sources. This is the definitive list of the UK's all-time biggest-selling singles, from 1952 to the end of May 2012 (the cut-off point owing to publishing deadlines).

In practice, the first officially recognised singles chart in the UK was that which was compiled from 1969 by the British Market Research Bureau, supported by the BBC and trade newspaper *Record Retailer*. Before this time, there were a range of charts operating in the UK, compiled by different media outlets. However, the charts which are today widely recognised as being the UK's 'official' charts began with the *New Musical Express*-published charts from November 1952 until 1960, followed by the *Record Retailer* charts published from 1960 until 1969. For this book, we have taken these as the UK's 'Official Charts', even though they were not known by this name at the time.

The data banks accompanying every one of the 122 entries are based on the information commonly accepted to be correct at the time of publication, and do not take into account any disputes which may occur after the end of May 2012. Weeks on chart refers to weeks in the Top 75, as based on the Official Charts Company's own charts history database. All of the information in this databank (including peak chart positions, weeks in this position and weeks on chart) is correct up to this cut-off date (end of May 2012).

THE MILLION SELLERS

INTRODUCTION

Speculating about the future is an interesting but futile way of passing the time. At various times in the past we have been told that at some point soon our basic food requirements would be reduced to tablet form, that no one would have to work and even that computers would perfect the formula for writing successful songs. In fact, we are eating a greater quantity of food than ever before, more people are working longer hours than at any time in the past and creating chart hits remains an elusive human skill.

Since the UK Singles Chart was established in 1952, more than 32,000 records (none of them written by a computer) have passed through it. Some have spent a single week at number 75, others have topped the chart for long periods and stuck around for more than a year. A mere 122 have sold more than a million copies. What they are, and how they did it, is the subject of this book.

As prestigious a group as the million sellers are, they were a smaller and even more elite selection 10 years ago. To mark the 50th birthday of the Singles Chart in 2002, the Official Charts Company prepared a TV programme called *The Ultimate Chart* for Channel 4. Only 76 of the Top 100 songs had achieved seven-figure sales at that point, and the prospect of any single ever again selling a million seemed unlikely.

After reaching a 15-year peak of 77.76 million in 1997, the singles market had collapsed. By 2002, sales slumped to 43.03 million, and the following year they plunged a further 30 per cent to 30.88 million – their lowest level since the 1950s.

But, from apparently terminal decline, the singles market has since achieved a remarkable turnaround. In 2011, sales reached nearly 178 million – almost six times their 2003 low point and by far their highest level in music history. With specialist bricks and mortar record shops closing at a rapid rate, the single's saviour was downloads.

The advent of broadband helped to precipitate a new era of digital deliveries, driven by a range of operators including Apple's iTunes, Amazon, HMV.com, Tesco.com, Play.com, 7digital Media, MyCokeMusic, Spotify and many others. Sales of physical formats now account for considerably fewer than one per cent of singles sales, with downloads – cheap, and delivered in seconds – monopolising the market.

In 1964, the seven-inch single was the dominant format. That year, The Beatles racked up three million sellers – 'Can't Buy Me Love', 'I Feel Fine' and 'We Can Work It Out'/'Day Tripper'. Singles were priced at the time at 6s 8d – the pre-decimal equivalent of 33.3p – so it would have cost a pound to buy all three. Today, most downloads are 99p, which is three times the 1964 cost, but to keep pace with overall price inflation since 1964, singles would actually need to cost £5.84.

The fact that they are now so cheap and readily available goes a long way towards explaining the explosion in sales of singles *and* the big increase in million sellers in recent years. Nine singles released in the two-year period immediately prior to the publication of this book have already sold upwards of a million copies apiece.

The digital age has also been a boon for older tracks. Many long-deleted singles – including Julie Covington's 'Don't Cry For Me Argentina' and 'Hit Me With Your Rhythm Stick' by Ian Dury & The Blockheads – came close to selling a million copies physically before being deleted and have finally reached the target thanks to digital sales. While they have sold fairly small quantities digitally, some vintage tracks have had a completely new lease of life from digital release, notably Survivor's 'Eye Of The Tiger', which has bagged more than 400,000 sales in the format since it was first embraced by chart compilers in November 2004.

In all probability, the fast expansion in the singles market – somewhat at the expense of albums, it has to be said, as buyers 'cherry-pick' the tracks they like rather than invest in an entire album – will result in more singles from the 2010s selling a million copies than any previous decade. For the present, however, it is the 1990s that is the dominant decade, providing 32 million sellers, five more than the second biggest decade – the 1970s.

Looking at the overall list, which includes songs from eight different decades, brings one no closer to establishing exactly what it is that makes a million seller. We can work out some figures – for example, the average million seller was released in 1985, is more likely to be by a group/duo (59.4 per cent are) of British or American extraction (84.6 per cent) and have a playing time of three minutes 46 seconds (give or take a second!).

The biggest-selling singles act in UK history, The Beatles, naturally also have more million sellers than any other act – six of them, all penned by John Lennon and Paul McCartney, each of whom also has another entry on the list from their solo canon. Beatles aside, the only artist on the list to have more than two entries is Rihanna, who appears three times.

The Beatles broke the mould in many respects, including having the first number one single to have a playing time of more than seven minutes. In the top spot in 1968, 'Hey Jude' was eventually replaced as the chart's longest number one by Oasis' 'All Around The World', which clocks in at over nine minutes. 'Hey Jude' is prevented from being the longest million seller by another Manchester group, New Order, whose ground-breaking 'Blue Monday' from 1983 was initially released only on 12-inch, in a version that ran seven minutes 29 seconds. The shortest million seller, at just one second over two minutes, is Frank Ifield's 1962 topper, 'I Remember You'. It is also the only million seller to feature yodelling.

Another curio, and a record that reached a million sales the hard way, is the 1961 TV theme 'Stranger On The Shore'. Although it never reached number one, the track – credited to Mr. Acker Bilk with the Leon Young String Chorale – spent 55 weeks on the chart. The only other instrumental to sell a million thus far was another TV theme, 'Eye Level' – from *Van Der Valk*, a TV drama about a Dutch cop – a 1972 number one for The Simon Park Orchestra.

But these are just some of the quirks, curiosities and facts which will feature in the 122 million seller profiles which you can read over the following pages, from the very first million seller, Bill Haley & His Comets' 'Rock Around The Clock', through to the most recent, Gotye's 'Somebody That I Used To Know', featuring Kimbra.

Vocal or instrumental, short or long, indigenous or foreign, and by a solo artist or group, the singles surveyed on the following pages have sold more than 165 million copies between them – and can rightly lay claim to the title of Britain's very greatest hits.

BILL HALEY & HIS COMETS 1955

ROCK AROUND THE CLOCK

WRITERS: Max C. Freedman, James E. Myers

PRODUCER: Milt Gabler

ALBUM: Rock Around The Clock

PEAK POSITION: Number 1 (5 weeks)

WEEKS ON CHART: 57
(1955, 19; 1956, 17; 1968, 11; 1974, 10)

SALES: 1.42m

Bill Haley's signature hit was the UK's very first million seller – and the record that launched rock'n'roll around the world.

Targeted at the teenage dancing crowd of the mid-Fifties, it was first registered in October 1952 and credited to veteran songsmith Max C. Freedman and middle-aged music business entrepreneur James E. Myers (aka Jimmy DeKnight), although it was reportedly solely written by Freedman.

Haley's version took less than half an hour to record, but is estimated to have sold close to 200 million copies worldwide on single and album.

Michigan-born, Pennsylvania-based Haley was no teenager when he scored this hit, either, at the age of 31. He had begun recording country & western music in the mid-Forties and had already tasted US Top 20 success with 'Crazy Man, Crazy' on Essex Records in 1953 – a groundbreaking track many cite as the first rock'n'roll record.

Although 'Rock Around The Clock' shared a title with earlier songs, it was penned with Haley & His Comets in mind. They had played it in their stage act for over a year before its release, although, due to a falling out between Essex and Myers, it was first recorded by Sonny Dae & His Knights and released on a label partly owned by Haley.

Haley's band studied Dae's rendition before recording their own 'cowboy jive' arrangement on April 12, 1954, four days after moving to Decca Records.

The session was booked for 11 a.m. to 5 p.m. at New York's Pythian Temple studios, but the ferry taking the band across the Delaware River got stuck on a sandbar and the group arrived over two hours late. They worked on the A-side, 'Thirteen Women', until 4.40 p.m., leaving only enough time for two takes of 'Rock Around The Clock'. On the first, the band's sound overpowered Haley, so only his vocal microphone was open on the second. There was no time for either track to be mixed, or for the group to hear them back, but Gabler made a composite tape using the best parts of both takes.

The musicians included session drummer Billy Gussack and session guitarist Danny Cedrone (who received a £7.50 fee). The latter was asked to repeat note-for-note a guitar break he had used on another Haley release, 'Rock The Joint' – which ironically resulted in the act being sued for 'lifting it' (subsequently settled out of court). The song also bore similarities to Hank Williams' 'Move It On Over', the blues number 'My Daddy Rocks Me With One Steady Roll' and Roy Milton's 'T-Town Twist'.

Sadly, Cedrone died in the summer of 1954, unaware of the monster he had helped to create, while three of the other Comets fell out with Haley and split in autumn 1955, just as the single headed up the US Best Sellers.

Released on May 6, 1954, *Billboard* called it a "good attempt at Cat Music" (the type of R&B music that white teenagers were starting to buy in the southern states of the US), but it was after DJs flipped the disc that 'Rock Around The Clock' reached the bottom rungs of both the US and UK charts (where it was released four months later).

As part of the promotion, Myers sent a copy to film studio MGM, where movie director Richard Brooks used it in *Blackboard Jungle* – and the rest is rock'n'roll history. Reissued in mid-1955, it rocketed to the top across the globe and remains the only non-Christmas single to reach the Top 20 of the UK's Official Singles Chart on five separate occasions (twice in 1955, then in 1956, 1968 and 1974). It also became a 1989 number one courtesy of Jive Bunny & The Mastermixers' 'Swing The Mood' mash-up.

One of the few recordings inducted into the Grammy Hall of Fame, 'Rock Around The Clock' may not have been the first rock'n'roll disc but it was *the* song that spread the genre around the world.

PAUL ANKA 1957
DIANA

WRITER: Paul Anka

PRODUCER: Don Costa

ALBUM: N/A

PEAK POSITION: NUMBER 1 (9 weeks)

WEEKS ON CHART: 25

SALES: 1.25m

With 'Diana', Paul Anka became the first Canadian to have a Gold record in Britain and the first teenager to either sing or write a UK million seller – Little Jimmy Osmond in 1972 being the only younger person to earn that accolade since. Britain's top-selling single of 1957, 'Diana' is estimated to have sold over 10 million copies to date globally.

Youthful as he was, 'Diana' was not Anka's first musical venture. He had sung in the Bobby Soxers trio at high school and, in 1956, while staying with an uncle in Los Angeles, recorded a single with noted producer/arranger Ernie Freeman (popular local doo-wop group The Jacks, also known as The Cadets, supplied backing vocals). It coupled Anka's own 'Blau-Wile-Deveest Fontaine' with a cover of 'I Confess', first recorded by another doo-wop group, The Dots. His first trade paper mention at that time described Anka as sounding like "a slightly older Frankie Lymon" – 13-year-old Lymon being the first teenager to top the UK chart, in 1956.

Perhaps "I'm so young and you're so old" is not the most romantic thing one could say to a girl, but that's exactly how 15-year-old Anka started his ditty, inspired by family babysitter Diana Ayoub, who was three years older and did not see him as boyfriend material. Anka wrote the song in the basement of his Ottawa home, and has said he offered it to several artists who appeared locally – including Frankie Lymon, The Platters and The Diamonds – but none spotted its potential.

Toronto group The Rover Boys (who had a US Top 20 hit in 1956 with 'Graduation Day') were friends with Anka, allowing him to share their New York City accommodation and helping arrange an audition with their label, ABC Paramount. Producer Don Costa loved 'Diana' and, in just one take, Anka nailed the vocal on an infectious chalypso (a combination of cha-cha and calypso rhythms) track that fellow teenagers found irresistible.

In August 1957, as it headed to the top of the US charts, 'Diana' was released in the UK. Radio Luxembourg instantly named it Record of the Week, while music paper *New Musical Express* called Anka "a teenager who should wow teenagers", adding that 'Diana' was "a dead cert" and their "buy of the week". Its nine weeks at number one in the Official Singles Chart proved them both right.

On December 22, 1957, EMI chairman Joseph Lockwood presented Anka with a Gold disc live on stage at the Regal Cinema, Edmonton, during his first UK tour. In the US, 'Diana' also went Gold, with Anka receiving that disc from Ed Sullivan on his TV show.

It is estimated that more than 300 different versions of 'Diana' have been recorded over the years (including an Anka duet with Ricky Martin), and its composer returned to the subject with his 1963 single 'Remember Diana'. Anka, who is in the US Songwriters Hall of Fame, went on to pen many other major hits including 'It Doesn't Matter Anymore', 'Puppy Love', 'Lonely Boy', 'She's A Lady' and 'This Is It' (co-written with Michael Jackson) and also wrote the English lyric to the perennial karaoke/wedding/funeral favourite, 'My Way', whose tune was taken from the French pop song 'Comme d'Habitude'.

HARRY BELAFONTE 1957
MARY'S BOY CHILD

WRITER: Jester Hairston	
PRODUCERS: Henri René, Dennis Farnon	
ALBUM: An Evening With Belafonte	
PEAK POSITION: Number 1 (7 weeks)	
WEEKS ON CHART: 19	
SALES: 1.18m	

The first Christmas song to sell over one million copies in the UK, 'Mary's Boy Child' also broke the record for the country's fastest million seller when it passed that magic mark within eight weeks of release.

In the US in 1956, even the phenomenally popular newcomer Elvis Presley could not surpass Harry Belafonte's albums chart dominance, but in the UK at the beginning of 1957 the latter was a stranger to the bestsellers lists. That year saw rock'n'roll become the most successful music style in Britain, while skiffle peaked – but Belafonte almost single-handedly launched the calypso music craze, which many thought would replace rock.

During 1957, Belafonte reached the UK Top Three with the 'Banana Boat Song (Day-O!)' and 'Island In The Sun', ending a spectacular year by spending seven weeks at the summit with 'Mary's Boy Child', which had been America's best-selling seasonal single a year earlier.

Born in Harlem, New York City, to West Indian parents, Belafonte was no newcomer to showbusiness when he enjoyed his first UK hit. He had attended acting classes with Marlon Brando and Tony Curtis in the late Forties, and was tipped for singing success as far back as 1949 when recording for the Roost and Capitol labels.

In 1950, he joined Jubilee Records, and two years later made the first of his many RCA recordings. Before finding his own calypso-styled niche, Belafonte sang both jazz (drawing comparisons with Billy Eckstine) and folk music.

The singer's 1956 album *Belafonte* topped the US chart for six weeks, while the follow-up, *Calypso*, headed that list for a record-breaking 31 weeks, making him the first act to have big album success in the US before achieving a top-selling single.

The majority of Christmas number ones can be categorised as good-time, party-type novelties, but in contrast 'Mary's Boy Child' was a beautiful religious ballad that told the tale of the birth of Jesus. It could have been a carol, and it has since become one of the world's best-loved Christmas compositions. Veteran African-American songwriter/actor Jester Hairston, who also penned the much-recorded gospel title 'Amen' and appeared in movies such as *To Kill A Mockingbird*, *In The Heat Of The Night*, *The Alamo* and *Lady Sings The Blues*, wrote the song.

'Mary's Boy Child' was also recorded at the time by legendary UK music hall singer/film actress Gracie Fields, Canadian vocal quartet The Four Lads and popular Danish duo Nina & Frederik (whose version made the Top 30 in 1959). However, it was Belafonte's flawlessly sung, moving rendition that caused the public to flock to their local record shops in unprecedented numbers.

'Mary's Boy Child' also returned to the UK Top Five in the sheet music chart in both 1958 and 1959, and the first chart-topper in the UK by an African-American singer returned to the Top 10 of the Official Singles Chart in 1958 – proving more successful than his similarly themed seasonal follow-up, 'Son Of Mary' (sung to the tune of 'Greensleeves').

This was not the end for 'Mary's Boy Child' either – it has subsequently been covered by a broad range of artists, from The Three Degrees, Charlotte Church and Rolf Harris to Connie Talbot, Joe McElderry and The Wiggles. But it was 20 years after Harry Belafonte's smash when the next biggest version arrived, Boney M. returning it to the UK number one spot, making it the first song to ever sell one million copies by two different artists.

ELVIS PRESLEY 1960
IT'S NOW OR NEVER

WRITERS: Eduardo di Capua (melody), Aaron Schroeder (lyrics), Wally Gold (lyrics)	
PRODUCERS: Steve Sholes, Chet Akins	
ALBUM: N/A	
PEAK POSITION: Number 1 (8 weeks)	
WEEKS ON CHART: 25 (1960, 19; 1977, 2; 2005, 4)	
SALES: 1.26m	

Although Elvis Presley remains the most successful singles artist in UK chart history, this was the only one of his 21 number one hits to sell more than one million copies.

'It's Now Or Never' used the melody of the turn-of-the-century Neapolitan semi-operatic song 'O Sole Mio' and, because the original was still in copyright in the UK, this new version almost didn't get a British release – in fact, it took several months of legal battles to solve the problem.

Presley had liked the song since he first heard it sung by American singer/actor Tony Martin in 1950 as 'There's No Tomorrow' (a version that seems to have been released in the UK with no obvious copyright problems). In 1959, while stationed in Germany with the US Army, Presley even recorded 'There's No Tomorrow', but asked his publishers if it was possible for a new English lyric to be written. They duly obliged by getting Aaron Schroeder and Wally Gold to pen 'It's Now Or Never' and had vocalist David Hill demo the song for Presley to hear. Hill, incidentally, had composed Presley's earlier chart-topper 'I Got Stung' and released a version of 'All Shook Up' before 'The King'.

Soon after Presley left the Army, one of his favourite singers, Jackie Wilson, had a US million seller with 'Night', based on a song from a French opera. Wilson's success convinced Presley that releasing a similar-styled song might not be the commercial risk he and his record label feared.

Cut in Nashville on April 3, 1960, 'It's Now Or Never' received a US release as Presley's second post-Army single in July. In America, it sold 700,000 copies in its first week and hit the top slot three weeks later, a position it held for five weeks.

The long wait for a UK release saw the single amass record advance orders of 548,000 copies. It entered the UK's Official Singles Chart at number one in late October 1960 and within a record-breaking 45 days sales had passed the one million mark. The single, which topped the bestsellers list for eight weeks, was the last number one to be available on a 78rpm record. It earned Presley a Gold disc, which was presented to him on the film set of *Wild In The Country* by leading UK DJ Jimmy Savile.

'It's Now Or Never' went on to become the biggest hit internationally for the world's top-selling recording artist. It was the song that introduced Presley to adult record-buyers, attracting many people to his music who had earlier dismissed Presley or rock'n'roll. The song's co-lyricist, Wally Gold, later remarked that it took just over 20 minutes to write a song that has sold over 20 million records.

In 2005, Presley's number one singles were all reissued chronologically in the UK and his original recording returned to the top of the Official Singles Chart, thus giving him a record three consecutive number one hits more than 27 years after he had died.

MR. ACKER BILK 1961
STRANGER ON THE SHORE

WRITER: Acker Bilk

PRODUCER: Dennis Preston

ALBUM: Stranger On The Shore

PEAK POSITION: Number 2

WEEKS ON CHART: 55

SALES: 1.16m

Britain's biggest-selling single of 1962 not only spent over a year on the UK chart, but also became the first British recording to top the *Billboard* Hot 100 in the US and earned jazz musician Acker Bilk a *Billboard* award as Top Instrumentalist of the Year in America.

Bilk, like skiffle pioneer Lonnie Donegan, had played with the UK's Ken Colyer's jazz band before successfully branching out and finding fame on his own. Many jazz purists looked down on the bearded clarinettist with the fancy striped waistcoat and bowler hat who, with his Edwardian-dressed Paramount Jazz Band, attempted to make jazz fun. However, it was Bilk's colourful ensemble, along with the bands of Kenny Ball and Chris Barber, that helped turn traditional jazz into a musical craze that briefly replaced skiffle in the hearts of numerous UK teenagers.

Bilk's first Official Singles Chart entry in the UK, his self-penned 'Summer Set' (a punning reference to Bilk's home county), was also a US Top 30 hit, but in a cover version by American musician Monty Kelly, which outsold the original recording. Undeterred, his US label, Atco, asked Bilk for an album. On it he included a beautiful, breathy clarinet instrumental (a far cry from his usual trad offerings) called 'Jenny', which Bilk named after his baby daughter, saying it was based on the sound of her crying.

The album, *Sentimental Journey*, sold relatively few copies at the time. However, in 1961, the BBC was looking for a theme tune for a new five-part children's TV series about a French au pair girl working in Brighton. They came across Bilk's recording of 'Jenny' and asked him if they could rename it and use it as the theme. Initially, they planned to re-title it Marie Hélène after the leading character in the show, but it was decided instead to give it the name of the actual series, *Stranger On The Shore*.

Bilk's recording of the song was produced by Dennis Preston and featured the Leon Young String Chorale rather than his regular Paramount Jazz Band. It was released in October 1961, but didn't start selling in large quantities until the BBC TV series had finished, after which it rapidly climbed to number two in January 1962. It stayed at number two for three weeks and remained on the Official Singles Chart for a record-shattering 55 weeks. In the US, it hit number one in May 1962 and also spent seven weeks at the summit of the *Billboard* Easy Listening chart.

The song was so popular that several vocal versions were successfully released, including US hits by The Drifters and Andy Williams. In the UK, Williams' rendering was a minor hit, and vocalist Michael London issued a version on which Acker also played.

Trad jazz's top showman picked up *Billboard*'s Most Popular International Artist award in the US in 1962, and the readers of music paper *Melody Maker* named his Grammy-nominated record Top Instrumental Single of 1962.

Since its initial chart-topping success, Bilk's most famous track has been heard on several film soundtracks, has amassed over four million plays on US radio and logged an estimated four million sales around the globe – and even beyond. In 1969, 'Stranger On The Shore' was taken around the moon as part of a mixtape by one of the crew of the Apollo 10 spacecraft.

CLIFF RICHARD & THE SHADOWS 1962

THE YOUNG ONES

WRITERS: Sid Tepper, Roy C. Bennett

PRODUCER: Norrie Paramor

ALBUM: The Young Ones (soundtrack)

PEAK POSITION: Number 1 (6 weeks)

WEEKS ON CHART: 21

SALES: 1.06m

Cliff Richard has sold more singles in the UK than any British act (other than The Beatles) and has had more chart entries than anyone else. He also has the longest span of UK hit singles and has sold more singles around the globe than any other British solo star. Despite this, like his early hero Elvis Presley, he has only achieved one UK million seller – the title song from his third film, *The Young Ones*.

Although several British singers, including Lonnie Donegan, David Whitfield and Vera Lynn, had previously received Gold discs for worldwide sales, Richard was the first UK vocalist to sell one million copies of a single domestically.

Richard's career began in late 1958 with a record regarded as the best early British rock'n'roll single, 'Move It!', and in 1960 he received a worldwide Gold record for his chart-topper 'Living Doll', which was also the first of his relatively few US Top 40 entries. By the time 'The Young Ones' was released, Richard and his group, The Shadows, were by far the biggest-selling and most successful British act.

In the film *The Young Ones* (retitled *Wonderful To Be Young!* in the US), Richard's youth club is in danger of closing and he has the idea of raising money to save it by staging a rock'n'roll concert; Robert Morley plays the villain, who is also Cliff's father. Prior to the film's launch on December 19, 1961, the featured ballad, 'When The Girl In Your Arms Is The Girl In Your Heart', had reached the UK Top Three; it appears that Richard insisted the title song was not released until people had been given the chance to see it in the film.

Noted American songsmiths Sid Tepper and Roy C. Bennett, who wrote both of the film's hit singles, penned the title track in a couple of hours after reading the script, the film being named after the song – not the other way around. The idea for the track's distinctive string arrangement came after it was recorded, with the parts overdubbed at a later session.

The veteran composers' CV includes songs from Presley movies and a string of novelty hits including 'The Naughty Lady Of Shady Lane', 'Twenty Tiny Fingers' and 'Nuttin' For Christmas'. They also wrote Top 10 entries for Perry Como and Frankie Vaughan and had composed Richard's earlier chart-topper, 'Travellin' Light'.

'The Young Ones' was the first British record to secure advance orders in excess of 500,000 and by the end of its first week had sold 634,500 copies, entering the UK's Official Singles Chart at number one in the first week of January – the first British record to achieve that feat.

The film was also one of 1962's top UK box-office hits, helping Richard earn the Most Popular Male Film Actor award from *Motion Picture Herald* magazine, and being variously hailed as "the best musical Britain has ever made" and "the finest teenage screen entertainment produced for a long time – anywhere". Both the single (holding off Chubby Checker's dance craze-making 'Let's Twist Again') and *The Young Ones* soundtrack album headed the UK charts for six weeks, while the EP *Hits From The Young Ones* led that list for two weeks.

'The Young Ones' was voted Single of the Year by *Melody Maker* readers, and the album became the first UK soundtrack to sell over one million copies around the globe. It was also the first UK million seller that was not a hit in the world's biggest market, the US, but despite this fact, it is estimated to have sold more than 2.6 million copies internationally.

In 1982 *The Young Ones* became the title of an anarchic TV comedy featuring Rik Mayall as a Cliff-loving student. That led, in 1986, to Richard and the show's stars recording a chart-topping revival of 'Living Doll'.

Richard retains massive popularity, as does this song. In 2010, when he rejoined The Shadows for a sell-out reunion tour, 'The Young Ones' and its B-side, the show-opener 'We Say Yeah', were frequently the best-received numbers.

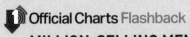

MILLION-SELLING MEMORIES

SIR CLIFF RICHARD

You have recorded many number ones in your career – did the likes of 'The Young Ones' feel more important than your number one singles in later years?

When you go back in time to those Fifties, Sixties, Seventies, Eighties, even Nineties hits, when you had a number one, they were big sellers. But I think every number one is special. What I've learned over the years is that it's not always possible to have number ones from every record you release. If it was possible, of course, I'd take up the formula and use it, but there is no formula [laughs].

Are the charts still important to you?

The charts are very important to me after 50 odd years as a recording artist, and I still consider myself a recording artist. In many ways, I know I'll never be able to do what I did before; I'm not supported in the same way as I used to be by radio stations, for example, and with the internet, people have usually heard a track on the radio before, otherwise, how do you know what to download? So people like myself have a big problem when it comes to how to sell music these days, but it is still possible. My last album, *Soulicious*, went into the Official Album Chart at number 10 and the record before that, *Bold As Brass*, went in at number three. If you record anything, you should be aiming at the top of the charts. You just have to be prepared to be number two or less.

Which modern stars do you like?

That's a difficult question for me, because I find it hard to remember who's in the charts [laughs]. There's a couple of names who spring to mind because I've worked with them; obviously Kelly Rowland and all the *X-Factor* people, but I really love Will Young. A lot of these reality TV singing contest winners are great, and so are the runners-up actually, but you need that support. It's like when I started out; you can't do it on your own, you need the record company to get behind you and go for it. Will Young's been around for 10 years now and he's still having success, he's still touring and he's still making music. I really applaud him. I also think Leona Lewis is fantastic; she's been around for five years now, so it shows that it still can happen. And long may it last.

You are the third biggest-selling singles artist in 60 years of the Official Singles Chart, just behind The Beatles and Elvis Presley – and you're still making music today. To what do you attribute your longevity?

Sixty years? I can almost remember when the charts started [laughs]. I think what's helped me is, when I first started singing, it wasn't to get rich. It's because I heard music by Elvis and Little Richard and Buddy Holly and Jerry Lee Lewis, and longed to sing the stuff they sang myself. Then, by trying it I realised I could sort of do it and I got my audition with EMI, I got a contract and I was off and running. It wasn't to become rich, it wasn't just even to become famous – it was just to be able to make these records. Of course, what happens is your record goes to number one in the charts and you become famous; everybody knew who I was, and my band The Shadows. We became known everywhere in the world, except America funnily enough, and then you find that the royalty cheques start turning up. But it was always a by-product of what I really wanted, and I think that's helped.

Now, regardless of whether one is going to make money or not, I still want to do it. I like singing and I like performing. And as long as the public accepts me, I'll continue to do it until I fall over. You've got to love what you're doing, so whatever happens with your next record, you're still prepared to make the third one.

FRANK IFIELD 1962

I REMEMBER YOU

WRITERS: Victor Schertzinger (music), Johnny Mercer (lyrics)

PRODUCER: Norrie Paramor

ALBUM: I'll Remember You

PEAK POSITION: Number 1 (7 weeks)

WEEKS ON CHART: 28

SALES: 1.1m

Singers from 'Down Under' have often found that they can find worldwide fame by using the UK as a springboard. Although in many cases, like Olivia Newton-John, the Bee Gees and Frank Ifield, this was actually more a case of coming home, as they had been born in the British Isles and, as children, had been taken to the Antipodes by their parents.

In the early chart years, Australia had given us hit-makers such as Jimmy Parkinson, Slim Dusty, Rolf Harris and Marie Benson (solo and fronting The Stargazers in their most successful years). However, the first to reach the top in their own right – and the earliest Gold disc winner – was Coventry-born, New South Wales-bred Ifield.

After making a name for himself in Australia (touring there with Buddy Holly, Jerry Lee Lewis and Paul Anka in 1958), Ifield returned to the UK in 1959 and such was his status that chart regular Tommy Steele hosted a 'Welcome to the UK' party for him. However, British success did not come overnight. Ifield released seven singles in the UK before his career really took off, including minor successes with 'Lucky Devil' (from the composers of Elvis Presley's 'It's Now Or Never') and 'Gotta Get A Date', and overlooked versions of later hit songs 'Unchained Melody' and 'Tobacco Road'.

After a failed attempt to represent the United Kingdom in the 1962 Eurovision Song Contest, Ifield's Columbia Records producer Norrie Paramor threatened to drop his contract if his next release flopped.

For his potentially final attempt, Ifield came up with the idea of recording the 1942 song 'I Remember You', from the Dorothy Lamour film *The Fleet's In*. He planned to give it a country-style treatment, complete with yodelling and falsetto effects (soon to become his trademark sound) and incorporating a 'Waltzing Matilda'-influenced harmonica phrase.

Paramor was not convinced that this treatment of the old Jimmy Dorsey hit worked, and even considered distancing himself from it by not having his name on the record as producer. However, it was an instant hit with the public in the last months before The Beatles changed the face of popular music. It topped the Official Singles Chart for seven weeks and was the last UK million seller prior to 'She Loves You'. The readers of the premier music paper *New Musical Express* duly named it Disc of the Year and Ifield New Act of the Year.

American country & western performers such as his heroes Hank Snow and Slim Whitman had influenced Ifield's style of music, and he was delighted when the single also took off across the Atlantic, becoming one of the very rare UK-produced singles to reach the US Top Five in the pre-Beatles era. The single also topped *Billboard*'s Easy Listening chart in the US, leading to Ifield recording in Nashville and even appearing on the popular country & western radio programme *Grand Ole Opry*, where he was introduced by Snow.

Despite Ifield's records bearing no resemblance to the Merseybeat sounds that ruled the charts in 1963, he continued to clock up number one hits with revivals of Hank Williams' 1949 hit 'Lovesick Blues' (which amassed advance orders of over 200,000), Tex Ritter/Gogi Grant's 1956 hit 'The Wayward Wind' and the 1930 hit 'Confessin' (That I Love You)'. Ifield even beat The Beatles by becoming the first British-based act to amass three successive UK number one singles.

THE BEATLES 1963

SHE LOVES YOU

WRITERS: John Lennon, Paul McCartney

PRODUCER: George Martin

ALBUM: The Beatles' Second Album (US-only release)

PEAK POSITION: Number 1 (6 weeks)

WEEKS ON CHART: 36 (1963, 33; 1983, 3)

SALES: 1.9m

The first Beatles record to sell more than one million copies in the UK spent six weeks at the chart summit and was the biggest-selling single in Britain in the Swinging Sixties. The single amassed unprecedented advance orders of 310,000 copies and was the UK's top seller until 1977, when 'Mull Of Kintyre' by ex-Beatle Paul McCartney's band Wings overtook it.

The Liverpool quartet's debut single 'Love Me Do' had just cracked the Top 20 in September 1962 and the follow-up, 'Please Please Me' (the title track of their debut album), made number two on the UK's Official Singles Chart in early 1963. Their third single in May, 'From Me To You', was their first chart-topper, but this, their next release, was the one that really launched Beatlemania and helped change pop music forever.

'She Loves You' (partly inspired by a Tony Hatch-composed Bobby Rydell hit, 'Forget Him') was written by John Lennon and McCartney on a coach after a Beatles show at the Majestic Ballroom, Newcastle-upon-Tyne, on June 26, 1963, then finished by them at McCartney's home in Forthlin Road, Liverpool.

Recording took place at Abbey Road five days later. It was producer George Martin who suggested they start with the "She loves you, yeah, yeah, yeah" chorus, while the falsetto "wooooo" exaltation was borrowed from The Isley Brothers' 'Twist And Shout', a song the group had covered on their debut album.

Released on August 23, 'She Loves You' had sold 500,000 copies by September 3 and reached the magical one million milestone by late November, when it returned to number one after an eight-week absence. Simultaneously, the band's second album, *With The Beatles*, replaced their debut (which had held the number one slot since May) at the top of the albums chart. 'She Loves You', like most of The Beatles' singles, didn't appear on the band's contemporary studio album, boosting its sales even further.

In the US, the single sold few copies in 1963, but it subsequently replaced their first US hit 'I Want To Hold Your Hand' at number one for two weeks in March 1964 – the first time an act had consecutive US number ones since Elvis Presley in 1956.

The band also recorded a German version, 'Sie Liebt Dich', in Paris. In Germany, both versions made the Top 10, while the German version also charted in the US. Appropriately, among the other artists to record 'She Loves You' were US rock'n'rollers The Crickets, whose 'That'll Be The Day' was the first song Lennon and McCartney ever recorded together.

The Beatles famously performed 'She Loves You' at a Royal Variety Show on October 13, 1963, and again on their February 9, 1964 inaugural appearance on US TV's *The Ed Sullivan Show*, which attracted an estimated viewing audience of over 70 million.

In 1963, 'She Loves You' was voted Top Record of the Year by *New Musical Express* and *Melody Maker* readers and in 2005 it was named one of the three records that most changed the world. It remains The Beatles' biggest-selling single of all time in the UK.

THE BEATLES 1963

I WANT TO HOLD YOUR HAND

WRITERS: John Lennon, Paul McCartney

PRODUCER: George Martin

ALBUM: Meet The Beatles! (US-only release)

PEAK POSITION: Number 1 (5 weeks)

WEEKS ON CHART: 24 (1963, 22; 1983, 2)

SALES: 1.77m

This was the record that kick-started the 'British Invasion' of the US charts, capturing the American audience's collective imagination and providing the foundation for the Fab Four's seven-year domination of the global music scene.

Topping the *Billboard* Hot 100 for seven weeks, it was the first of The Beatles' 20 US number one singles. It was no mean performer in the UK either, where it amassed an unprecedented 940,000 advance orders, spent five weeks at the top of the Official Singles Chart and was the first of the group's four Christmas number ones. It also replaced the band's own previous release, 'She Loves You', at the top of the chart – the first time anyone had accomplished this feat in the UK.

'I Want To Hold Your Hand' was written by Lennon and McCartney in the downstairs cellar of the latter's then-girlfriend Jane Asher's house. Lennon later said it was written "one-on-one, eyeball-to-eyeball", with the pair both playing the piano at the same time. Lennon recalled: "We had, 'Oh you-u-u... got that something...' and then Paul hit this chord [E minor] and I turned to him and said, 'That's it!'. It was that chord that made the song." The recording took place at Studio 2 at Abbey Road on October 17, 1963; it was The Beatles' first session using four-track technology and took 17 takes to get it perfect.

Before its UK release, The Beatles' manager, Brian Epstein, played the track to EMI's US company, Capitol Records, and they clearly heard something they felt was missing from the four previous Beatles singles (all of which Capitol had rejected and were released on other labels). An almost unprecedented $50,000 promotion campaign (using the tagline 'The Beatles Are Coming') was put into place prior to the release of the single, big features on Beatlemania appeared in *Time*, *Life* and *Newsweek* magazines and, to build even more of a buzz, film of the group's live British shows appeared on several top US TV news programmes.

US demand for the single was so great that the release date was brought forward to December 26, and on January 18, 1964 it became The Beatles' first US chart entry. By the time of their debut on *The Ed Sullivan Show* on February 9, it was at number one and a week later, when they re-appeared on the show, their US album, *Meet The Beatles!*, had followed suit. That set went on to shift over 3.5 million copies in its first two months, topping the US chart for 11 weeks.

Album-wise in the UK, *With The Beatles* and *Please Please Me* held the top two slots on the chart for the first four months of 1964, the former clocking up 21 weeks at the top and giving them a record 51 consecutive weeks at number one.

It is no exaggeration to suggest that 'I Want To Hold Your Hand' opened the floodgates for British acts Stateside. In the first nine years of the rock era (1955–1963), UK artists had accounted for a total of only 1.25 per cent of US Top 20 hits, but after 'I Want To Hold Your Hand' broke down the invisible barriers, battalions of British bands followed The Beatles into the US charts.

That resulted in UK artists accounting for an incredible 26 per cent of all Top 20 US hits during 1964.

Although not a Grammy winner at the time, 'I Want To Hold Your Hand' was added to the Grammy Hall of Fame in 1998 and remains The Beatles' biggest-selling single worldwide, with sales exceeding an estimated 15 million copies.

THE BEATLES 1964
CAN'T BUY ME LOVE

WRITERS: John Lennon, Paul McCartney

PRODUCER: George Martin

ALBUM: A Hard Day's Night

PEAK POSITION: Number 1 (3 weeks)

WEEKS ON CHART: 17 (1964, 15; 1984, 2)

SALES: 1.53m

Even by The Beatles' high standards, 'Can't Buy Me Love' raised the bar – both for themselves and their chart competitors.

In the UK, it was the first ever single to amass one million advance orders. The group's first simultaneous transatlantic number one, it also set a new record in the US with more than 1.7 million copies ordered prior to its March 16 release date.

In America, where it was the first record to jump to number one from outside the Top 20, 'Can't Buy Me Love' also completed an all-Beatles Top Five – a feat unlikely ever to be equalled. It gave the band a record-breaking third consecutive chart-topper Stateside and, one week later, it was one of an unprecedented (in the pre-digital days, in any case) 14 different Beatles entries in the *Billboard* Hot 100. At the same time, the 'Mop Tops' also had the Top Six singles in Australia and the Top Nine in Canada.

In the UK, the single spent three weeks at the top of the Official Singles Chart before being replaced by Peter and Gordon's recording of another Lennon and McCartney composition, 'A World Without Love'. In America, it reached number one on April 4, followed on that week's chart by the band's 'Twist And Shout' (two), 'She Loves You' (three), 'I Want To Hold Your Hand' (four) and 'Please Please Me' (five).

The single stayed at number one for five weeks and, by the first week of May, the band had three albums in the American Top Four;

US-only compilations *The Beatles' Second Album*, *Meet The Beatles!* and *Introducing... The Beatles*, which had been totally ignored by the American record-buying public on its original July 1963 release.

At the time, 'Can't Buy Me Love' was only available in the UK as a single, and the track did not make its Official Albums Chart debut until it appeared on *A Hard Day's Night* in July 1964.

The song was composed on an upright piano in the sitting room of The Beatles' suite in the George V Hotel, close to the Champs-Élysées in Paris, during the band's famous 18-night stand at the Olympia Theatre in January 1964. Lennon later admitted: "That's Paul's completely. Maybe I had something to do with the chorus but I don't know. I always considered it his song."

George Martin flew over from London on January 29, 1964 to produce the song at the Pathé-Marconi Studios, Paris, where the band started the recording. The final vocal tracks had to wait until they returned from their first successful US trip. On February 25, McCartney laid down the lead vocal at Abbey Road, and it was decided that, for the first time, they would not include their usual Beatles backing harmonies.

'Can't Buy Me Love' is a rare million seller in that The Beatles' legions of fans bought it on trust, since the vast majority had not even heard the song when they placed their orders – proving, perhaps, that you can't buy love (or loyalty) like that!

THE BEATLES 1964

I FEEL FINE

WRITERS: John Lennon, Paul McCartney

PRODUCER: George Martin

ALBUM: Beatles '65 (US-only release)

PEAK POSITION: Number 1 (5 weeks)

WEEKS ON CHART: 14 (1964, 13; 1984, 1)

SALES: 1.41m

The Beatles' problem in 1964 was how to end a year in which they had not only broken countless sales and chart records but also set records that will never be equalled. Their solution was, quite appropriately, a song called 'I Feel Fine'.

A Christmas number one on both sides of the Atlantic, the single sold over one million copies in both the UK and US. In Britain, 'I Feel Fine' continued the band's unprecedented run of consecutive chart-toppers, racking up advance orders of 750,000 and spending five weeks at the Official Singles Chart summit. In the US, it enjoyed three weeks at number one, while it was coupled with 'She's A Woman', which reached the Top Five in its own right, making it their highest-placed B-side (an achievement made possible by the US tendency to calculate the A-side and B-side sales separately).

'I Feel Fine' was the band's sixth US chart-topper of the year and, unbelievably, pushed their total number of Top 100 entries in 1964 to 30. It was the first of six consecutive singles by the act to reach number one in the US – a record that stood until 1988, when it was surpassed by Whitney Houston.

'I Feel Fine' and 'She's A Woman' were actually written at Abbey Road Studios during a nine-hour session on Sunday October 18, 1964, with the A-side needing nine takes to get it right. In retrospect, this was the start of the band's experimentation in the studio with its distinctive and deliberate amplified feedback opening – often hailed as the first use of it on a record.

Arguably the most memorable moment in the record, that unique sound came about purely by accident, as McCartney later recalled: "We were just about to walk away to listen to a take when John leaned his guitar against the amp. I can still see him doing it. He had forgotten to turn the guitar off and it went 'nnnnnwahhhh', and we went 'Wow, what a great sound!' Producer George Martin was there so we asked: 'Can we have that on the record?' 'Well, I suppose we could edit it on the front,' he said."

The A-side was basically Lennon's composition, while the flip side was McCartney's. They sang lead on their own songs, with McCartney supplying harmonies on 'I Feel Fine', which featured both Lennon and George Harrison playing lead guitar. Lennon wrote the distinctive guitar riff, which he admitted was inspired by Bobby Parker's 1961 song 'Watch Your Step', an R&B song The Beatles had often performed before they were famous. Lennon also noted that the drum sound on the record was influenced by Milt Turner's work on the Ray Charles classic 'What'd I Say'.

Not unusually for The Beatles, neither side of the single was available on a UK album. In Britain, at the time 'I Feel Fine' was at number one, the group's *Beatles For Sale* album replaced *A Hard Day's Night* at the top of the Official Albums Chart (a position it had held for 21 weeks).

In the US, where Beatles albums differed from the UK in that they included singles and fewer tracks, both sides appeared on the album *Beatles '65*, which joined *A Hard Day's Night* and *The Beatles' Story* in the Top 10, leaping from number 98 to number one on January 9, 1965.

THE RIGHTEOUS BROTHERS 1965
UNCHAINED MELODY

WRITERS: Alex North (music), Hy Zaret (lyrics)

PRODUCER: Phil Spector

ALBUM: N/A

PEAK POSITION: Number 1 (4 weeks)

WEEKS ON CHART: 26 (1965, 12; 1990, 14)

SALES: 1.04m

Bill Medley and the late Bobby Hatfield's 'Unchained Melody' was not the first rendition of this song to reach the Official Singles Chart summit (that honour went to Jimmy Young in 1955), but it was the first of three different versions to pass the one million sales mark.

Having met in their native California in 1962, when Medley was singing in small clubs, the duo joined Los Angeles quintet The Paramours that year, but first recorded as a duo under the Righteous Brothers name in 1963, producing songs such as 'Little Latin Lupe Lu' and 'My Babe' for the Moonglow label.

That brought them to the attention of producer Phil Spector, who, enthused by their distinctive 'blue-eyed soul' sound, signed them to his Phillies imprint. They scored a transatlantic number one with 'You've Lost That Lovin' Feelin'' and subsequently continued to dent the Top 10 in their homeland. However, follow-up 'Unchained Melody' found only moderate success in the UK in the summer of 1965, peaking at number 14 in the Official Singles Chart in early September as The Rolling Stones' '(I Can't Get No) Satisfaction', Sonny & Cher's 'I Got You Babe' and The Walker Brothers' 'Make It Easy On Yourself' ruled the roost.

It took another 25 years for 'Unchained Melody' to reach its peak, becoming a surprise hit all over again as the signature song for the blockbuster movie *Ghost*, featuring prominently in a steamy pottery wheel scene with Demi Moore and the late Patrick Swayze. Three months after the film's release, a reissued 'Unchained Melody' was sitting pretty atop the chart, where it remained for four consecutive weeks before the very antithesis of Alex North and Hy Zaret's classic took over as 'Ice Ice Baby' by Vanilla Ice sashayed into town.

The success of 'Unchained Melody' spawned a Righteous Brothers greatest hits collection (their first ever Official Albums Chart entry) and a fourth stab at UK chart success for that first US million seller, 'You've Lost That Lovin' Feelin'', which reached number three at the tail-end of 1990.

'Unchained Melody' was ideally suited to The Righteous Brothers' inimitable vocal styling; Medley's deep, soulful bass and Hatfield's soaring tenor were a match made in heaven. Written in 1964, 'Melody' was born out of the need for a theme song for American prison film *Unchained*. The Oscar-nominated film version was performed by Kentucky-born actor/opera singer Todd Duncan, but within six months of the film's release he had been overshadowed by a string of hit versions from Jimmy Young, Al Hibbler, Les Baxter and Liberace.

After the hits dried up in 1966, Medley and Hatfield went their separate ways, but reunited to score three US-only hits, including 'Rock And Roll Heaven', on Haven Records in 1974. Medley also enjoyed some solo success, most notably on US chart-topper '(I've Had) The Time Of My Life' with Jennifer Warnes, from the soundtrack to 1987 film *Dirty Dancing* (again starring Swayze).

The Righteous Brothers were inducted into the Rock and Roll Hall of Fame in 2003, eight months before Hatfield died, aged 63, from a heart attack brought about by an overdose of cocaine. After this time, his soaring "I ne-ee-ed your love" vocal took on added poignancy. In 2009, producer Phil Spector was sentenced to 19 years to life for the second-degree murder of actress Lana Clarkson at his LA home.

In the years since 'Unchained Melody' was first a hit in 1955, the karaoke bar favourite has become one of the most recorded songs in history, with hundreds of cover versions in many different languages. Even Elvis Presley was seduced by the song's charms and reportedly sang it on the last night of his life in August 1977.

What links every version of the song? The absence of the word 'unchained' in the lyrics.

KEN DODD 1965
TEARS

WRITERS: Frank Capano, Billy Uhr

PRODUCER: Norman Newell

ALBUM: Tears Of Happiness

PEAK POSITION: Number 1 (5 weeks)

WEEKS ON CHART: 24

SALES: 1.52m

For many mid-century comedians, ending their act with a serious song was a chance to show how versatile you were and a way of trying to win over people who perhaps weren't that keen on your jokes... While Harry Secombe, Des O'Connor and Charlie Drake enjoyed hit records as a result, the most successful of the bunch was arguably 'Mr Tickling Stick', Ken Dodd.

Dodd, like the fictional Diddy Men characters he created for his stage and TV shows, came from Knotty Ash, Liverpool, and was born in 1927 – some three years before 'Tears' was composed. He made his professional debut at the Nottingham Empire in 1954 and was one of the brightest new comedy stars to emerge in the late 1950s, first appearing on television in 1957 in the *Six-Five Special*.

In his own phraseology, how tickled Dodd must have been when he reached the UK Top 10 in 1960 with 'Love Is Like A Violin', his version of the French song 'Mon Coeur Est Un Violon', which Bing Crosby had sung in the 1953 film *Little Boy Lost* as 'Violets And Violins'. He scored another half-dozen chart entries before 'Tears', including three successive hits written and initially recorded by US country singer/songwriter Bill Anderson – 'Still', 'Eight By Ten' and 'Happiness' – the latter becoming Dodd's theme song.

Legend has it that Jimmy Phillips, a music publisher friend of Dodd's, had a dream about the 1931 Rudy Vallee bestseller 'Tears', inspiring him to send a copy to the comic. Dodd's recording, accompanied by Geoff Love & His Orchestra, was released in August 1965. The sing-along lament for lost love was composed by Billy Uhr and Frank Capano.

To many, Dodd's dated ditty looked decidedly doomed at a time when The Rolling Stones were flavour of the month and groundbreaking tracks such as '(I Can't Get No) Satisfaction', Bob Dylan's 'Like A Rolling Stone' and 'Help!' by The Beatles (who had supported Dodd at a 1961 charity show in Liverpool) were riding high.

Nonetheless, Dodd had the last laugh. 'Tears' shot to the top of the Official Singles Chart at the end of September and headed the UK chart for five weeks (before being dethroned by The Stones' 'Get Off Of My Cloud'), spending six months on the bestsellers list. Such was its success, in October top pop TV show *Thank Your Lucky Stars* decided that "good music" was back. They banned "long-haired groups" and introduced a new policy of just two "easy on the ear" acts a week – the first being Dodd and Petula Clark.

There was no sign of 'Tears' dropping at Christmas. In fact, it was joined in the Top Five by Dodd's follow-up, 'The River', and such was Dodd's success in 1965 that the buck-toothed baritone was named Top Show Business Personality of the Year.

Therefore, despite the fact that 1965 was one of the most important years in rock music, it was 'Tears' that was the year's biggest-selling single. In fact, it was the UK's third biggest seller of the whole Swinging Sixties. Perhaps not surprisingly, in the US, where he was a complete unknown, a cover version of 'Tears' by chart regular Bobby Vinton easily outsold Dodd's disc, which stalled just outside the Hot 100.

Over the next five years, Dodd added another half-dozen Top 20 hits to his collection. Although later years saw his star wane in terms of music and TV, he remained an in-demand live phenomenon. In 2006, over 50 years after his showbiz debut, he once again starred in a Royal Variety Show, and in 2009 a statue of 'Doddy', complete with tickling stick, was unveiled at Liverpool's Lime Street Station. Famously, Dodd was acquitted of tax evasion in 1989. During the trial it emerged that he had £336,000 in cash hidden in suitcases in his attic.

Dodd, like his biggest hit, is a throwback to the music hall days. It is perhaps ironic that the entertainer who never lost the knack of making people laugh may be best remembered for his 'Tears'.

THE SEEKERS 1965

THE CARNIVAL IS OVER

WRITER: Tom Springfield (lyrics)

PRODUCER: Tom Springfield

ALBUM: N/A

PEAK POSITION: Number 1 (3 weeks)

WEEKS ON CHART: 17

SALES: 1.41m

'The Carnival Is Over' was the most successful single by The Seekers – making them the first Australian group to both top the Official Singles Chart and the only one to claim a UK million seller.

Good musicians and vocalists that guitarists Keith Potger and Bruce Woodley and bass player Athol Guy were, it was lead singer Judith Durham's distinctive soprano that set The Seekers apart from the many other folk-oriented groups of the early Sixties and also saw them become the first non-UK or non-US act to ever top the UK Albums Chart.

Durham was a budding Australian jazz star when she joined The Escorts in 1962. Renamed The Seekers, they released their debut single, 'Waltzing Matilda', and their album *Introducing The Seekers* the following year. On March 28, 1964, they set sail for Southampton on the SS *Fairsky* (as that cruise ship's entertainment) to seek UK fame, giving themselves 10 weeks to achieve it.

During their first weeks on UK shores, they appeared on TV's *Tonight Show*, supported Freddie & The Dreamers and secured a two-album deal with World Record Club. Their big break came when they appeared at Blackpool Opera House alongside singer Dusty Springfield, which brought them to the attention of her brother, producer/songwriter Tom Springfield (born Dionysius O'Brien).

Springfield produced The Seekers' recording of his own composition 'I'll Never Find Another You', which topped the UK chart in January 1965 and reached the US Top 10. The act was the first Aussie group to achieve that feat Stateside, and in May 1965 the single became one of an unprecedented nine UK-produced records in the US Top 10.

The Seekers soon returned to the UK Top Five with another Springfield composition, 'A World Of Our Own', with their album of that name repeating the feat. Then, in October 1965 – shortly after being named Top New Group of the Year by *New Musical Express* readers – they released their most famous single, the haunting 'The Carnival Is Over'.

The song's melody was taken from a 19th-century Russian folk song, 'Stenka Razin (Dmitri Volnitsa)' that told the tale of folk hero Stepan Timofeyevich Razin, who in 1670 defeated the Tsar's forces and established a Cossack republic along the Volga River before being captured and brutally murdered. Springfield's English lyric tells of a lover going to battle, with references to Pierrot and Columbine suggesting that perhaps it was a love that was never meant to be.

Released in late October, four weeks later it was sitting at number one in the UK, a position it held for three weeks. At its peak it was selling over 90,000 copies a day, enough to stop even The Who's timeless 'My Generation' from reaching the top. Despite the hefty rock competition The Seekers faced in 1965, no act spent longer than them on the chart that year.

In April 1969, the recording returned to the top of the UK chart on *The Best Of The Seekers* album (released after the group split up), and it was once again in the Top 10 in 1994 on their album *A Carnival Of Hits*.

In Australia, 'The Carnival Is Over' is considered an ideal closing song for major events. The Seekers sang it at the end of Expo '88 in Brisbane, and they were intended to be the closing act in the 2000 Olympics in Sydney. Unfortunately though, Durham broke her hip and the group was unable to perform. They did, however, close that year's Paralympics with the song – even though the singer was in a wheelchair.

Keith Potger would go on to form The New Seekers, who in 1971 scored a number one UK hit with 'I'd Like To Teach The World To Sing', adapted from a Coca-Cola jingle.

THE BEATLES 1965

WE CAN WORK IT OUT/DAY TRIPPER

WRITERS: John Lennon, Paul McCartney

PRODUCER: George Martin

ALBUM: Yesterday And Today (US-only release)

PEAK POSITION: Number 1 (5 weeks)

WEEKS ON CHART: 12

SALES: 1.39m

The penultimate Beatles single to go Gold in the UK was also the band's first double-sided chart-topper and their third successive Christmas number one in the Official Singles Chart. In America, where the two tracks' sales were calculated separately, both sides made the Top Five, with 'We Can Work It Out' being their 11th number one single in less than three years.

'Day Tripper' was recorded in three takes at Abbey Road on October 16, 1965. It was written at Kenwood, John Lennon's house in Weybridge, Surrey. On the verses, McCartney sang lead and Lennon handled the harmony, while on the chorus their roles were reversed.

According to McCartney, "Acid was coming in on the scene – and this song was to do with tripping. It was just a tongue-in-cheek song about a girl who was a day tripper, a Sunday painter, in other words, a weekend hippy, someone who is only partly committed to the idea of tripping.

"It was a co-written effort," he added, "but I would give John the main credit. One of the great things about collaborating is that you could nudge-nudge, wink-wink a bit. We thought that'd be fun to put in that 'big teasers' bit – we liked including references that we knew our friends would get, but the mums and dads wouldn't."

As 'Day Tripper' was intended as a kind of homage to the Memphis R&B label Stax, Lennon and McCartney said they were honoured when that label's top artist, Otis Redding, recorded it.

'We Can Work It Out' was recorded at the same sessions as The Beatles' *Rubber Soul* album. In all, they spent 11 hours on the track, with the main parts put down on October 20 and overdubs added on October 29. It was the most time they had spent on a single track up until then.

McCartney wrote 'We Can Work It Out' at the house he had bought for his father in Heswall, Cheshire. "I wrote it as a more up-tempo thing, country & western," he said. "I had the idea, the title, and a couple of verses when I took it to John to finish off."

The lyrics are thought to have been inspired by McCartney's relationship with his then-girlfriend Jane Asher and he wrote the upbeat, optimistic verses, while Lennon contributed the more mournful "Life is very short... " middle eight. McCartney also recalled that it was fellow Beatle George Harrison's suggestion to make the middle section sound like a German waltz, with the idea of using a harmonium on the track only occurring to them when they found one in the studio.

Since The Beatles stopped playing live around the time this single was released, they made groundbreaking promotional films of them singing both tracks, which helped the single become their biggest seller since 'Can't Buy Me Love'. It was released in the UK on December 3, 1965 – the same day as *Rubber Soul* (which did not include either track) – and it topped the UK Singles Chart for five weeks. In the US, both sides debuted on December 18 and 'We Can Work It Out' headed the *Billboard* Hot 100 for three weeks.

As with many other Beatles songs, 'We Can Work It Out' had a chart life outside the band; five years later, Stevie Wonder had a Top 20 hit with it and in 1981 it was a transatlantic Top Three hit as part of Starsound's 'Stars On 45' medley.

TOM JONES 1966

GREEN, GREEN GRASS OF HOME

WRITER: Claude 'Curly' Putman, Jr.

PRODUCER: Peter Sullivan

ALBUM: Green, Green Grass Of Home

PEAK POSITION: Number 1 (7 weeks)

WEEKS ON CHART: 22

SALES: 1.23m

Tom Jones has been mining Welsh gold across five decades, but never struck a richer vein than with this song, which is not just unusual, but unique. 'Green, Green Grass Of Home' is, to date, the only million-selling UK single by a Welsh artist.

The song that gave the man with 'The Voice' his biggest hit had an unlikely subject for a million seller, being about the dream of a prisoner on Death Row, awaiting execution the following morning. 'Green, Green Grass Of Home' was written by noted country music composer Claude 'Curly' Putman, Jr. – the man who inspired his one-time house guest, Paul McCartney, to write Wings' single 'Junior's Farm'.

Putman wrote Jones' chart-topper after watching 1950 movie *The Asphalt Jungle* on late-night TV. The film, which gave Marilyn Monroe her start, starred Sterling Hayden as a crook who bit the dust on the green grass of home, while looking up at the old house where he used to live. Putman also composed another UK chart-topper, Tammy Wynette's 'D-I-V-O-R-C-E', and Dolly Parton's first country hit, 'Dumb Blonde', as well as the much-covered country song 'My Elusive Dreams' (penned with Jones in mind).

'Green, Green Grass' was first recorded in 1965 by country vocalist Johnny Darrell, who was also the first person to cut the hits 'The

Son Of Hickory Holler's Tramp' and 'Ruby, Don't Take Your Love To Town'.

In the US, Porter Wagoner took the song into the *Billboard* Country Top Five in summer 1965, but the rendition that first brought it to Jones' attention was by one of his favourite singers, Jerry Lee Lewis. A few years later, Jones and his early idol reportedly recorded the song together for a still-unreleased proposed album project, tentatively titled *Tom And Jerry*. Such diverse artists as Elvis Presley, Johnny Cash, Joan Baez, Katherine Jenkins and Joe Tex have also recorded the golden death ditty.

Jones' version charted on the Official Singles Chart in November 1966 and three weeks later replaced 'Good Vibrations' by The Beach Boys as the UK's official number one. It held that position for seven weeks, stopping such big hits as Donovan's 'Sunshine Superman' and The Seekers' 'Morningtown Ride' from reaching the top spot. The single was also a Top Five entry in many European countries, but narrowly missed the US Top 10. It also spawned an album of the same name, which climbed to number three in the UK in early 1967 – the year Jones was voted Top Male Singer by the readers of *New Musical Express*, *Record Mirror* and *Disc*.

Knighted in 2003, the appeal of the former Thomas John Woodward seems timeless. Jones had his first number one single ('It's Not Unusual') in 1965 and his most recent chart-topper came in 2009, through his 'Islands In The Stream' collaboration with Robin Gibb and *Gavin & Stacey* TV characters Vanessa Jenkins and Bryn West (aka comic actors Ruth Jones and Rob Brydon). He was also part of the all-star team on the million-selling UK number one 'Perfect Day' in 1997.

Jones has certainly endured – having picked up his first Grammy in 1965, he was still picking up BRIT Awards in the 21st century. And he is the only solo act to have scored a UK number one single and album after the age of 60.

Indeed, in recent years, he has gained some of his strongest critical acclaim through two albums which have mined his love of gospel and roots music, 2010's *Praise & Blame* and 2012's *Spirit In The Room*, while gaining a brand new generation of fans in 2012 via BBC TV's *The Voice*.

In June 2012, Jones was among the performers at the Queen's Diamond Jubilee concert in front of Buckingham Palace in London.

ENGELBERT HUMPERDINCK 1967

RELEASE ME

WRITERS: Eddie Miller, James Pebworth, Robert Yount	
PRODUCER: Charles Blackwell	
ALBUM: Release Me	
PEAK POSITION: Number 1 (6 weeks)	
WEEKS ON CHART: 57 (1967, 56; 2004, 1)	
SALES: 1.38m	

Engelbert Humperdinck was the name of the 19th-century German composer best known for writing an opera based on the children's story 'Hansel and Gretel'. In 1966, in true fairytale fashion, recording artist Gerry Dorsey borrowed his name and went on to become one of the world's biggest-selling and most popular vocalists.

Like Cliff Richard, Humperdinck was born in India and returned with his family to his parents' homeland as a child. Coincidentally, both singers recorded their first singles in late 1958 and impressed TV producer Jack Good enough for him to let them perform on the top pop TV show of the time, *Oh Boy!*

However, it took another seven years and a handful of different record labels before fame came to the singer with the superstar looks.

His manager, Gordon Mills, also looked after Tom Jones and was convinced that he had another worldwide superstar on his hands. He was surprised when Jones' label, Decca, said Dorsey was "old hat and would never make it". Undeterred, Mills decided a name change might help and he played the same demo to a different Decca A&R man, who reportedly acclaimed, "That's fabulous, that's great. This Engelbert Humperdinck is going to be as big as Tom Jones!"

At the end of 1966, with Jones enjoying the biggest hit of his career with a song that started in the US country & western field, 'Green, Green Grass Of Home', it seemed good sense for Humperdinck and

Mills to take the country road too.

Humperdinck first heard 'Release Me' as an instrumental by UK saxophonist Frank Weir (who had the US Top Five version of 'The Happy Wanderer' in 1954). He told Mills: "This is a hit melody. Let's find the words." He was even more convinced this was the song to break him when, at his suggestion, noted arranger Charles Blackwell incorporated a three-tone key change.

The song that finally put Humperdinck on the musical map was by no means a standard love song. It was about a married man who wanted a divorce – a subject most singers would stay well clear of, and there were many at the time who doubted the commercial possibilities of such a record.

In Sixties US country music, songs about the 'three d's' (divorce, death and diesels) were commonplace, but back in 1950 when co-writer Eddie Miller and his group The Oklahomans put out the original version of 'Release Me', many radio stations refused to play it.

However, four years later, with the subject less taboo in country music, the divorce ditty became a US Top 10 hit on the *Billboard* country chart for three different acts: Ray Price, Jimmy Heap and Kitty Wells. The song finally found pop success Stateside in 1962, when one-time child star Esther Phillips, with help from producer Lelan Rogers (Kenny Rogers' brother), turned it into an American pop and R&B hit. If Humperdinck's arrangement owes anything to an earlier rendition, it would be that of Phillips; he also later had a big hit with her follow-up, 'Am I That Easy To Forget'.

'Release Me' was not an instant hit; after influential TV show *Juke Box Jury* voted it a miss, it took a standout performance on the even more popular *Sunday Night At The London Palladium* to kick-start it. It took six weeks to climb to the top of the Official Singles Chart, where it stayed for six weeks, going on to spend 56 consecutive weeks on the UK Singles Chart in 1967 and 1988, more than any other single before or since.

'Release Me' proceeded to sell well over one million copies in both Britain and America and topped charts in 11 countries. Most famously, in the UK it kept The Beatles' 'Penny Lane'/'Strawberry Fields Forever' off the top spot, stopping the Fab Four from extending their sequence of seven consecutive number one singles.

Humperdinck was elated and told the *New Musical Express*: "I don't care if I never get another hit. I've achieved my ambition of getting a number one, and now I'm happy."

MILLION-SELLING MEMORIES

ENGELBERT HUMPERDINCK

You're one of the few artists to have two million-selling singles. What do you remember about the early part of 1967 when 'Release Me' and 'The Last Waltz' first went to number one on the Official Singles Chart?

It felt great! 'Release Me' made history because it stopped The Beatles from getting their eighth consecutive number one [with 'Penny Lane'/'Strawberry Fields Forever'] and it stayed on the singles chart for 56 weeks [in 1967 and 1968]. 'The Last Waltz' went to number one a few months later and was my first number one around the world; it was played in dance halls all around the world and it's really stayed in people's minds.

Even fewer artists can say they kept The Beatles off number one. Were you a Beatles fan?

Definitely. To this day I still love the work of Paul McCartney; he's an amazing performer, and if I want to learn anything I still watch his videos. He's a real master of showbusiness and a great, great songwriter.

It didn't matter to them that they weren't number one; they had already had 12 number ones, and have had many, many since. They've sold millions and millions of albums and then this poor lad from Leicester came along and ruined it for them [laughs]! No, it didn't really matter; they are all very wonderful people. I've met Ringo and Paul over the years... I didn't get to meet George in the end, but I did meet John.

You released your Eurovision single in 2012 – what do you think about the charts today? How would you feel if you had to start your career now?

It's a whole different ball game now. It's very, very different. I'm very proud of the Gold and Platinum albums I've released; they're on the wall in my home alongside my trophies. When I look at them, it makes me proud that so many people have supported me over the years and bought my music. I've sold around 150 million albums, so I've been very, very fortunate.

What was the first single you bought?

It was 'When I Fall In Love' by Nat King Cole. The reason I bought it was because I was courting my now wife, and I needed a song that had a nice message behind it, and that was the song I bought for her.

Throughout the history of the Official Chart, is there a number one single that secretly you wish you'd written?

I can't answer that question; it's too difficult! I'm just very happy that I've been fortunate enough to record the kind of songs I've recorded over the years. They have been a big part of my life. Wherever I go, people request my music and that makes me feel very proud. It's been a good life, a good journey, and I hope to carry it on for as long as possible.

ENGELBERT HUMPERDINCK 1967

THE LAST WALTZ

WRITERS: Les Reed, Barry Mason

PRODUCER: Peter Sullivan

ALBUM: The Last Waltz

PEAK POSITION: Number 1 (5 weeks)

WEEKS ON CHART: 27

SALES: 1.17m

After his massive success with 'Release Me' turned the newly named Engelbert Humperdinck into the worldwide star his manager Gordon Mills always claimed the former Gerry Dorsey could be, the hunt for a suitably huge follow-up began.

The single's immediate successor was country song 'There Goes My Everything', which stalled for a month in the UK at number two behind Procol Harum's 'A Whiter Shade Of Pale', but Humperdinck ended the year by earning his second UK Gold disc, for a million sales of 'The Last Waltz'.

This ultimate end-of-evening dance-floor filler entered the UK chart on August 23, 1967, and just two weeks later replaced hippy anthem 'San Francisco (Be Sure To Wear Some Flowers In Your Hair)' at number one. It stayed there for five weeks and even stopped fellow Mills client Tom Jones from grabbing another chart-topper with 'I'll Never Fall In Love Again'. On the album front, the track's parent album, *The Last Waltz*, was a Top 10 entry on both sides of the Atlantic.

'The Last Waltz' was the first of many standout songs written especially for Humperdinck by top UK songsmiths Les Reed and Barry Mason, the latter happily admitting that "The song that has earned us a lifetime of royalties took us just 20 minutes to write!"

Humperdinck, unknown to British record-buyers at the start of 1967, was voted Top New Artist of the Year by *New Musical Express* readers. The year may now be best remembered for giving us psychedelic music and the Summer of Love, but 'The Last Waltz' helped give him the last laugh over the flower children's favourite artists, as no one had a more successful year on the UK's Official Singles Chart than Humperdinck.

Whether or not its composers intentionally set out to do so, 'The Last Waltz' has probably closed more dances than any other record or song in history. Such is the song's across-the-board appeal, it came as no surprise when it collected the Ivor Novello Award for the Highest Certified British Sales of the Year. Reed and Mason, who are one of the most successful British writing partnerships of all time, also penned later Humperdinck winners such as 'Les Bicyclettes De Belsize' and 'Winter World Of Love', as well as 'Delilah' by Tom Jones and Des O'Connor's number one, 'I Pretend'.

The 'King of Romance', as the Vegas veteran is often tagged, is still making news. Humperdinck, who belongs to the select 100 million-plus sales club, saw his career go full circle in 2012 when he was called upon to represent Britain in the Eurovision Song Contest with 'Love Will Set You Free'.

That harked back to 1966, when, with the aim of breaking him in Europe first, Humperdinck had represented Britain in the Knokke-Heist music festival in Belgium. The plan paid off in November 1966, when his second Decca single, 'Dommage Dommage', became the first of his six number ones in Belgium.

THE BEATLES 1968
HEY JUDE

WRITERS: John Lennon, Paul McCartney
PRODUCER: George Martin
ALBUM: N/A
PEAK POSITION: Number 1 (2 weeks)
WEEKS ON CHART: 27 (1968, 16; 1976, 7; 1988, 2; 2010, 2)
SALES: 1.06m

'Hey Jude' was The Beatles' first release on their own Apple label, their 18th UK single and their 15th number one in the Official Singles Chart. In the US, it was the most popular group of all time's biggest ever hit, as well was America's most successful single of the Sixties.

Although jointly credited to John Lennon, the song was solely composed by Paul McCartney. It had started life as 'Hey Jules', and McCartney began writing it while driving to visit Lennon's then-wife Cynthia and their five-year-old son Julian, hoping that the song might help Jules get through his parents' pending divorce. However, when McCartney first played it to Lennon, the latter was convinced that he was the titular Jude and said, "Ah, it's me" – to which McCartney replied, "No, it's me."

It was recorded during the sessions for *The Beatles* (aka 'The White Album'), but was never intended for inclusion on it. On July 29 and 30, 1968, The Beatles reportedly did 25 rehearsal takes of 'Hey Jude' at Abbey Road Studios, and the following day relocated to Trident Studios in London's Soho to record the master (as Trident had an eight-track machine and EMI's studios still only had a four-track). Eagle-eared listeners may note that around the three-minute mark, McCartney can be heard swearing when he hits a bum note on the piano.

The recording was completed on August 1 when a 36-piece orchestra was added (although McCartney had originally envisioned a 100-piece orchestra). While in the studio, the extra musicians were recruited to clap and sing along on the chorus (for a second session fee, naturally).

The first public performance of 'Hey Jude' was when McCartney played it at a listening party hosted by The Rolling Stones to launch their *Beggars Banquet* album. A promotional film was shot at Twickenham Studios on September 4, the group being joined by a small, well-behaved crowd who sang and clapped along.

'Hey Jude' entered the UK Singles Chart on September 4, 1968 at number 21 and the following week leapt to the top. Surprisingly, it only managed two weeks at the summit before being relegated to the runner-up slot by the second release on Apple, the McCartney-produced 'Those Were The Days' by Mary Hopkin.

A month later those same singles held the top two slots Stateside. 'Hey Jude' entered the *Billboard* Hot 100 at number 10, then the highest ever entry position, and at seven minutes and 11 seconds it was the longest single to top the UK or US chart at the time. It headed the Hot 100 for a then-record nine weeks, while the B-side, 'Revolution', reached number 12 in its own right.

'Hey Jude' was a huge international hit and on November 30 it was announced that world sales had passed six million (it would go on to top eight million), thus making it the biggest-selling first release ever by a record label.

No sooner had The Beatles' version left the chart, soul man Wilson Pickett returned 'Hey Jude' to the Top 20. In 1976, the original Beatles recording returned to the UK Top 20, and briefly re-charted in 1988 and 2010.

The song was nominated for three Grammy Awards (Record of the Year, Song of the Year and Best Pop Performance by a Group) but, somewhat surprisingly, won none of them. Nevertheless, it was later inducted into both the Grammy and Rock and Roll Halls of Fame. It won an Ivor Novello Award for Best-Selling Song, while the readers of *New Musical Express* and *Disc* named 'Hey Jude' Best Single of the Year. Since then, of course, it has appeared in countless 'all-time greatest hits' lists.

In 1996, Julian Lennon paid £25,000 at an auction for the recording notes from the session. Commenting then that he and McCartney hung out "… more than dad and I did", he said of 'Hey Jude': "It's very strange to think that someone has written a song about you", adding that whenever he hears it, "it still touches me".

THE ARCHIES 1969

SUGAR, SUGAR

WRITERS: Jeff Barry, Andy Kim

PRODUCER: Jeff Barry

ALBUM: Everything's Archie

PEAK POSITION: Number 1 (8 weeks)

WEEKS ON CHART: 26

SALES: 1.02m

In the late 1960s, US music publisher/producer Don Kirshner had an unusual problem: how do you follow an act like The Monkees? It was Kirshner who had produced all that manufactured-for-TV group's big hits.

In terms of chart hits, the band had fared far better when 'the man with the golden ear' (as Kirshner was known) was calling the shots than when they began demanding more input. After The Monkees insisted on more artistic freedom, Kirshner's idea for a trouble-free follow-up was to act as music supervisor for the top-rated Saturday morning CBS cartoon series *The Archies* – after all, what problems could you have with animated artists?

At that time in Britain, the name Archie Andrews would have conjured up images of ventriloquist Peter Brough's dummy of that name – their radio series *Educating Archie* had attracted 15 million listeners every week in the 1950s. However, across the Atlantic, Andrews was the star of the *Archie* comic books.

The redheaded, freckle-faced perennial teenager first appeared in *Pep Comics* in 1941 and soon became so popular that he and his 'typically American' school friends from Riverdale High got their own comic book and radio show. *The Archies* reached a peak of popularity in the late Sixties when it transferred to the small screen and sales of the comic rocketed from about 300,000 a month to over one million. As the *World Encyclopedia Of Comics* said, "Archie, like

Batman, Superman and a small handful of others, has transcended comic books into pure Americana."

With such a large potential youth market already in place, it seemed only natural for the animated teenagers to make Monkees-styled records – and who better to organise that than Kirshner?

After encountering US radio resistance to the first two Archies singles, the third release, 'Sugar, Sugar', was played to top media people without disclosing the act's identity. That did the trick. Radio play helped the single rocket to the top of the *Billboard* Hot 100, where it spent four weeks. It was still number one there at the time of its UK release and within three weeks had repeated its US success, leaping from number 11 to number one in the Official Singles Chart.

The bubblegum classic fought off all-comers for eight weeks, preventing The Tremeloes' '(Call Me) Number One' from living up to its title before handing the Christmas crown to Rolf Harris and his 'Two Little Boys'. 'Sugar, Sugar' outsold all other singles in the UK, US and Germany in 1969 and amassed worldwide sales of more than six million – not bad for a song The Monkees reportedly rejected. In the UK, it sold just under one million copies in 1969, but has subsequently passed that mark through download sales.

The Archies line-up was supposedly Andrews, Jughead Jones, Veronica Lodge, Betty Cooper, Reggie Mantle and Hot Dog, but the actual voices heard on 'Sugar, Sugar' were those of session singer Ron Dante (who at the same time was singing lead on The Cuff Links' Top 10 hit 'Tracy', and later co-produced many Barry Manilow hits) and Toni Wine (whose compositions include 'A Groovy Kind Of Love' and 'Candida'). Dante handled all the male vocals, while Wine took the "I'm gonna make your life so sweet" line.

The Archies' only UK chart hit was produced and co-written by Jeff Barry, whose wife and regular co-writer Ellie Greenwich sang on other Archies tracks, as did session vocalist Tony Passalacqua plus 'Sugar, Sugar' co-writer – and later hit-maker in his own right – Andy Kim.

Producer and singer/songwriter Jonathan King took the song back to the Top 20 in 1971, performing under the name Sakkarin, while Ron Dante created a disco version under his own name in 1975 before 'Sugar, Sugar' became a transatlantic Top three hit again in 1981 as part of Starsound's 'Stars On 45' medley.

Dan Kirshner died aged 76 in January 2011.

THE NEW SEEKERS 1971

I'D LIKE TO TEACH THE WORLD TO SING (IN PERFECT HARMONY)

WRITERS: Roger Cook, Roger Greenaway, Bill Backer, Billy Davis

PRODUCER: David Mackay

ALBUM: We'd Like To Teach The World To Sing

PEAK POSITION: Number 1 (4 weeks)

WEEKS ON CHART: 21

SALES: 1.01m

When the carnival truly proved to be over for Australian folk/pop group The Seekers, it was guitarist Keith Potger, rather than the group's star vocalist Judith Durham, who had the most immediate impact, launching the group that taught the world to sing TV commercials.

Potger formed The New Seekers shortly after his original band's demise in 1969, initially as a full member of the group. However, by 1971 he had taken more of a behind-the-scenes role as their manager and vocal arranger.

The new band came close to claiming their first UK number one in the summer of '71 with 'Never Ending Song Of Love', which spent five weeks waiting in the runner-up spot, mainly behind Diana Ross' aptly-titled 'I'm Still Waiting'. However, they did not have to wait long for their own chart-topper.

The song started life as a TV commercial for Coca-Cola as 'I'd Like To Give The World A Coke', a title thought up by McCann-Erickson advertising executive Bill Backer, who is credited as composer alongside regular McCann-Erickson writer Roquel 'Billy' Davis and the noted British songwriting duo of Roger Cook and Roger Greenaway.

The tune comes from an earlier Cook and Greenaway composition, 'True Love And Apple Pie', which had slipped out unnoticed a couple of months earlier by Susan Shirley. The pair were one of Britain's most successful songwriting teams, having composed countless hits including 'Something's Gotten Hold Of My Heart', 'Melting Pot', 'My Baby Loves Lovin'' and 'You've Got Your Troubles'. Davis also had an impressive CV, featuring such favourites as 'Reet Petite', 'Rescue Me' and 'Hello Summertime'.

The TV advert, known as 'the Hilltop commercial', featured a vast multicultural group of teenagers on a hill singing the praises of Coca-Cola and international friendship; the drinks company gave all its publishing royalties from the hit to UNICEF. The commercial, which cost an unprecedented £100,000, was first aired in July 1971. The earliest version released was the original recording by session group The Hillside Singers, and this was already starting to sell well in the US when The New Seekers' rendition was issued.

The New Seekers' line-up at the time was also multi-national, with members Eve Graham, Lyn Paul, Marty Kristian, Peter Doyle and Paul Layton hailing from the UK, Australia and Germany (Potger himself was born in Sri Lanka).

The New Seekers' version soon shot to number one in the UK's Official Singles Chart, while in the US it reached the Top 10 and was nominated for a Grammy. At the time, British sales were just under one million, but it has since passed that magic mark. The track was produced by Australian David Mackay, who has also worked with such notables as Cliff Richard, Dusty Springfield and Bonnie Tyler.

In the UK, it was the first new number one of 1972, replacing Benny Hill's 'Ernie' at the top, and during its four-week stay at the summit it stopped 11-year-old Neil Reid from becoming the youngest ever Brit to hit the top. It was also the featured track on The New Seekers' *We'd Like To Teach The World To Sing*, which climbed to number two on the Official Albums Chart.

In 2007, the advertising trade magazine *Campaign* named the advert "one of the best loved and most influential ads in TV history". It was not the first TV commercial to be turned into a musical bestseller, but it was the one that taught the music world that commercials could be perfect launching pads for huge hits.

THE SIMON PARK ORCHESTRA 1972

EYE LEVEL

WRITER: Jack Trombey (Jan Stoeckart)

PRODUCER: Uncredited

ALBUM: Eye Level

PEAK POSITION: Number 1 (4 weeks)

WEEKS ON CHART: 24 (1972, 2; 1973, 22)

SALES: 1.01m

In 1973, slap bang in the middle of a run of UK number ones from hit-making machines Donny Osmond, Wizzard, David Cassidy, Slade and Gary Glitter, up popped an instrumental orchestral piece by an act with no previous hits, who would never trouble chart compilers again and that many could not identify. In fact, the only chart-topping million-selling instrumental was credited to an act that did not really exist. Welcome to the mysterious world of library music.

Production music libraries specialise in tracks that capture various moods and musical styles which can then be licensed 'off the peg' for inclusion in programmes and advertisements, saving broadcasters time and money by eliminating the need to commission new compositions. De Wolfe Music – where 'Eye Level' originated – is the owner of one of the most renowned library music catalogues, controlling over 80,000 tracks.

'Eye Level' began life as a track on the 1971 album *Double Or Quits*, released on the De Wolfe Music label. Its mood was described on the sleeve as "easy-going tempo, melodic", the writer was listed as Jack Trombey (Dutch composer/arranger Jan Stoeckart) and the album was credited to The International Studio Orchestra, a generic name used by De Wolfe to describe the various groups of musicians that performed on their orchestral releases, although generally each track's composer was also its arranger/conductor.

When Thames Television was seeking a theme track for new

series *Van Der Valk*, set in the Netherlands and based on the detective thrillers of Nicolas Freeling, the broadcaster selected 'Eye Level'. Columbia released it in November 1972, coinciding with the show's first broadcast, and the single reached number 41 during an initial two-week chart run. Other than being in stereo, the recording was identical to the mono 1971 library track.

Oxford music graduate Simon Park was working at De Wolfe and several of his compositions had appeared on their albums (many under the alias Simon Haseley), although there was no orchestra performing exclusively under his name.

To this day, there remains some doubt about the level of Park's involvement with the track. Park claims that Trombey sent him snippets of a tune probably based on an old Dutch folk song, which he then arranged into 'Eye Level' and conducted himself. De Wolfe concur that Trombey's role was as composer of the piece and nothing more (he had written, arranged and conducted his own recordings for the company since the early Sixties). Regardless of Park's involvement, the act was named The Simon Park Orchestra.

Eight months after its initial release, with the second series of *Van Der Valk*, a re-promoted 'Eye Level' sped to the top of the Official Singles Chart, becoming the first TV theme to reach pole position. Its number one reign began at the end of September 1973, 307 days after its chart debut – at that time, the only single to have taken longer to reach the summit was Bill Haley's 'Rock Around The Clock' (322 days in 1955).

Although instrumentals topped the Singles Chart at an average of one per year during its first 20 years, 'Eye Level' remains the most recent chart-topper to contain no vocals of any description (discounting the title vocalese on Doop's eponymous number one and the spoken intro on Mr. Oizo's 'Flat Beat') and is only the second million-selling instrumental, after Acker Bilk's 'Stranger On The Shore'.

The Simon Park Orchestra, along with The Archies and Teletubbies, are the only million-selling one-hit wonders to date – all three, essentially, TV creations.

Inevitably, an album credited to Park followed, although it seemed largely a hastily thrown together selection of 12 previously released tracks from De Wolfe, only four of them having any apparent connection to Park himself. However, evidence from the album sleeve indicates that 'Eye Level' was "arranged by Jack Trombey".

LITTLE JIMMY OSMOND 1972

LONG HAIRED LOVER FROM LIVERPOOL

WRITERS: Christopher Kingsley
(incorrectly credited as Christopher Dowden)

PRODUCERS: Mike Curb, Perry Botkin, Jr.

ALBUM: Killer Joe

PEAK POSITION: Number 1 (5 weeks)

WEEKS ON CHART: 27

SALES: 1m

Looking back, 1973 may be recalled as a year when Elton John, David Bowie and Rod Stewart ruled. However, a survey of the first six months' charts shows that, in fact, teen idol Donny Osmond was the top male albums act and Little Jimmy the top male singles act – reflecting a period when the Osmond family was amazingly successful in the UK, with no fewer than seven of George and Olive Osmond's nine children reaching the Top Three on the Official Singles Chart.

During the early Seventies, the all-male five-member Osmonds group clocked up six Top 20 entries, while teen pin-up Donny had seven in his own right plus three with his sister Marie, whose solo smash 'Paper Roses' made number two. It was, however, the youngest Osmond, Little Jimmy, who earned the family its only UK million seller – at the very tender age of nine.

Some 40 years later, Little Jimmy Osmond remains the youngest artist to ever top the UK chart (at nine years and 251 days old), yet surprisingly this was not the first sales award that the schoolboy star had earned – his single 'My Little Darling', precociously sung in Japanese, had earned him a Gold record in Japan during 1970, when he was just seven.

On paper, the idea of recording a song about a Beatles-like 'Long Haired Lover From Liverpool' long after Beatlemania had peaked would seem well past its sell-by date. That thinking seemed correct when its composer Christopher Kingsley's 1969 version went nowhere. To release the same song two years after The Beatles had actually split, and when long hair was so usual that it did not merit any special mention, could have seemed like commercial suicide.

However, factor in the 'so cute' singer's membership of the best-known musical family of the time, add a chorus that everyone in the family could sing along to and top it off by releasing it in time for the Christmas silly season and you had a million seller.

The single was produced by regular Osmonds collaborator Mike Curb, in this case assisted by Perry Botkin, Jr., who had previously worked with such diverse talents as Barbra Streisand, Bobby Darin, Carly Simon, The Righteous Brothers and Sammy Davis, Jr.

Little Jimmy's debut UK hit entered the Official Singles Chart in November 1972 and four weeks later replaced another novelty record, Chuck Berry's 'My Ding-A-Ling', at the top. It held pole position for five weeks, leading for most of that time a Top 10 that included both 'Crazy Horses' by The Osmonds and Donny Osmond's 'Why', while stopping David Bowie's 'Jean Genie' from becoming a chart-topper.

In the US, the single only briefly entered the Top 40, but it reached the number two slot in Australia and Holland and number three in Belgium. Interestingly, it was coupled with 'Mother Of Mine', the song that had given 11-year-old TV talent show winner Neil Reid a UK Top Three hit earlier in the year.

The British public has always had a soft spot for Jimmy Osmond, who over the years has appeared in UK stage shows such as *Grease*, *Chicago* and *Jimmy Osmond's American Jukebox Show* as well as the pantos *Cinderella* and *Aladdin*. He has also appeared on TV shows including *Come Dine With Me* and *I'm A Celebrity… Get Me Out Of Here!* When not performing, he now runs Osmond Entertainment, which organises all the family's merchandising and live shows – including, in 2012, The Osmonds' biggest ever UK tour.

DAWN FEAT. TONY ORLANDO 1973

TIE A YELLOW RIBBON ROUND THE OLE OAK TREE

WRITERS: Irwin Levine, L. Russell Brown

PRODUCERS: Hank Medress, Dave Appell

ALBUM: Tuneweaving

PEAK POSITION: Number 1 (4 weeks)

WEEKS ON CHART: 40

SALES: 1m

1973 was a classic year for teen-targeted pop.However, the year's most successful chart single in the UK (as well as the US and Australia) was 'Tie A Yellow Ribbon Round The Ole Oak Tree'.

Larry Brown and Irwin Levine were inspired to write the song when they read the story of a man called Vingo in the June 1972 issue of *Reader's Digest.* Hailing from Brunswick, Georgia, Vingo had been jailed in New York on a fraud charge. He told his wife he would understand if she and his kids could not wait for him, asked her not to write, and, three years later, when he was being paroled, he wrote to tell her that he would get the Greyhound bus from New York to Atlanta, and that if she wanted him to come home she should put a yellow ribbon on the big oak tree in their town centre. The story also inspired the ABC-TV drama *Going Home,* starring James Earl Jones.

New York-born Tony Orlando, who credits pop svengali Don Kirshner (manager and creator of both The Monkees and The Archies) as the man who discovered him, had been a genuine teenage idol in the early Sixties. He released his first recording ('Ding Dong') aged 15 and in 1961 had his first US hit with his original version of 'Halfway To Paradise' (a UK hit for Billy Fury).

Several months later he was touring the UK promoting 'Bless You', which was not only his first British hit but also the first hit for one of the most successful writing duos of the Sixties, Barry Mann and Cynthia Weil.

In 1970, Orlando had switched to the business side of the industry and was working as a top executive at Columbia US. When he was asked to record a new song, titled 'Candida', he only agreed on the understanding that it would be released under the name Dawn – inconveniently, the single became a Top 10 UK and US hit, while its follow-up, 'Knock Three Times', topped both charts.

There was little alternative but to put together an actual group, with Telma Hopkins and Joyce Vincent Wilson becoming Tony's Dawn chorus, both in the studio and on the road. Looking for new material in 1973, Orlando came across 'Tie A Yellow Ribbon', which he initially thought was "a corny novelty" that would stand out like a sore thumb on his R&B-oriented *Tuneweaving* album.

Produced by Orlando's long-time friend Hank Medress (a member of The Tokens, who made the original recording of the UK million seller 'The Lion Sleeps Tonight') and noted US bandleader Dave Appell, the track was dashed off in just two takes – and then went on to become the signature tune of Orlando's career. A number one across the world (including the US and UK), the single sold more than six million copies and is among the most covered songs of the rock era, with versions by such legends as Frank Sinatra, Bing Crosby and Perry Como, not to mention an answer version ('Should I Tie A Yellow Ribbon Round The Ole Oak Tree?') by Connie Francis.

This single made its UK chart debut in March 1973, taking six weeks to get to number one, and became a fixture on the Official Singles Chart for a remarkable 40 weeks. Nominated for two Grammy Awards, it was while singing at the US awards show that Dawn came to the attention of CBS TV, who gave them their own series from 1974 to 1976.

Dawn broke up in late 1977 and Orlando has remained busy ever since – with that yellow ribbon his enduring motif. In 1991, he recorded a Gulf War-inspired sequel, 'With Every Yellow Ribbon (That's Why We Tie 'Em)', and soon after opened the Tony Orlando Yellow Ribbon Music Theater in Branson, Missouri.

I LOVE YOU LOVE ME LOVE

WRITERS: Gary Glitter, Mike Leander

PRODUCER: Mike Leander

ALBUM: Remember Me This Way

PEAK POSITION: Number 1 (4 weeks)

WEEKS ON CHART: 14

SALES: 1.14m

Scandal may have seen Gary Glitter almost airbrushed out of pop music history in recent years – and this single may well be the least played million seller on today's radio – but there is no hiding the fact that this ever-extrovert character was one of the UK's most popular entertainers during the 1970s.

Glitter, born Paul Gadd, started his recording career under the name Paul Raven with a single on Decca in 1960, before releasing two George Martin-produced singles on Parlophone in 1961 (including a cover of Frankie Vaughan's chart-topper 'Tower Of Strength'). At that time, he was best known as the protégé of radio's *The Goon Show* star Spike Milligan, but despite appearances on top TV pop shows such as *Cool For Cats* and *Thank Your Lucky Stars*, his career went nowhere.

During the mid-1960s, he sang with the Mike Leander Show Band, fronted a group called Boston International (which later evolved into his backing group, The Glitter Band) and acted as a 'warm-up' man on TV shows *Ready, Steady, Go!* and *Top Of The Pops*. He joined MCA in 1968 and, over the next couple of years, put out releases under the names Paul Raven, Rubber Bucket and Paul Monday. He can also be heard playing a priest on MCA's 1972 studio cast album of the *Jesus Christ Superstar* musical.

Success finally came in summer 1972 when, after a slow start, his first single as Gary Glitter, 'Rock And Roll' (parts one and two), took off. It narrowly missed the top slot on the UK singles chart and gave him his only major success in the US, where it has since been added to the Rock and Roll Hall of Fame.

Hit followed hit in his homeland and Glitter's tongue-in-cheek glam rock performances gained him superstar status. In November 1973, 'I Love You Love Me Love' entered the Official Singles Chart in the top position, thus giving Glitter membership to the then extremely exclusive 'in at number one' club, whose only members at that time were Elvis Presley, Cliff Richard, The Beatles and Glitter's glam-rock rivals Slade.

'I Love You Love Me Love', like all his previous hits, was co-written by Glitter and his old boss Mike Leander, and its anthemic sing-along quality helped make it the year's biggest-selling single in the UK. It held the top spot for four weeks before Slade's seasonal classic 'Merry Xmas Everybody' dislodged it just in time to claim the Christmas number one crown.

In Germany, where Glitter also sold millions of records, the single gave him his sixth successive Top 20 hit. However, in the US he was always considered to be a bit of a curiosity or novelty act and this record, like all the previous ones since 'Rock And Roll', went nowhere. Even a cover version by Tommy James failed to sell Stateside.

Up to that moment in time, Glitter had the best chart start of any act ever in the UK, with his first nine chart entries making the Top Five, and his first 11 gracing the Top 10.

On the day that this single charted, Glitter, complete with huge silver platform boots and his obligatory tight-fitting glitter suit, performed at London's Rainbow Theatre, a show that was filmed and later seen on the big screen as *Remember Me This Way*. Today, however, it is fair to say that most people don't.

SLADE 1973

MERRY XMAS EVERYBODY

WRITERS: Noddy Holder, Jim Lea	
PRODUCER: Chas Chandler	
ALBUM: N/A	
PEAK POSITION: Number 1 (5 weeks)	
WEEKS ON CHART: 59 (1973, 9; 1980, 2; 1981, 4; 1982, 3; 1983, 5; 1984, 4; 1985, 3; 1986, 1; 1998, 3; 2006, 5; 2007, 4; 2008, 4; 2009, 4; 2010, 4; 2011, 4)	
SALES FIGURES: 1.19m	

When Slade recorded this track in New York on a hot July day in 1973, it must have seemed hard for the Black Country quartet to envisage it becoming as important a part of the Christmas build-up in the UK as buying presents, sending cards and hanging decorations.

The song's story dates back to 1967, when Noddy Holder, lead singer of The 'N Betweens (Slade's original name), wrote a psychedelic song called 'Buy Me A Rocking Chair'. Although it did not merit a release at the time, the chorus' distinctive melody remained in Holder and bass player Jim Lea's mind.

Fast forward to 1973, when, after a few false starts, Slade had ridden the glam rock wave to become one of the UK's biggest acts with a series of guitar-driven, amiably loutish singles. When the band's label, Polydor, suggested they write a Christmas song, Lea recalled that great chorus and, while taking a shower, came up with an equally good melody for a verse to go with it.

After burning the midnight oil at his mum's house in Walsall, Holder wrote the finished lyric, complete with the uplifting chorus hook, which he hoped would bring cheer to a country riven by industrial disputes and tough times.

The track was recorded with Slade's producer/manager Chas Chandler over five days at Record Plant Studios in New York. To get the full echoing chorus sound they wanted, Chandler miked up the corridor outside the studio, much to the surprise of the office workers who were using it. The harmonium was borrowed from the next studio where John Lennon was using it for the recording of his *Mind Games* album.

1973 was a truly golden year for Slade. They started it with 'Gudbuy T'Jane' in the Top Five of the Official Singles Chart and followed with 'Cum On Feel The Noize', which entered at number one – a feat only Elvis, Cliff and The Beatles had achieved before. Then came 'Skweeze Me Pleeze Me', which made them the first UK act to have two records chart in pole position, before they capped it off with this seasonal smash, making Slade the very first act in history to see three of their releases achieve that feat. The record is even more remarkable considering that the three were consecutive singles and that Holder and Lea penned them all. On the album front, it was also a banner year with both *Slayed* and the compilation *Sladest* topping the UK LP chart.

The most-charted UK Christmas record of all time had over 300,000 advance orders, sold over 500,000 in its first week and made its debut in December 1973. It knocked Gary Glitter's 'I Love You Love Me Love' off the summit of the Official Singles Chart, staying there for five weeks.

Although recorded in the US, the track never spent a single week on the *Billboard* Hot 100 – indeed, the Wolverhampton wonders never graced the US Top 40 with any of their huge 1970s UK hits.

Slade's re-recording of 'Merry Xmas Everybody' entered the UK chart in 1980 and a remix reached the Top 40 in 1998. Between those two entries, the original version returned to the chart in 1981, 1982, 1983, 1984, 1985 and 1986 – a remarkable feat pre-digital. And exactly 16 years after Slade's version entered at number one, Holder joined Jive Bunny on a version of the song, included on the latter's 'Let's Party' single, which also entered in the top position.

Slade disbanded in 1992 and Noddy Holder has since become a radio DJ in Manchester and TV personality. Following the inclusion of digital sales towards chart positions, their Christmas classic has returned to the UK Top 40 every year since 2006. It could well be that its sales have only just begun.

ROD STEWART 1975
SAILING

WRITER: Gavin Sutherland	
PRODUCER: Tom Dowd	
ALBUM: Atlantic Crossing	
PEAK POSITION: Number 1 (4 weeks)	
WEEKS ON CHART: 34 (1975, 11; 1976, 20; 1987, 3)	
SALES: 1.02m	

If asked to name the most anthemic, scarf-waving, arms-flailing rock songs of all time, chances are that Rod Stewart's 'Sailing' would be among the very first to spring to mind.

The song was written by Gavin Sutherland and originally released by his group The Sutherland Brothers Band in June 1972, as a single and a track on their album *Lifeboat*. Stewart, a huge football fan, was attracted to it because he thought it would be "one for the terraces". He was proved correct, and it became a hugely popular song at football grounds around the country. Stewart's success helped draw attention to the song's writer, whose band (at that time, The Sutherland Brothers & Quiver) enjoyed a major hit in their own right with 'Arms Of Mary' in 1976.

Born in north London to a Scottish father and English mother, one-time grave-digger Stewart's musical career began when he was hired for singer Long John Baldry's band in 1964. However, his major breakthrough came when he joined the Jeff Beck Group in 1967. That volatile band's aggressive blues-rock provided a blueprint for the similarly inclined Led Zeppelin, but Stewart and bandmate Ronnie Wood exited in 1969 for The Faces, joining Ronnie Lane, Ian McLagan and Kenney Jones, the three members of The Small Faces stranded after vocalist/guitarist Steve Marriott left to form Humble Pie. Stewart simultaneously re-launched his solo career, successfully juggling hit solo and Faces albums and singles for the next five years.

On quitting The Faces in 1975, R&B and soul music fan Stewart opted to utilise both Muscle Shoals Sound Studios in Alabama and Hi Records studios in Memphis to make his first US-recorded album, *Atlantic Crossing*, his debut solo album for Warner Bros. and the first not to feature any of his old bandmates.

Not only did the album feature the famed Muscle Shoals rhythm section that had appeared on countless soul classics (Jimmy Johnson, Barry Beckett, David Hood, Roger Hawkins) but also many of Stax Records' finest musicians including Booker T. & The M.G.'s members Steve Cropper, 'Duck' Dunn and Al Jackson, along with the unmistakable Memphis Horns. In addition, Stewart brought in veteran producer Tom Dowd, who had worked with many of his favourite soul stars at Atlantic Records.

Additional work on the album, which also included the later hits 'This Old Heart Of Mine' and 1977 UK chart-topper 'I Don't Want To Talk About It', took place at Wally Heider Studios in San Francisco and Criteria in Florida. *Atlantic Crossing* gave Stewart his fifth of six successive number one solo albums in the UK, and earned him a Gold album and a Top 10 placing in the US.

'Sailing' topped the Official Singles Chart for four weeks from September 6, 1975, stopping veteran folk singer Roger Whittaker from getting his only number one with 'The Last Farewell' and Leo Sayer from scoring his first chart-topper with 'Moonlighting'. Exactly one year later, it returned to the chart after being heard as the theme to the BBC series *Sailor*, a documentary about six months at sea on the HMS *Ark Royal*. This time, the single climbed as high as number three, helping push its sales over the one million mark.

It also sailed to the top in many other countries including Norway, where it spent a record-breaking 17 weeks at the summit. Surprisingly, in the US, where Stewart has always been one of the most successful UK acts, it did not crack the Top 40.

'Sailing' was reissued in 1987 after the Zeebrugge ferry disaster, narrowly missing the Top 40. Some 20 years later, Stewart's rendering of the song at the July 2007 Concert For Diana (10 years after the Princess Of Wales had died) at the then-new Wembley Stadium proved one of the most memorable moments of the all-star show, watched by an estimated 500 million people in 141 countries.

Recently Stewart has released albums of American standards and appeared in Las Vegas.

JOHN LENNON 1975

IMAGINE

WRITER: John Lennon

PRODUCERS: John Lennon, Yoko Ono, Phil Spector

ALBUM: Imagine

PEAK POSITION: Number 6 (1975)
Number 1 (4 weeks, 1980)

WEEKS ON CHART: 43 (1975, 11; 1980, 13; 1988, 5; 1999, 14)

SALES: 1.6m

John Lennon once said that 'Imagine' was "as good as anything I had written with The Beatles" and many would still suggest it is as important as any song he ever composed.

Certainly, unlike many pop songs, the appeal and standing of this song and its deceptively sugar-coated "anti-religious, anti-nationalistic, anti-conventional and anti-capitalistic message" (to use Lennon's own words) seems to have increased over the years – something even Lennon may not have imagined.

A message of worldwide peace and brotherhood presented in an easy-on-the-ear, melodic manner, the song's main theme was inspired by 'Cloud Piece', a short poem from Lennon's wife Yoko Ono's 1964 book *Grapefruit*. Ono said the lyric was "just what John believed – that we are all one country, one world, one people". He famously wrote the lyric on the back of a hotel bill in an aeroplane, although he composed the music at home.

Ono recalled: "John was elated about that particular song – he thought it was really important for the world to hear. He wanted to keep it very simple and easy, so even children could sing it – and then the message would get across."

It was first recorded at Lennon's home studio, Ascot Sound, in February 1971, and then worked on at Abbey Road in June and completed at Record Plant in New York in July. Musicians on the track were Klaus Voormann (a friend from The Beatles' Hamburg days) on bass, drummer Alan White (who would go on to join Yes) and the Flux Fiddlers. The album's production chores were shared between Lennon, Ono and Phil Spector.

Lennon and Ono directed a memorable promotional film for the song, set in their home at Tittenhurst Park in Berkshire, featuring Lennon on a white grand piano in his white living room. The title track of Lennon's globally chart-topping October 1971 album *Imagine*, it was released as a single in 1971 in the US. It entered the *Billboard* Hot 100 at number 20 – at that time, the highest entry ever for a solo singer – and eventually reached the Top Three.

In the UK, it was not issued in single form until November 1975, after Lennon took a break from music to bring up his and Yoko's son, Sean. It then reached number six on the UK Singles Chart, while *Shaved Fish*, the greatest hits album it featured on, made the Top 10 on the UK Albums Chart. They were his last chart entries for five years.

Lennon's murder on December 8, 1980 sparked demand for his past recordings and three weeks later 'Imagine' re-entered the UK Top 10, jumping to number one on the next Official Singles Chart, where it stayed for four weeks before being replaced by 'Woman', a single from his and Yoko's new album *Double Fantasy*. Sales at this time helped push 'Imagine' past the one million mark. When, 19 years later, it narrowly failed to become the UK's end-of-millennium number one, 'Imagine' became the only record ever by a solo artist to reach the UK Top 10 on three separate occasions.

The song, which has been accepted into both the Grammy and Rock and Roll Halls of Fame, has been named one of the greatest records of all time in countless music paper, radio and TV polls around the world.

Its popularity can be judged by the words of former US President Jimmy Carter, who remarked in 2006: "In many countries around the world, you hear John Lennon's 'Imagine' used almost equally with national anthems."

QUEEN 1975

BOHEMIAN RHAPSODY

WRITER: Freddie Mercury

PRODUCERS: Roy Thomas Baker, Freddie Mercury, John Deacon, Brian May, Roger Taylor

ALBUM: A Night At The Opera

PEAK POSITION: Number 1 (9 weeks, 1975)/ Number 1 (5 weeks, 1991)

WEEKS ON CHART: 31 (1975, 17; 1991, 14)

SALES: 2.36m

It could well be that more people in the UK own a copy of 'Bohemian Rhapsody' than any other track.

Not only did the marathon single top the Official Singles Chart on two separate occasions (1975 and 1991), selling over one million copies each time, but it also features on the biggest-selling UK album ever (Queen's six million-selling *Greatest Hits*).

As Queen guitarist Brian May points out, "Whenever polls for all-time greatest records are conducted around the globe, it still always crops up at, or near, the top of the list." Indeed, it was named Best Single Since 1952 at the first BRIT Awards and was voted the number one all-time favourite single by readers of the *Guinness Book Of British Hit Singles*.

Queen frontman Freddie Mercury wrote 'Bohemian Rhapsody' at his house in Kensington, London. He said he might shatter some people's illusions when he recalled, "In the early stages I almost rejected it. There was a time when the others wanted to chop it around a bit, but I refused. If it was going to be released, it would be in its entirety.

"We knew it was risky," admitted Mercury about releasing a six-minute single, and his record label, EMI, had doubts. "However, I had confidence in the song and felt that if it was successful it would earn us a lot of respect."

Recording started at Rockfield Studios in Wales on August 24, 1975 and in the end four other studios were also used. It was put together over three weeks; group members had to sing for 10-12 hours a day and in places there were 180 separate vocal overdubs. At the time it was said to be one of the most expensive singles ever recorded.

The video was shot in four hours on November 10, 1975 and took just five hours to edit, at a total cost of £4,500. It was aired on *Top Of The Pops* for the first time on November 20, the groundbreaking promotional clip helping to kick-start the video age.

The single entered the chart on November 8, 1975 and reached number one just three weeks later. It became the first record since Paul Anka's million-selling 'Diana' to spend nine weeks at the summit of the Official Singles Chart and its sales not surprisingly passed the one million mark.

That alone would make it one of the most successful UK singles ever. However, in late December 1991, a month after the death of Freddie Mercury (on November 24), the record re-entered the Official Singles Chart at number one, fought off all-comers for five weeks and again sold in excess of one million copies. It therefore became the only single to be a Christmas number one on two separate occasions and the only one to claim the top spot in four different calendar years (1975, 1976, 1991 and 1992). To date, the song has charted on four separate occasions, racking up 31 weeks on the UK Singles Chart (33 if you include 2009's version with The Muppets).

In the US, it was a Top 10 hit in 1976 and again in 1992, when it featured in the film *Wayne's World*, the soundtrack of which topped the albums chart and drove the re-released single to number two on the *Billboard* Hot 100. American sales are also well over one million, and it is one of only a handful of singles to be included in both the Grammy and Rock and Roll Halls of Fame.

The influence of 'Bohemian Rhapsody' lives on. On the occasion of the 50th anniversary of the Official Singles Chart in November 2002, a poll of music fans brought 188,357 responses, with the resounding result being that 'Bohemian Rhapsody' was named the nation's favourite number one of all time – with 117 per cent more votes than John Lennon's second-placed 'Imagine'.

BROTHERHOOD OF MAN 1976
SAVE YOUR KISSES FOR ME

WRITERS: Tony Hiller, Martin Lee, Lee Sheriden

PRODUCER: Tony Hiller

ALBUM: Love And Kisses From Brotherhood Of Man

PEAK POSITION: Number 1 (6 weeks)

WEEKS ON CHART: 16

SALES: 1.01m

The Eurovision Song Contest is the most popular music competition the world has ever known. Every year since it started in 1956, it has attracted huge TV audiences right across Europe and has provided countless pan-European hits. For many years, a British chart placing was taken as read for the UK entry – several of which have topped the chart – but only one has managed to sell over one million copies in the UK alone: 'Save Your Kisses For Me' by Brotherhood Of Man, which won the competition in 1976.

The original Brotherhood Of Man had been put together by songwriter/producer/publisher Tony Hiller in 1969. The group, which included top session singers Tony Burrows, John Goodison, Roger Greenaway, Sue Glover and Sunny Leslie, enjoyed a major international hit with 'United We Stand' in 1970, but, in 1972, after failing to score similar success, Hiller unveiled a new line-up with Lee Sheriden, Martin Lee and Nicky Stevens, adding Sandra Stevens (no relation).

Signed to Pye Records' new Dawn label, the revamped act's first recordings, 'Lady' and 'Kiss Me Kiss Your Baby', sold few copies in the UK but charted in several European countries. The act proved especially popular in Belgium and the Netherlands.

'Save Your Kisses For Me' had been written by Sheriden in August 1974. At first the rest of the group were not over-keen, even after it was rewritten as 'Oceans Of Love'. However, one year later, when another song was needed for their new album, Sheriden submitted the original again and with some added input from Lee and Hiller, it was accepted.

The song initially seems to be the tale of a man going to work and saying goodbye to his wife – only at the very end does it emerge he is singing to his three-year-old daughter. Initially in the studio, Sheriden took lead vocals, but group consensus decided that Lee's voice was better suited. Hiller had always been a Eurovision fan and, when a change to UK selection competition rules allowed acts to submit their own compositions, he entered 'Save Your Kisses For Me'.

The group beat 11 other UK acts to win the UK's A Song For Europe competition at the Royal Albert Hall on February 25, 1976. The single entered the Official Singles Chart on March 13, and two weeks later stood at number one, a position it held for six weeks until replaced by earlier Eurovision winners ABBA, with 'Fernando'.

It was at number one in the UK when the Eurovision Song Contest took place on April 3 at The Hague in Holland. Performing, the guys in the group wore suits (one white, one black) and the girls wore jumpsuits (one white, one red, with matching berets). They stood still, but eye-catching arm and leg choreography helped make them memorable and they were easy winners, scoring an exceptional 164 points. That was an average of 9.65 points per jury – 80.4 per cent of the total possible vote – and seven countries gave them a maximum 12 points.

'Save Your Kisses For Me' went on to top many European charts and is estimated to have sold over five million copies worldwide. It was the top-selling single of 1976 in the UK, and in the US it headed the *Billboard* Easy Listening chart (also reaching the pop Top 30), outselling a cover version by four-time chart-topper Bobby Vinton.

It was the first of a hat-trick of UK number ones for Brotherhood Of Man, while the long-player it appears on, *Love And Kisses From Brotherhood Of Man*, gave them the first of four UK Top 20 albums.

ABBA 1976

DANCING QUEEN

| WRITERS: Stig Anderson, Benny Andersson, Björn Ulvaeus |
| PRODUCERS: Benny Andersson, Björn Ulvaeus |
| ALBUM: Arrival |
| PEAK POSITION: Number 1 (6 weeks) |
| WEEKS ON CHART: 20 (1976, 15; 1992, 5) |
| SALES: 1.06m |

ABBA are the most successful mixed-sex group of all time and the biggest-selling non-UK or non-US act ever, with a staggering 11.2 million singles sales in the UK, nine number one singles and eight successive number one albums. And 'Dancing Queen' is their biggest-selling UK single.

The Scandinavian group opened the UK market to records from mainland Europe. ABBA's greatest hits collection, *Gold*, which is the only record to have topped the UK chart on three separate occasions, is the third biggest seller in UK history and one of only three albums to have sold more than five million copies – alongside The Beatles' *Sgt. Pepper's Lonely Hearts Club Band* and Queen's *Greatest Hits*.

Recording started at the Glen Studio in Stocksund, Sweden, on August 4, 1975, with the song originally called 'Boogaloo' (named after a 1960s R&B dance), while group members/composers Benny Andersson and Björn Ulvaeus said it was inspired by the rhythm of George McCrae's 1974 chart-topper 'Rock Your Baby'.

In September 1975, Agnetha Fältskog and Anni-Frid Lyngstad added their lead vocals but the track was not completed until a few months later. Andersson called it "one of those songs where you know during the session that it's going to be a smash hit".

ABBA first performed 'Dancing Queen' for King Carl Gustaf and Queen Silvia of Sweden on the eve of their wedding on June 18, 1976, at an all-star Royal Variety Show.

On September 4, 1976, the song jumped from number 16 to the top slot on the Official Singles Chart, their third successive chart-topper that year following 'Mamma Mia' and 'Fernando'. It was also a featured track on the group's album *Arrival*, which topped the British bestsellers for 10 weeks in 1977. 'Dancing Queen' remained at the top for six weeks and stopped both Wings ('Let 'Em In') and Rod Stewart ('The Killing Of Georgie [Part I and II]') adding to their table-topper tallies. It also headed the charts in over a dozen other countries around the world.

Ulvaeus and Andersson were already veterans of the Swedish music scene when they joined forces with their respective romantic partners Fältskog and Lyngstad – both of whom had their own solo careers – and renamed themselves ABBA in 1973. After domestic success, the act broke internationally with their Eurovision Song Contest entry 'Waterloo' in 1974, which topped the UK chart that April.

Although the group considered themselves relative failures in the US, they amassed 10 Top 20 singles there, with 'Dancing Queen' selling over one million copies and giving them their only number one. The Scandinavian superstars never managed a Top 10 US album entry; however, eight of their albums earned a Gold record or better, and *Gold: Greatest Hits*, although failing to even make the Top 40 at the time, has since sold over six million copies Stateside.

In June 1992, Erasure's version of 'Dancing Queen', from their EP *ABBA-esque*, topped the UK chart, and three months later ABBA's original rendering was reissued and again reached the Top 20, while *Gold* (which, of course, includes the track) topped the chart. The arrival of the digital age helped push UK sales of 'Dancing Queen' past the one million mark in September 2010, and US digital sales alone are reported to be over 500,000.

Interest in ABBA has been maintained by the musical *Mamma Mia* (in which 'Dancing Queen' plays a major part), which has grossed more than £1.2 billion worldwide and has been seen by over 42 million people since it was launched in 1999. The 2008 film version is the most successful British-made movie of all time and was the world's highest-grossing musical film ever, taking over £300 million. Equally impressive is the fact that in the UK, where the soundtrack album topped the chart, it was the highest-grossing film ever, with over £69 million taken at the box office.

SHOWADDYWADDY 1976

UNDER THE MOON OF LOVE

WRITERS: Tommy Boyce, Curtis Lee

PRODUCER: Mike Hurst

ALBUM: Greatest Hits

PEAK POSITION: Number 1 (3 weeks)

WEEKS ON CHART: 15

SALES: 1m

Oddly, in the 1970s, there were more UK groups having hits in the late Fifties rock'n'roll/doo-wop style than there ever were in that actual era.

In the pre-Beatles rock years, Britain had only a handful of successful groups, mainly clean-cut pop acts like The King Brothers, The Mudlarks and The Springfields. In comparison, many more 1970s British bands adopted Fifties sounds and classic rock'n'roll images – including Darts, Matchbox and Shakin' Stevens & The Sunsets – even top pop acts such as Mud, Alvin Stardust and Wizzard nodded to Fifties styles.

Few of these rock'n'roll rejuvenators were more popular than Showaddywaddy, who clocked up 15 Top 20 entries on the Official Singles Chart in five years and have ultimately sold over one million copies of 'Under The Moon Of Love'.

In the early 1970s, Leicester's Choice and The Golden Hammers were two of countless similar-sounding rock bands playing the UK's club and pub circuits. While both were playing at the Fosse Way pub, they decided to get together one night a week and play old-style rock'n'roll. When this proved more popular than their usual rock sets, they permanently joined forces in 1973 and, like the similarly-inclined US band Sha Na Na, named themselves after an oft-used doo-wop vocal group nonsense phrase, 'Shoo-waddy-waddy'.

Bell Records signed the act after they came second on the top-rated TV talent show *New Faces*, and the band's first single, the self-composed 'Hey Rock And Roll', narrowly missed the top spot in May 1974. Hit then followed hit for the teddy boy-dressed octet, which featured two lead vocalists (Dave Bartram and Buddy Gask), two drummers (Malcolm Allured and Romeo Challenger), two bass players (Rod Deas and Al James) and two lead guitarists (Russ Field and Trevor Oakes).

Although they had other original hits, they are probably best remembered for their lively covers of oldies such as 'Three Steps To Heaven' (Eddie Cochran), 'When' (The Kalin Twins), 'You Got What It Takes' (Marv Johnson) and 'Dancin' Party' (Chubby Checker).

The catchy 'Under The Moon Of Love' was first released in 1961 by Curtis Lee as the follow-up to his US Top 10 hit 'Pretty Little Angel Eyes' (also a hit for Showaddywaddy, in 1978), although it only reached number 46 in the US. Both songs were co-written by Lee and Tommy Boyce and the originals were produced by the then up-and-coming Phil Spector.

Boyce later went on to co-write (with Bobby Hart) numerous songs for The Monkees, and after the success of this Showaddywaddy track he relocated to the UK and produced another successful British retro act, Darts.

'Under The Moon Of Love' climbed to number one on the Official Singles Chart in December 1976 and, during its three-week stay at the summit, prevented Queen from reaching the top with 'Somebody To Love'. Like most of their singles, it was produced by Mike Hurst, who had previously discovered Cat Stevens and worked with acts including Marc Bolan, The Move and Manfred Mann.

'Under The Moon Of Love' – number one when the Sex Pistols made their UK chart debut with 'Anarchy In The UK' – started a run of seven successive Top 10 hits for the group and helped push Showaddywaddy's *Greatest Hits* album into the Official Albums Chart Top Five in December 1976.

Despite spending 209 weeks on the UK Singles Chart and scoring five Top 10 albums (including their chart-topping second volume of *Greatest Hits* in 1978), Showaddywaddy have never received the critical acclaim or respect their success might seem to merit.

But their music clearly endures – this single tipping over the edge to become a million seller by virtue of the downloads sold since 2004.

DON'T GIVE UP ON US

WRITER: Tony Macaulay

PRODUCER: Tony Macaulay

ALBUM: David Soul

PEAK POSITION: Number 1 (4 weeks)

WEEKS ON CHART: 16

SALES: 1.16m

David Soul was not the first US actor to have a number one hit in the UK – Tab Hunter and Lee Marvin had managed it before – and he was not even the first TV cop to top the pops, as Telly Savalas (aka 'Kojak') had headed the list a year earlier. He was, however, the first to sell over one million copies of a single in the UK alone.

Born David Solberg in Chicago in 1943, Soul's first record was 'Covered Man', released in April 1966, and he performed under that name on Merv Griffin's US TV talk show, singing with his face covered by a ski mask.

A 1967 appearance in US kids TV series *Flipper* kick-started his acting career and, over the next few years, Soul had parts in many top TV shows, including *Star Trek*, *I Dream Of Jeannie* and *All In The Family*, before winning a starring role in the popular US series *Here Come The Brides*.

However, he found wider fame in 1975, starring alongside Paul Michael Glaser as Detective Ken 'Hutch' Hutchinson in the series *Starsky & Hutch*, a cop show which became a global hit, despite Soul's own reservations about it being "formula TV".

The show continued until 1979 and, in the middle of its run, Soul signed to Private Stock Records. He had already finished recording an album when label head Larry Uttal received a demo of 'Don't

Give Up On Us' from British composer/producer Tony Macaulay. He thought it could be an ideal Soul single, so quickly arranged a session for the singer with Macaulay. Within days they were in the studio and it was rush-released as Soul's first single in the UK. His album was also re-cut, with this song replacing Neil Sedaka's composition 'One More Mountain To Climb'.

Composer Macaulay's previous compositions included UK number ones 'Baby Now That I've Found You' (The Foundations), 'Let The Heartaches Begin' (Long John Baldry), 'Love Grows (Where My Rosemary Goes)' (Edison Lighthouse) and 'You Won't Find Another Fool Like Me' (The New Seekers).

The single first reached the Official Singles Chart on December 18, 1976 and was number one by January 15, 1977, a position it held until being replaced by Julie Covington's 'Don't Cry For Me Argentina' – another million seller by another actor.

'Don't Give Up On Us', which was also big in Europe and a number one record in Australia, topped the *Billboard* Hot 100 three months later. However, Soul is regarded as a one-hit wonder in his homeland as the follow-ups, 'Going In With My Eyes Open' and 'Silver Lady', failed to reach the Top 40. In the UK, the former reached number two, while the latter gave him a second UK chart-topper.

1977 was a bumper year for Soul. 'Don't Give Up On Us' was the year's top-selling single and he was the top-selling solo artist, appearing in the Silver Jubilee Royal Variety Show. In total, Soul scored five UK Top 20 singles and two Top 10 albums. He said at the time: "I don't want to sell a few million singles and then disappear – I want to be an album artist with longevity."

Soul, who now has dual US and UK citizenship, may never have attained that status, but he enjoyed an enviable track record as a singer and has continued to work on stage and TV or in movies.

JULIE COVINGTON 1976

DON'T CRY FOR ME ARGENTINA

WRITERS: Andrew Lloyd Webber, Tim Rice

PRODUCERS: Andrew Lloyd Webber, Tim Rice

ALBUM: Evita

PEAK POSITION: Number 1 (1 week)

WEEKS ON CHART: 18 (1976, 15; 1978, 3)

SALES: 1.01m

The biggest-selling single by a British female solo artist in the first 50 years of the Official Singles Chart had a fairly inauspicious start to its career.

Julie Covington made her singles chart debut at number 37; two weeks later, the record had still only clawed its way to position 25.

This was hardly the opening Tim Rice and Andrew Lloyd Webber might have expected from the first fruits of their latest musical project, *Evita*, a 'rock opera' and subsequent stage/film musical based on the life story of Eva Perón (Argentina's First Lady from 1946-1952), but by mid-February the single had climbed to the top of the pile.

Although Covington (born in London, in 1946) had years of theatre experience and had released an album in 1971, she was best known as 'rock chick' Dee, vocalist with fictitious band The Little Ladies from the 1976 TV drama *Rock Follies*. The programme's soundtrack topped the UK Albums Chart for three weeks and Covington was offered the principal role on Rice and Lloyd Webber's new album project.

For *Evita*'s big hit number, Rice had wanted a generic love song lyric that would work outside of the context of the musical. Various ideas were tried – at one point Covington recorded the title line as "it's only your lover returning" – but nothing sounded quite right.

In the end, the words "don't cry for me Argentina" were redeployed from elsewhere in the draft and assigned as the song's title.

The single was a global success, hitting the top spot in Belgium, Holland and Norway. It was also the number one single of 1977 in Australia, where it spent seven weeks in pole position. The album reached number four in the UK and produced a further Top 20 hit for Barbara Dickson ('Another Suitcase In Another Hall').

However, the more successful the project became, the more Covington seemed to back away from it. The actress declined to promote her hit single on *Top Of The Pops* during its nine-week run in the Top 10 and was replaced by a video collage featuring images of Perón. Similarly, when the album was to be made into a West End musical, Covington was not interested – a decision that launched the mainstream career of singer Elaine Paige, who took the stage role.

When *Evita* opened in 1978, in addition to providing a Top Three hit for one of its stars, David Essex, with 'Oh What A Circus', Covington's 'Argentina' charted again. By the stage show's opening night in London, she was back on UK TV screens, reprising her role in *Rock Follies Of '77*, the soundtrack of which produced a Top 10 hit, 'O.K.?', on which she was credited alongside co-stars Charlotte Cornwell, Rula Lenska and Sue Jones-Davies.

Covington made another TV appearance in October 1977 performing a cover of Alice Cooper's 'Only Women Bleed', at the inaugural BRIT Awards, where she won Best British Female Newcomer. The song would eventually reach number 12 and be Covington's final UK singles success, although she went on to become one of the featured performers on Jeff Wayne's *The War Of The Worlds* album, which has sold over 2.5 million copies in the UK alone.

Covington's signature anthem has continued to sell, rejuvenated by the digital age, with downloads helping to push it over the one million mark – making her one of only four UK female soloists to emulate the feat alongside *X Factor* winners Alexandra Burke and Leona Lewis, plus the world-conquering Adele.

Rice and Lloyd Webber's composition also remains the only million-selling recording in the UK to subsequently inspire as many as three Top 30 cover versions: The Shadows, Mike Flowers Pops and – most successfully – Madonna, who played the lead in the film version of *Evita*, which also starred Antonio Banderas and Jonathon Pryce.

MILLION-SELLING MEMORIES

SIR ANDREW LLOYD WEBBER

'Don't Cry For Me Argentina' was taken from your musical, *Evita* – did you ever think that it might become a number one when you were writing it, or when it was being recorded by Julie Covington?

Evita was always intended to be a stage show. And 'Don't Cry For Me Argentina' was very specifically written to be a key moment in the theatre, but the fact it became a hit was incidental. I couldn't really understand how it became such a big hit. It was six minutes long, it had a one-minute instrumental by the London Symphony Orchestra and Julie Covington refused to promote it. It even went to number one in the disco chart, which I just couldn't understand. I asked a friend of mine who was a DJ, why was it so popular – he said, "Because DJs are playing it to clear the dance floor" [laughs].

So, do you always look to write a chart hit for your musicals?

I always want great melodies in my shows, but I don't come from the view of, "Can I write a number one hit?" And I'm very proud to say I write songs with great melodies. Of course, it's great if those songs then get to number one – and, of course, with 'Sing' I'm back in the club.

When you were working on 'Sing' with Gary Barlow did you expect it to be another chart-topper?

I thought that it was one of those things that people might say, 'It's just the Jubilee single'. But what I was aiming to do was try to write a song that would travel. And in the last few months I have heard from people in Canada, South Africa and other Commonwealth countries, all of whom want to use the song in another guise. We have also had 15,000 downloads of the sheet music, which is fantastic.

Your other million seller, 'No Matter What', was different from 'Don't Cry For Me Argentina' in that it was recorded by an established pop act. How did the collaboration with Boyzone come about?

Yes, Boyzone recorded the song from *Whistle Down The Wind*. Stephen

Gately wanted to record it, so they did and it was finished and done. But Louis Walsh and Universal didn't want to release it. They just didn't. It is a very funny story, but I went out with [Capital radio programmer] Richard Park to see the Chinese Elvis in Lewisham, we had something to eat and then Richard came back to my home. He asked if I had anything to play him, so I played him 'No Matter What' by Boyzone – and Richard said, "It's an absolute smash. It will be on Capital Radio at 7 a.m. tomorrow morning." This was at 2 a.m. in the morning! But it went to number one just a few weeks later.

Very few artists can claim more than one million seller – is there a secret ingredient to a million-selling single?

No, of course not. The one thing that you have to have is a love of great pop records. I adore great songs; when I think back to when I was a kid, I loved great songs. The first single I remember buying was 'When' by The Kalin Twins. In those days, you didn't hear things on the radio, you just heard about records. I still have my vinyl collection – I think it's the biggest in the world. I've got a library of them, full of anything The Everly Brothers, The Beatles, Elvis has ever released.

So what do you think of modern music?

I can't miss what is going on at the moment, because my son is working at Island Records. I do find melody to be a little short right now, to be honest. I couldn't do a lot of what is connected to the production of the songs today, it just isn't something I could do. I think melody will have to come back at some point. I don't believe 'Don't Cry For Me Argentina' would even get airplay today.

DONNA SUMMER 1977

I FEEL LOVE

WRITERS: Pete Bellotte, Giorgio Moroder, Donna Summer

PRODUCERS: Giorgio Moroder, Pete Bellotte

ALBUM: I Remember Yesterday

PEAK POSITION: Number 1 (4 weeks)

WEEKS ON CHART: 27 weeks (1977, 11; 1982 (remix), 10; 1995, 5; 2012, 1)

SALES: 1.05m

Donna Summer's career was dominated by two singles – the controversial 'Love To Love You Baby' and the groundbreaking 'I Feel Love'. But it was the latter which became the American singer's biggest single in the UK.

Born LaDonna Gaines in Boston just after the Second World War, Summer began singing in public aged 10; by 19, she was living in New York and fronting rock band Crow. After failing to get a deal, she auditioned for the musical *Hair* and was offered the chance to take a role in the version being staged in Munich.

Over the next few years, Summer made Germany her home, learning the language, securing a short-lived solo deal with Decca and marrying Austrian actor Helmuth Sommer. When they divorced in 1976, she decided to keep his surname, but in its anglicised version: Donna Summer was born.

While working as a backing singer, she met Munich-based Italian producers Giorgio Moroder and Pete Bellotte and finally secured her own deal with the Ariola label. Her first album, *Lady Of The Night*, was a moderate success, but *Love To Love You Baby* (including its provocative title track, complete with heavy breathing and suggestive moaning) moved her to another level, embedding her deep in the world of disco.

But the biggest track of her career (certainly in the UK, where 'Love To Love You Baby' was banned by the BBC) was yet to come.

'I Feel Love' emerged from the recording of her concept album *I Remember Yesterday*, on which Summer ran through a range of stylistic changes, as she led the listener on a tour through musical history, from the Forties through to the present day and into the future, where 'I Feel Love' was presented as an anthem.

Until that time, disco had relied on predominantly acoustic instruments and sounds, and followed traditional verse-chorus-verse-chorus structures. 'I Feel Love' changed all of that, Moroder laying an otherworldly Summer vocal with minimal lyrics on top of a synthesized backing track full of mechanised beats and electronically sequenced rhythms. The producer had been a pioneer in introducing synthesizers on pop records back in early 1972 with Chicory Tip's UK number one 'Son Of My Father'.

Initially six minutes long, it was also released in an eight-minute extended version and even a 15-minute 53-second remix by Patrick Cowley, an underground classic on the New York club scene.

The record's impact was immense. It was a four-week number one on the UK's Official Singles Chart in July 1977 and a hit in clubs and in mainstream charts around the world. But it also influenced a range of artists over the following decades – from Brian Eno to New Order, through Duran Duran and Madonna to Moby.

While it was Summer's only UK number one, she continued to make hits for years to come. *Once Upon A Time* in 1977 was another concept album recorded with Moroder and Bellotte, as was 1979's *Bad Girls* (which tackles the knotty issue of prostitution). Replacing Moroder with Quincy Jones on 1982's *Donna Summer* produced further UK Top 20 hits in the form of 'State Of Independence' and 'Love Is In Control (Finger On The Trigger)'. 'She Works Hard For The Money' (1983) kept the hits flowing, while 1989's *Another Place And Time* represented a resurgence, with 'This Time I Know It's For Real' and 'I Don't Wanna Get Hurt' both breaking the UK Top 10.

But, throughout it all, 'I Feel Love' remained the dominant force in Summer's career, covered by artists like Bronski Beat and Red Hot Chili Peppers. In the 35 years since it appeared, the single charted on three separate occasions (in 1977, 1982 and 1995) and it has continued to sell more than 10,000 copies a year, without any promotion, the dawn of the digital age nudging it over the line to become one of the UK's most recent million sellers. Following her death from cancer aged 63 in May 2012, it once again reached the Top 50 on the Official Singles Chart.

BING CROSBY 1977

WHITE CHRISTMAS

WRITER: Irving Berlin	
PRODUCER: Uncredited	
ALBUM: Merry Christmas	
PEAK POSITION (SINCE 1952): Number 5 (2 weeks)	
WEEKS ON CHART (SINCE 1952): 16 (1977, 7; 1985, 2; 1998, 4; 2007, 3)	
SALES: 1.01m	

The world's biggest-selling single (according to Guinness World Records) is also the oldest UK million seller, recorded by the artist who has had more US chart entries than anyone. But it took until after Bing Crosby's death for this all-time classic to finally chart in the UK.

Back in the 1940s, Bing was King, reportedly banking an average annual record royalty cheque of around £150,000 (equivalent to more than £4 million in 2012). Before the UK's singles chart launched in 1952 he had numerous massive hits, the most successful being 'White Christmas', a huge seller every year between 1942 and 1950.

Irving Berlin was born Israel Baline in Belarus in 1888, his family moving to the US when he was five. By the time he penned 'White Christmas' he was arguably the world's best-known popular music songwriter. A list of his hits would fill this page, but they include 'Let's Face The Music And Dance', 'There's No Business Like Show Business' and 'God Bless America'.

As legend has it, Berlin wrote 'White Christmas' on January 8, 1940 (the fifth birthday of Elvis Presley, whose version he disliked so much he tried to get it banned from radio in 1957). Although Jewish, Christmas meant a lot to the songwriter, as it was on that day in 1928 that his only son, Irving Berlin, Jr., died when only a few days old.

Tacoma, Washington-born Harry Lillis 'Bing' Crosby was the first vocalist to become a superstar in the big band era, making his recording debut in 1926. His record sales (singles and albums) are estimated to be over 300 million. However, he was not just the top recording artist of the 1930s and 1940s but also among the top radio and movie stars of those decades – and one of the top-earning entertainers of all time.

Crosby reportedly first sang 'White Christmas' on US radio on Christmas Day 1941 and recorded it in just two takes during the summer of '42, backed by John Scott Trotter's orchestra and The Ken Darby Singers. Its appearance in his 1942 movie *Holiday Inn* saw it become an instant, unstoppable hit and a US number one two months before Christmas.

Other versions reached the US Top 20 in 1942, but it was Crosby's which passed the two million mark there and over one million copies of the sheet music were sold (now over five million). His rendering was also an overnight UK hit, with the song topping the Music Publishers Association sheet music chart in November 1942 and becoming Britain's best-selling single by mid-December. 'White Christmas' was awarded the Oscar for Best Movie Song in 1942, when presenter Irving Berlin had the unique experience of giving himself the award.

Every Christmas for the rest of the decade, Crosby's record returned to the top rungs of the US chart and was among the UK's top-sellers. That led to the 'masters' becoming so worn that, on March 18, 1947, Crosby had to re-record the song, this later version being used ever since. It was also a featured track on Crosby's *Merry Christmas* album, which topped the *Billboard* chart every Christmas from 1945 to 1950, spending a total of 39 weeks at number one.

Global sales of 'White Christmas' are now estimated to be in the region of 50 million, with a similar amount being sold on albums. Both the single and Crosby's *Merry Christmas* album have charted every year since 1963, on separate *Billboard* Holiday charts.

Things were very different in the UK however – until just after Crosby's death of a heart attack while playing golf on October 14, 1977. Buoyed by the nostalgia following his death at the age of 74, 'White Christmas' climbed to number five in Christmas week 1977.

'White Christmas', which contains just eight different lines of lyric, has been recorded over 500 times and has charted in the UK by eight different artists. Crosby's timeless recording is also in the Grammy Hall of Fame. The ever-modest Irving Berlin may have been right when he said: "It's not only the best song I've written, but the best song anyone has written!"

WINGS 1977

MULL OF KINTYRE/ GIRLS' SCHOOL

WRITERS: 'Mull Of Kintyre' – Paul McCartney, Denny Laine/'Girls' School' – Paul McCartney

PRODUCER: Paul McCartney

ALBUM: London Town

PEAK POSITION: Number 1 (9 weeks)

WEEKS ON CHART: 17

SALES: 2m

Paul McCartney is, quite rightly, best known for his Beatles work, yet this Wings single remains the biggest seller of his lengthy career. It was the biggest single of the Seventies and the fourth biggest of all time in the UK, outstripping any release by The Beatles or their members' solo projects.

The Mull of Kintyre is at the most southerly tip of the Kintyre peninsula in south-west Scotland, but is most significant to McCartney as a location near to his home, High Park Farm, which he had bought during the *Revolver* era. Today, the area remains best known as the subject of this track, recorded at Abbey Road Studios during sessions for Wings' sixth album *London Town*.

In 1977, Wings were fighting their corner in an era when punk rock was dominating the headlines in the UK. Paul was the hardest working ex-Beatle and his band the most prolific – although rarely the most critically acclaimed – producing almost an album a year from 1971 onwards, and in 1976 their *Wings At The Speed Of Sound* album and Wings Over The World tour had both proved hugely popular.

'Mull Of Kintyre' (and its double A-side, 'Girls' School') emerged in late 1977 after what had been a turbulent year for the group. Initial sessions in the Virgin Islands and at London's Abbey Road became complicated by Linda McCartney falling pregnant (with son James). In turn, drummer Joe English and lead guitarist Jimmy McCulloch left the band – albeit after making their contributions to what would become two record-breaking tracks.

Recording for the album was abandoned in summer 1977, with Wings by now comprising the two McCartneys plus band stalwart, guitarist Denny Laine (ex-Moody Blues). However, 'Mull Of Kintyre'/'Girls' School' was released on November 11, 1977. Featuring bagpipes from a local Mull pipe band on the A-side, it entered the Official Singles Chart one week later and held the top spot for nine weeks. It became 1977's Christmas number one, the biggest-selling single of all time at that point and the first two million-selling single in the UK.

It also topped the charts in Australia, as well as Germany, Benelux and Scandinavia. But in the US, 'Mull Of Kintyre' never quite took off – there, 'Girls' School' was the lead track and attracted more airplay, although it reached a relatively lowly 33 on the *Billboard* Hot 100.

'Mull Of Kintyre'/'Girls' School' ultimately proved the beginning of the end for Wings. Parent album *London Town* followed the iconic single in March 1978, but never came close to achieving anything like the same level of success, peaking at number four in the UK and two in the US.

The commercial failure of 'Mull' and the under-performance of *London Town* in the US resulted in the collapse of McCartney's relationship with Capitol Records there; Wings subsequently signed to Columbia, who released the next – and final – Wings album *Back To The Egg* in the US, although the act and McCartney remained with EMI for the rest of the world.

Through much of 1979, McCartney recorded a follow-up to his 1970 solo album *McCartney* (the imaginatively titled *McCartney II*), before reforming Wings for a US tour. However, in January 1980 on the eve of Japanese dates, he was arrested for possession of marijuana at Tokyo Airport, jailed for nine days and then deported. Further touring plans were scrapped, then Wings' recording sessions later that year were abandoned following the December murder of John Lennon in New York.

Wings had effectively folded, a fact confirmed officially by McCartney in April 1981. The longest standing post-Beatles solo band was over – but left, as its legacy, the biggest non-charity single of all time.

BONEY M. 1978

RIVERS OF BABYLON/ BROWN GIRL IN THE RING

WRITERS: 'Rivers Of Babylon' – Brent Dowe, Trevor McNaughton, Frank Farian, Reyam/ 'Brown Girl In The Ring' – Frank Farian

PRODUCER: Frank Farian

ALBUM: Nightflight To Venus

PEAK POSITION: Number 1 (5 weeks)

WEEKS ON CHART: 40

SALES: 2m

Boney M. were the outstanding singles act in the biggest pre-digital year in history for singles sales – the only act to have recorded two of the 10 biggest singles in the history of the UK's Official Singles Chart.

The star of Boney M. was, in reality, the Svengali who stood out of the limelight – German producer, songwriter and vocalist Frank Farian. He created Boney M. in 1974 when he stepped into the studio in Offenbach, Germany, to record his song 'Baby Do You Wanna Bump'. It was a moderate hit in continental Europe for Farian, who at that point called himself Zambi.

However, TV wanted a live act. Reluctant to take the limelight, Farian decided to recruit a band that could 'represent' his music. Over a period of 18 months, he ran through a series of line-ups for Boney M., before settling on the best-known grouping of Marcia Barrett, Bobby Farrell, Liz Mitchell and Maizie Williams.

Signed to the West German label Hansa Records, Farian began recording Boney M. in 1976. He and Jamaican-born British resident Mitchell laid down most of the vocals, with Barrett also contributing, for what became *Take The Heat Off Me*. The album's biggest hit was 'Daddy Cool', which was their breakthrough track, first in Germany and then in the UK, where it reached the Top 10. Another extracted hit single, the Bobby Hebb cover 'Sunny', followed in 1977, as did the album *Love For Sale* and the further chart success 'Ma Baker'.

But 1978 was Boney M.'s monster year, as 'Rivers Of Babylon'/'Brown Girl In The Ring' became an absolutely huge international hit. The single became the group's first UK number one in May, staying at the top for five weeks. The two records are currently the UK's fifth and sixth biggest-selling singles of all time, with a sales total of more than four million between them.

Adapting the words of a Biblical psalm, 'Rivers Of Babylon' was a Rastafarian song written by Brent Dowe and Trevor McNaughton and recorded by The Melodians in 1970, but little known in Europe at the time. 'Brown Girl In The Ring' was a West Indian children's song named after a playground game, which had previously been recorded by Mitchell, but this time saw Farian take the writing credit.

The single occupied the top slot on the UK's Official Singles Chart for five weeks but was slipping down the chart as it began its fourth month on the listing (and fifth on air). At that point, weary of the lead song, UK radio reverted to play-listing the flip side, 'Brown Girl In The Ring'.

By this time it was mid-July and, after dropping to number 20 in its 13th week on the chart, the single (now widely credited as a fully-fledged double A-side) began to climb again. By mid-September, it found itself back at number two, in its 20th week on the singles chart. By the time it had slipped out of the Top 10 again, in its 23rd week on the Top 40, it was primarily because of the arrival of the band's next single, 'Rasputin'.

It was not until the end of October 1978 that 'Rivers Of Babylon'/'Brown Girl In The Ring' finally slipped out of the Top 40, for the first time in the 27 weeks since its April entry – a journey that had followed the path 21-2-1-1-1-1-1-2-3-6-10-18-20-18-10-6-5-4-3-2-3-5-10-21-28-37.

In the midst of this remarkable chart story Boney M.'s third album, *Nightflight To Venus*, also took them to new heights, giving the band their first number one album. But 'Rivers Of Babylon', 'Brown Girl In The Ring' and 'Rasputin' were not the end of the story. There was another two million seller still to come at Christmas.

MILLION-SELLING MEMORIES

LIZ MITCHELL
(BONEY M.)

How does it feel to have been involved in two of the top 10 biggest singles in British musical history? And do you have a favourite?

It makes me feel really happy, but it feels a little unbelievable. People love the songs – they have their own personal connection to the songs, they remember particular moments because of particular songs. And that makes me feel very proud. I don't really have a favourite. They all have their own special meaning. When you are creating a song, when you are giving life to that song, you are bringing it into the present so that whoever hears it can feed from it, because music is the food of our soul. Afterwards, you don't dissect your own work – but when I go out to work [at live gigs] and I see what the songs do, that is amazing.

How did you become involved in Boney M.?

I actually didn't know Frank Farian. I was in Germany playing in the musical *Hair* and did about a year and a half in the show. Then I joined a choir called the Les Humphries Singers, but after that I launched a solo career. That didn't go very well, so I went back to college and had a call from someone trying to do a show, of mostly Les Humphries' repertoire. Someone told Frank and he made his way to see me in Berlin and got me to demo the following morning. And the record company must have liked me…

What are your greatest memories of that time?

There were so many wonderful moments. But the most outstanding memory has to be going to Russia in 1978. We were invited by the government and to be involved in something so momentous was really quite special. Our going there really was the beginning of the whole change in Russia – the Russian people never let me forget that. And 'Rivers Of Babylon' played a huge part – it was a song which meant so much to many Russian Jews.

When did you first realise how huge Boney M. had become?

When 'Daddy Cool' became a hit, I was very happy because it meant we weren't going to waste the year. Even Frank wasn't sure it was going to continue. Our first two albums were really successful, but nobody anticipated how big *Night Flight To Venus* would become [the parent album of 'Rivers Of Babylon', 'Brown Girl In The Ring', 'Rasputin' and 'Mary's Boy Child'].

I didn't really know how big we were until later, in the Nineties really. I was sitting in an airport in Singapore and talking to someone, and all of a sudden a voice said from nowhere, "I don't know who it is, but that's the voice of Boney M." He hadn't even seen me. That was just amazing.

Frank Farian is viewed in different ways by different people, through his work with Boney M. and then, notoriously, with Milli Vanilli. What was he like to work with?

Frank's name became such a focus for the band because the Germans were so proud to have a successful producer working with foreign artists on international music. Even Bobby [Farrell] was uplifted by the Dutch [his home nation], but it was very sad that, rather than us getting the credit for what we had done, it was the producer. I am a British singer and have always been disappointed I have never received any recognition in the UK for what I was involved in, even now.

Who were your heroes and inspirations back at the start of your career?

That is such a huge question. Between 14 and 17, I listened to the radio – I liked rock-steady reggae and my parents' music like Jim Reeves and Sam Cooke. Plus The Supremes were fantastically important.

What are you doing now?

I have the Let It Be Foundation, which supports young people in this country. We take them on a trip to Gambia once a year, although we would like to do it more often. And I still love performing.

JOHN TRAVOLTA & OLIVIA NEWTON-JOHN 1978

YOU'RE THE ONE THAT I WANT

WRITER: John Farrar

PRODUCER: John Farrar

ALBUM: Grease (soundtrack)

PEAK POSITION: Number 1 (9 weeks)

WEEKS ON CHART: 35 (1978, 26; 1998, 9)

SALES: 2m

No artist can top actor-turned-singer John Travolta's UK chart debuts – his first two hits not only topped the Official Singles Chart, but both also sold more than one million copies.

In Britain, New Jersey boy Travolta first tasted success in 1977 as the star of the disco movie *Saturday Night Fever*. However, in his homeland, he initially found fame in the role of high school rebel Vinnie Barbarino in popular TV comedy series *Welcome Back, Kotter*, which first aired in September 1975. This led to him getting a record deal with Midland International and scoring a US Top 10 single in July 1976 with his version of UK singer/songwriter Gary Benson's 'Let Her In'.

Before relocating to the West Coast in search of a movie career, Travolta had toured and played on Broadway in the stage musical version of *Grease* before *Saturday Night Fever* (1977) turned him into a worldwide star (at the tender age of 24, he was nominated for an Oscar for his *Fever* role as Tony Manero).

His first singing role in a film came in *Grease*, when he was teamed with Olivia Newton-John in the respective roles of Danny Zuko and Sandy Olsson.

English-born, Australian-raised Newton-John had already amassed half-a-dozen UK Top 20 entries since making her debut in 1971 with

'If Not For You'. She was also not a movie virgin, having starred in the Don Kirshner (The Monkees, The Archies) and Harry Saltzman (James Bond) 1970 sci-fi musical *Toomorrow*, which was intended to launch a group of that name featuring Olivia.

Most of the songs in *Grease* had been featured in the stage musical that originally opened Off Broadway on Valentine's Day 1972. However, when it became apparent that a couple more songs were needed, 'You're The One That I Want' was written especially for the movie by ex-Shadows member John Farrar, who also produced the track.

The single was released shortly before the film and was an instant hit on both sides of the Atlantic. In the UK, where it became the first million seller by a duo, it dethroned Boney M.'s two million-selling 'Rivers Of Babylon'/'Brown Girl In The Ring', and held the top slot for two months in summer 1978.

In the US, despite selling two million copies, it only managed one week at the top in June, replacing another male/female duo, Johnny Mathis and Deniece Williams, who had been on top with 'Too Much, Too Little, Too Late'.

It was also a number one hit right around the globe, passing the one million sales mark in both France and Germany, spending 18 weeks at number one in Norway and becoming the year's biggest-selling single in both Germany and Australia.

Grease premiered in the US on June 16, 1978 and Travolta went on to pick up a Golden Globe award for Best Actor in a Musical or Comedy for his role. The soundtrack album topped the Official Albums Chart for 13 weeks and has continued to sell well ever since, with total sales in excess of 2.5 million. In the US, it stood at number one for 12 weeks, notching up total sales to date of over eight million copies.

'You're The One That I Want' has also been a UK hit for comic actors Hylda Baker & Arthur Mullard (1978) and Craig McLachlan & Debbie Gibson (1993).

The original Travolta and Newton-John recording also reached the Official Singles Top Five on another two other occasions: in 1990 it was part of 'The Grease Megamix' (along with 'Summer Nights' and Travolta's solo smash, 'Greased Lightnin''), and in 1998 it climbed all the way to number four. It is without doubt one of the most popular and timeless film or show songs ever.

JOHN TRAVOLTA & OLIVIA NEWTON-JOHN 1978

SUMMER NIGHTS

WRITERS: Warren Casey, Jim Jacobs	
PRODUCER: Louis St. Louis	
ALBUM: Grease (soundtrack)	
PEAK POSITION: Number 1 (7 weeks)	
WEEKS ON CHART: 19	
SALES: 1.59m	

Not only did John Travolta and Olivia Newton-John become the first duo to sell one million copies of a single in the UK, but they repeated that feat soon afterwards. In fact, there was a gap of just two number ones at the top of the UK's Official Singles Chart between their previous single, 'You're The One That I Want', and 'Summer Nights'.

The idea of making a film from the hit musical *Grease* was already well advanced before Newton-John got involved. Initially, producer/screenplay writer Allan Carr had considered Marie Osmond for the part of Sandy and Henry 'The Fonz' Winkler for Danny. However, Winkler was worried about being typecast and dropped out, and Osmond considered the role of Sandy a little too raunchy for her.

Carr signed Travolta as the male lead and, after meeting Newton-John at a Hollywood party thrown by fellow Australian singer Helen Reddy, he asked her to audition for the part.

Newton-John said the audition was "the most important thing I've done in my career", and admitted being "very mixed up and frightened". She was not worried about playing the pony-tailed, innocent, sweet, demure Sandy, but was not sure how fans would take to her metamorphosis into a leather-clad, gum-chewing biker's chick – so she phoned Travolta on the set of *Saturday Night Fever* and he soothed her fears.

Once Newton-John was on board, she introduced her regular

backing musician and good friend John Farrar to the *Grease* team and he composed two songs for the film, 'Hopelessly Devoted To You' (a transatlantic Top Three hit for Newton-John) and the multi-million-selling 'You're The One That I Want'.

'Summer Nights' was written by Jim Jacobs and Warren Casey, who wrote the story for *Grease* and most of the songs in the original stage musical. Before making it to the big screen, their musical had played a record-breaking 3,883 performances on Broadway – which, to put it in perspective, means that 'Summer Nights' was sung more times on Broadway than there were actual summer nights in the whole of the 1950s. As for the film, it is one of the all-time most successful musicals, having taken over £205.2 million at the box office.

The single entered the UK's Official Singles Chart in September 1978, and two weeks later leapt from number 11 to the top slot, where it remained for seven weeks, ensuring that in total the duo spent 16 weeks at number one during the summer and autumn of 1978.

'Summer Nights' not only stopped Boney M. achieving three successive number ones by halting the progress of 'Rasputin' – it also prevented John Travolta having his only solo chart-topper with the *Grease* track 'Sandy'. Although a little less successful internationally than 'You're The One That I Want', 'Summer Nights' was a Top Five hit in most major territories around the globe, including the US.

On the downside, it could be noted that the duo's next film and single together – *Two Of A Kind* and 'Take A Chance', in 1984 – had few takers. But on the upside, if you're going down in music history as two-hit wonders, then the hits just don't get bigger than those enjoyed by John Travolta and Olivia Newton-John on those summer nights and days back in 1978.

VILLAGE PEOPLE 1978
Y.M.C.A.

WRITERS: Henri Belolo, Jacques Morali, Victor Willis	
PRODUCER: Jacques Morali	
ALBUM: Cruisin'	
PEAK POSITION: Number 1 (3 weeks)	
WEEKS ON CHART: 26 (1978, 16; 1993, 7; 1999, 3)	
SALES: 1.46m	

As 1978 drew to a close, having been stuck at number two in the Official Singles Chart behind Boney M.'s second UK million seller of the year ('Mary's Boy Child – Oh My Lord'), it looked as if the Village People's ode to the Young Men's Christian Association may have peaked. However, when the New Year came, demand for the track continued to grow, with reported sales of more than 150,000 copies in a single day over the festive period and it broke through to claim a three-week slot at number one.

The Village People (a reference to New York City's Greenwich Village) was the brainchild of French-born producer Jacques Morali, who enlisted vocalist Victor Willis to perform songs about US gay capitals, with a backing dance troupe of macho moustachioed models.

The act's first single release, 'San Francisco (You've Got Me)', spent six weeks on the lower rungs of the UK Top 50 at the tail-end of 1977 but did not chart in the US, although it bubbled under the *Billboard* Hot 100 for 30 weeks, selling 100,000 copies in the process.

A year on, Morali had replaced the models with guys who could sing as well as pose and launched the act's most successful line-up, casting each member as a gay stereotype or fantasy. Willis took the role of a cop, joined by Felipe Rose as an American Indian, construction worker David Hodo, G.I. Alexander Briley, cowboy Randy Jones and 'Leather Man' Glenn Hughes. The band's third album, *Cruisin'*, was ready to hit the shops and lead single 'Y.M.C.A.' was unleashed.

Willis' lyrics worked on two very different levels, with some hearing the song as a genuine attempt to encourage disaffected young males to spend time engaging with like-minded individuals in the range of activities provided, while others – aware of the Y.M.C.A.'s reputation as a popular meeting location among the gay community at the time – perceived a less innocent level to lines such as "You can hang out with all the boys."

Whatever the lyrical intent, 'Y.M.C.A.' went Gold in France and Germany, also topping charts in Australia, Holland and Belgium and selling two million copies in the US, despite only reaching number two there (it was kept off the top spot initially by Chic's 'Le Freak' then Rod Stewart's 'Da Ya Think I'm Sexy?'). It was the second of the group's three consecutive million-selling singles in America (between 'Macho Man' and 'In The Navy'), each one of which was also accompanied by a million-selling album release Stateside.

A perennial wedding disco/Christmas party favourite, 'Y.M.C.A.' returned to the UK chart as a 1993 PWL remix and again as a Millennium Mix by Almighty in 1999. Billy Connolly parodied the song and the band's UK number two follow-up, 'In The Navy', on his summer 1979 hit 'In The Brownies' and, more recently, it was adapted for a TV advertising campaign by insurance company confused.com.

However, the band will likely be remembered most for their use of elaborate arm movements in performance to spell out the letters Y, M, C and A. Although copied across the globe, it was not the group's idea; the formation of the Y was part of   the dance routine in the song's video, but the remaining letters were first added by the audience during a January 1979 edition of US TV music show *American Bandstand*, on which the Village People were guesting.

The group's other legacy, which could be taken as a delicious irony, is the fact that the Village People's June 1979 Official Singles Chart number 15 hit, 'Go West' (subsequently taken to number two by the Pet Shop Boys in 1993), interpreted by many as a paean to a gay utopia, has been used for many years as the tune to chants by fans at UK football grounds.

BONEY M. 1978

MARY'S BOY CHILD/
OH MY LORD

WRITERS: 'Mary's Boy Child' – Jester Hairston, Frank Farian, Fred Jay/'Oh My Lord' – Frank Farian

PRODUCER: Frank Farian

ALBUM: N/A

PEAK POSITION: Number 1 (4 weeks)

WEEKS ON CHART: 10 (1978, 8; 2007, 2)

SALES: 1.85m

As Christmas 1978 approached, Boney M. had already logged one million-selling single for the year, in 'Rivers Of Babylon'/'Brown Girl In the Ring'. 'Mary's Boy Child – Oh My Lord' made it a double.

Comprising German producer/songwriter Frank Farian and performers Marcia Barrett, Bobby Farrell, Liz Mitchell and Maizie Williams, Boney M. had been a consistent presence on the UK Singles Chart for an unbroken run of 34 weeks during 1978 (through 'Rivers Of Babylon'/'Brown Girl In The Ring' and 'Rasputin') when 'Mary's Boy Child/Oh My Lord' was released.

Earlier in the year, the band's *Nightflight To Venus* album project had attracted unwelcome press coverage after Boney M. creator Farian admitted in German tabloid magazine *Bravo* that Williams and Farrell did not sing on the records and that he was not only their producer, but also the main vocalist alongside Mitchell.

At the time, the revelation sparked something of a furore, yet unlike a similar Farian confession 10 years on, which destroyed his later act Milli Vanilli, the controversy blew over and fell well short of damaging the act. After 'Rivers Of Babylon'/'Brown Girl In the Ring', 'Rasputin' kept Boney M. in the UK chart. And then came 'Mary's Boy Child – Oh My Lord'.

The single was a medley of the established Christmas song 'Mary's Boy Child' and Farian's own new composition 'Oh My Lord'. 'Child' had previously been recorded by a range of singers, including UK music hall/film star Gracie Fields, but was made a hit by US singer Harry Belafonte in 1957. It is one of the very few songs to sell one million UK copies in more than one recording.

Recorded hurriedly in the autumn, the single did not appear on *Nightflight To Venus* (unlike its two predecessors and its spring 1979 successor 'Painter Man'), but immediately maintained Boney M.'s chart presence. It hit the number one spot in the UK in its second week on the Official Singles Chart and remained at the summit for four weeks before giving way to Village People's 'Y.M.C.A.'. Falling away after Christmas, the single chalked up eight weeks in the Top 40 before dropping out and ending Boney M.'s unbroken 42-week presence in the Singles Chart.

While Boney M. would never again reach the heights of 'Rivers Of Babylon'/'Brown Girl In The Ring' or 'Mary's Boy Child – Oh My Lord', they continued to have hits in 1979 – 'Painter Man' and 'Hooray! Hooray! It's A Holi-Holiday' both reached the Top 10, while 'Holiday''s parent album, *Oceans Of Fantasy*, hit number one.

But things then began to slide. While Europe continued embracing new material, the UK public's interest began to wane. Although greatest hits album *The Magic Of Boney M. – 20 Golden Hits* became a number one and racked up 26 weeks in the chart, the group never again scored a Top 10 with new material. By 1982, Bobby Farrell had been fired (replaced by Reggie Tsiboe who, unlike Farrell, actually sang on subsequent recordings) and the act's UK chart career was finished.

Varying versions of the group have returned at different times in the intervening 30 years, and a range of remixes, remix albums, megamixes and greatest hits has appeared, but no new material emerged with enough appeal to make the UK charts. In December 2010, Bobby Farrell died following a heart problem, ending any prospect of the 'original' Boney M. coming back together.

Boney M.'s light shone for a relatively short period on the UK scene, but did so with incredible intensity as they became the only band with two singles among the UK's Top 10 biggest sellers of all time.

Frank Farian, meanwhile, went on to work with many other artists, eventually amassing more than 800 gold and platinum records.

IAN DURY & THE BLOCKHEADS 1978
HIT ME WITH YOUR RHYTHM STICK

WRITERS: Ian Dury, Chaz Jankel

PRODUCER: Laurie Latham

ALBUM: N/A

PEAK POSITION: Number 1 (1 week)

WEEKS ON CHART: 20 (1978, 15; 1985, 4; 1991, 1)

SALES: 1.11m

Crippled by polio as a child, Ian Dury was the most unlikely pop star, an irresistible musical force whose emergence was made possible by the punk rock revolution of the mid to late Seventies. In the form of 1978 chart-topper 'Hit Me With Your Rhythm Stick', he and his band The Blockheads gave new wave arguably its most mainstream signature tune.

Born in wartime Harrow, north-west of London, Dury was seven when he contracted polio from an open-air swimming pool in Southend. He was already in his late twenties – working as a teacher – when he formed his first band, Kilburn & The High Roads, who made their live debut in 1971.

Favourites on the London pub rock circuit, Dury drew attention to himself with a stage act that saw him flaunting his disability, a confrontational style which was a direct extension of his own personality and predated the spirit of punk by half a decade. After unsuccessful spells with the Raft and Dawn labels, the band broke up in 1975. The singer carried on as Ian Dury & The Kilburns, recruiting pianist and guitarist Chaz Jankel, with whom he developed a lasting songwriting partnership.

The pair began to assemble a line of songs which would form the heart of Dury's debut solo album, *New Boots And Panties!!* (1977).

Without a label, and passed on by a string of major record companies, their managers Peter Jenner and Andrew King popped to the label next door, Stiff Records (then home to Elvis Costello, Nick Lowe and Wreckless Eric).

Impressed with what they heard, Stiff released 'Sex & Drugs & Rock & Roll' as Dury's debut solo single, following it with *New Boots And Panties!!* However, it was only after a successful slot on a Stiff 'package' tour that the label began to really put marketing effort into the project.

The 1978 single 'What A Waste' saw Dury & The Blockheads in the Official Singles Top 10, but it was 'Hit Me With Your Rhythm Stick' that took him from being a major name on the pub rock scene to the top of the chart.

The single had not featured on *New Boots*, but was put together by Dury and Jankel during a rehearsal session and based on old lyrics from a couple of years before. Recorded in the Workhouse Studio in south London, it was instantly recognised by the pair as a potential hit and was scheduled for release with 'There Ain't Half Been Some Clever Bastards' as its B-side.

The single arrived at the end of a year dominated by a queue of monster number ones including Wings' 'Mull Of Kintyre', Kate Bush's 'Wuthering Heights', 'Rivers Of Babylon'/'Brown Girl In The Ring' and 'Mary's Boy Child – Oh My Lord' by Boney M., 'You're The One That I Want' and 'Summer Nights' by John Travolta & Olivia Newton John and the Commodores' 'Three Times A Lady'.

It was a highly competitive market, and 'Hit Me With Your Rhythm Stick' took seven weeks to reach the top of the Official Singles Chart, eventually usurping Village People's 'Y.M.C.A.' to hit the summit at the end of January 1979. While the single only held the number one spot for a week (it was unseated by Blondie's 'Heart Of Glass'), it retained a Top 10 position for seven weeks and stayed at number two for three weeks.

The success drove the subsequent 1979 album *Do It Yourself* to the act's highest albums chart position of number two, with accompanying single 'Reasons To Be Cheerful (Part 3)' peaking at number three.

Further albums followed, including 1981's solo *Lord Upminster* (featuring the controversial 'Spasticus Autisticus') and 1988's *Mr Love Pants* (a reunion with The Blockheads), but 'Rhythm Stick' was easily Dury's career sales high point in any territory.

BLONDIE 1979
HEART OF GLASS

WRITERS: Deborah Harry, Chris Stein	
PRODUCER: Mike Chapman	
ALBUM: Parallel Lines	
PEAK POSITION: Number 1 (4 weeks)	
WEEKS ON CHART: 12	
SALES: 1.27m	

Blondie's fifth UK hit, 'Heart Of Glass', was the first of six Official Singles Chart number ones for the US new wave/pop act – the first five of which would top the chart within a 21-month period.

Fronted by Debbie Harry, the band had emerged from the fledgling New York City punk scene in 1975, although one-time Playboy Bunny Harry had made her recording debut in 1968 as a member of an unsuccessful psychedelic folk band, The Wind In The Willows. She met her future Blondie partner Chris Stein in her next band, The Stillettoes.

By the time of Blondie's third album, *Parallel Lines,* in 1978, the band's sound had lost most of its punk edge, thanks in part to the involvement of Australian-born, UK-based producer Mike Chapman (co-producer of The Sweet, Suzi Quatro, Smokie, Mud), and had made its Singles Chart breakthrough with 'Denis' in February 1978.

Blondie had actually demoed 'Heart Of Glass' in 1975 under the title 'Once I Had A Love' and recorded another arrangement in 1978. It was referred to by the band as 'The Disco Song', as it marked a departure from the group's New Wave sound.

'Heart Of Glass' was the third single from *Parallel Lines*, following 'Picture This' and 'Hanging On The Telephone', which had charted at 12 and five respectively in the UK Singles Chart. However, the album had managed just two weeks in the Official Albums Chart Top 10 following a September 1978 release. The following January, as demand for 'Heart Of Glass' grew, it went stratospheric, going on to spend 35 weeks in the Top 10, spawning a further chart-topping single ('Sunday Girl') and becoming the UK's best-selling album of 1979.

The track was written by Harry with her long-term partner, the band's guitarist Chris Stein, and was the first of three UK number ones on which she received a writing credit (the others being 'Atomic' and 'Call Me'), making her the first female to do this. The band's *Parallel Lines* line-up was completed by Frank Infante (guitar), Jimmy Destri (keyboards) and Clem Burke (drums), along with lone Brit bass player Nigel Harrison.

A lyric change took place in the transition from album track to UK single release to guarantee all-important daytime radio play, with the potentially controversial "Soon turned out to be a pain in the ass" being dropped in favour of a more radio-friendly repeat of the title line from the first verse, although foreign imports soon started to appear featuring album version edits.

'Heart Of Glass' spent four weeks as Britain's number one and also sold one million copies in the US, becoming the first of three transatlantic chart-toppers for Blondie. 'Heart Of Glass' and 'Sunday Girl' each hit the UK number one spot in their second week on the chart, particularly unusual for the third and fourth single releases from an album, and both were among the UK's Top 10 best-selling singles of the year. No act clocked up more weeks on the singles chart in 1979 and only Art Garfunkel's 'Bright Eyes' outsold 'Heart Of Glass'.

For two weeks in February 1979, Blondie was number one in both the Official Singles Chart and Official Albums Chart in the UK, a feat only Elvis Presley, The Shadows, Cliff Richard, The Beatles, The Rolling Stones, The Monkees, Simon & Garfunkel, Rod Stewart, T. Rex, The Stylistics, Queen and ABBA had achieved thus far. Blondie were also the only US act to have UK number one singles in the Seventies, Eighties and Nineties, while a remix by Diddy (UK producer Richard Dearlove) returned 'Heart Of Glass' to the UK Top 20 in 1995.

Blondie's span of just over 20 years from this track's first week at number one to the band's last week at the top of the Official Singles Chart with a newly recorded track ('Maria' in February 1999, by which time Harry was 53 years old) is an accomplishment reflecting success and longevity that has been bettered only by Cliff Richard and the Bee Gees.

I WILL SURVIVE

WRITERS: Dino Fekaris, Freddie Perren

PRODUCERS: Dino Fekaris, Freddie Perren

ALBUM: Love Tracks

PEAK POSITION: Number 1 (4 weeks)

WEEKS ON CHART: 25 (1979, 15; 1993, 10)

SALES: 1.02m

"The first true superstar of the disco era" is how *Billboard* magazine described Gloria Gaynor – the singer best remembered for the dance floor anthem and timeless karaoke classic 'I Will Survive'.

Born into a poor household in Newark, New Jersey in 1949, Gaynor had a string of low-paid jobs before releasing her first single in 1965, subsequently touring with various bands as a featured singer. After a couple of false starts, her first real success came in 1974, the year the disco music craze really took off in the US.

That year, the first ever *Billboard* Disco Action chart showed Gaynor at number one with her revival of The Jackson 5's 'Never Can Say Goodbye'. The following year, she again topped that listing with 'How High The Moon'/'Casanova Brown', and was named the Queen of Disco by America's National Association of Discotheque DJs.

Gaynor would be the first to admit that for the next couple of years she lost that crown to Donna Summer – but she was, indeed, a survivor and, in 1979, bounced back with one of disco's biggest ever hits.

Before teaming with Gaynor, writer/producer Freddie Perren had co-written The Jackson 5's first three million sellers, produced three albums for Tavares and was a producer on the *Saturday Night Fever* film soundtrack.

In 1978, Polydor asked Perren to produce Gaynor's version of a Righteous Brothers recording, 'Substitute'. Perren agreed on the understanding that he could provide the B-side (which would earn him extra income). Perren's writing partner Dino Fekaris consulted Gaynor about the sort of subject matter she would like to sing about, and together the writers penned the uplifting 'I Will Survive'.

Legend has it that, at the recording session, Perren and Fekaris provided Gaynor with the words written on a brown paper bag, having left the original lyric sheet at home. Unlike most other disco-targeted tracks it had a relatively clean, uncluttered sound and did not feature backing vocalists. Somewhat appropriately, given the song's sentiment, Gaynor recorded it wearing a back brace, having had a serious fall on stage in Europe shortly before the session.

The singer was taken with the track, saying she liked to give listeners "songs that would have a positive impact on their lives". However, since neither Polydor nor the composers saw its potential, it remained as the B-side when the single was released on October 27, 1978.

Undeterred, Gaynor promoted 'I Will Survive' during her many club appearances and encouraged disco DJs to play it. After 'Substitute' failed to climb higher than number 107 in the US, the label bowed to pressure from discos and flipped it. To promote 'I Will Survive', a video was made at Xenon Discotheque in New York that showcased Sheila Reid-Pender of local roller-skating group The Village Wizards.

'I Will Survive' took off and on March 17, 1979 simultaneously topped the UK and US singles charts, heading the UK Official Singles Chart for four weeks and the *Billboard* Hot 100 for three. In Britain, it replaced the Bee Gees' 'Tragedy' at number one and held Village People's 'In The Navy' at number two. In the US, where it sold over two million copies, it took over from Rod Stewart's 'Da Ya Think I'm Sexy?' before being dethroned by 'Tragedy'.

Disco albums were not normally big sellers, but in Gaynor's homeland the single's parent album, *Love Tracks*, reached the Top Five and sold over one million copies. The Grammy-winning single went on to become a big hit in many other countries and has become, arguably, the best-known anthem for both feminists and gay rights campaigners. It returned to the UK chart at various points over the coming years, in versions by country singer Billie Jo Spears (1979), Diana Ross (1996), Chantay Savage (1996) and alternative rock band Cake (1997).

ART GARFUNKEL 1979

BRIGHT EYES

WRITER: Mike Batt

PRODUCER: Mike Batt

ALBUM: Fate For Breakfast

PEAK POSITION: Number 1 (6 weeks)

WEEKS ON CHART: 19

SALES: 1.2m

Taken from a tear-jerking 1979 animated movie depicting the internecine battles among rabbits living on Watership Down, 'Bright Eyes' is arguably one of the most sentimental (and heart-rending) songs ever recorded.

Six months after Simon and Garfunkel's *Greatest Hits* album had finally dropped off the Official Albums Chart, record-buyers were probably in need of a gentle reminder why Art Garfunkel had been 50 per cent of the most successful recording duo of all time with his childhood friend and fellow New Yorker Paul Simon.

On the face of it, however, 1979 appeared not to be the year in which to make a triumphant return to the UK chart with a poignant ballad. The kids were down with disco and new wave, and the number ones before 'Bright Eyes' that year were the Village People's 'Y.M.C.A.', 'Hit Me With Your Rhythm Stick' by Ian Dury & The Blockheads, Blondie's 'Heart Of Glass', 'Tragedy' by The Bee Gees and Gloria Gaynor's 'I Will Survive'.

Garfunkel's dreamy melodies, however, had once before captured the hearts and minds of the British public, when 'I Only Have Eyes For You' crowned the chart at the height of Bay City 'Rollermania' in 1975. He duly repeated the trick when 'Bright Eyes' not only locked down number one in the Official Singles Chart for six weeks but also became the biggest-selling single of 1979. That was quite an achievement, with the likes of Queen, ABBA, The Police, Michael

Jackson and the aforementioned Blondie providing some tough competition.

The song was the creation of musician/producer/songwriter (and, lest we forget, Wombles group creator) Mike Batt. Up to this point, Batt's resumé was eclecticism personified. It included four trips to the Top 10 as the writer and main performer behind The Wombles, the ecologically sound furry characters from a popular kids' TV and book series. He'd also enjoyed success as a producer with Steeleye Span's 'All Around My Hat' and Elkie Brooks' 'Lilac Wine' and scored a Top 10 hit under his own name, 1975's 'Summertime City'.

Offered the chance to add another string to his bow by *Watership Down* director Martin Rosen, Batt put pen to paper, enlisted the help of his hero, Arthur 'Art' Garfunkel, and the rest is history – just like those poor bunnies.

Garfunkel himself was said to be "knocked out" by 'Bright Eyes' after being sent a demo of the "surreal, lovely, dark" song. "I knew my own tone of voice has a quasi-religious pop element to it and I knew that I could create goose bumps with this mysterious enquiry into 'what is this life and what is death for all of us?'", proclaimed Garfunkel in a 2009 interview with the BBC.

Batt's composition was a perfect fit for *Watership Down*, featuring prominently in the film when rabbit leader Hazel (voiced by award-winning British actor John Hurt) cheats death after being peppered with shotgun pellets on Nuthanger Farm. It also provided a shot in the arm for Garfunkel's album *Fate For Breakfast*, which was only kept off the top spot by ABBA's *Voulez-Vous* in May 1979, and remains his best-performing solo album.

'Bright Eyes' was denied a shot at the *Billboard* Hot 100 after it was omitted from the US version of *Fate For Breakfast*, but it was included on the Stateside release of Garfunkel's 1981 album *Scissors Cut*.

'Bright Eyes' has been interpreted by a number of artists, starting with The Shadows the same year, but most notably by the late Boyzone singer Stephen Gately for the animated TV series (1999–2001) of *Watership Down*, and perhaps most surprisingly by the Manic Street Preachers (their live version appears on the group's compilation album *Lipstick Traces*). But nobody comes close to matching Garfunkel's dreamy delivery and his ability to enhance the song's tear-welling potency, as he did so successfully on such Paul Simon compositions as 'America' and 'Bridge Over Troubled Water'.

PINK FLOYD 1979

ANOTHER BRICK IN THE WALL (PART II)

WRITER: Roger Waters

PRODUCERS: David Gilmour, Bob Ezrin, Roger Waters, James Guthrie

ALBUM: The Wall

PEAK POSITION: Number 1 (5 weeks)

WEEKS ON CHART: 12

SALES: 1.08m

It is probably understating matters to say that Pink Floyd are the antithesis of 'a singles act' – and prime evidence, if it were needed, is the 12 years and 260 days which elapsed between their first Official Singles Chart hit in March 1967 and their second with December 1979's 'Another Brick In The Wall (Part II)'. But when Pink Floyd took the number one spot, they did it with style – their five-week spell at the top racking up a number of firsts and curiosities.

For a start, that gap represents the longest wait any UK group has had between entering the chart and topping it with newly recorded material. In turn, 'Brick' became the band's only UK single release of the decade, the final number one of the 1970s, as well as the first of the 1980s, while also becoming their final Top 20 single (up to the present day, that is).

Curiously, it was also the first Official Singles Chart-topper to include a part number in its title, its parent album, *The Wall*, featuring three tracks with the same title suffixed by the relevant sequence number.

And it became that year's Christmas number one, holding off Top Five hit 'Rapper's Delight' by The Sugarhill Gang, the first UK chart hit to feature rapping.

Founded in 1965, Pink Floyd consisted of four university students – Syd Barrett, Nick Mason, Roger Waters and Richard Wright – who were joined by Dave Gilmour in 1967, before Barrett's departure the following year. The Floyd's only hit singles had been their debut 'Arnold Layne' (number 20) and 'See Emily Play' (number six) in 1967, but the departure of Barrett had seen the previously quirky psychedelic band from Cambridge evolve into one of the bastions of the album-oriented progressive rock movement.

Conceived by Pink Floyd bassist Roger Waters, who had increasingly taken the mantle of the band's main writer post-Barrett, *The Wall* is a concept album exploring, principally, the theme of personal isolation, this particular track commenting on disillusionment with the education system.

Initially consisting of just one verse and a chorus, producer Bob Ezrin saw commercial potential in the track and, having earlier performed production duties on another school-related anti-establishment UK chart-topper (Alice Cooper's 'School's Out', from 1972), he arranged for children from Islington Green School in north London to go to Pink Floyd's nearby Britannia Row Studios and record the vocals for the repeated second verse and chorus in their best Cockney accents.

Cartoonist Gerald Scarfe created an accompanying video combining live action of kids in a London playground overseen by a menacing, cane-wielding, teacher-hammer puppet with animation depicting school as a meat mincer for young minds. The result was a global success, not least in America where the single topped the *Billboard* Hot 100 for four weeks and sold one million copies, becoming the second biggest seller of the year Stateside, trailing only Blondie's 'Call Me'. *The Wall* had a consecutive 15-week run at the top of the US albums chart and was 1980's best-selling album.

When *The Wall* was translated into an Alan Parker-directed film starring Bob Geldof in 1982, 'Brick' won a BAFTA for Original Song, but it also achieved fame of a different kind when it was banned in South Africa at the start of the 1980s after being adopted by supporters of a school boycott in protest against racial inequalities in the education system under apartheid.

Although subsequent releases by the band failed to hit the UK Top 20, a remix of this track by Swedish DJ/producer Eric Prydz, billed as 'Proper Education' and credited to Eric Prydz vs. Floyd, reached number two in January 2007.

ADAM & THE ANTS 1981

STAND & DELIVER!

WRITERS: Adam Ant (Stuart Goddard), Marco Pirroni

PRODUCER: Chris Hughes

ALBUM: Prince Charming

PEAK POSITION: Number 1 (5 weeks)

WEEKS ON CHART: 15

SALES: 1.03m

On the UK pop scene, 1981 was definitely the Year of the Ant, with a veritable insect infestation of both the UK's Official Singles and Albums Charts, resulting in two of the year's Top Three best-selling singles and two of its Top 10 albums. Adam & The Ants' total of 91 weeks on the Official Singles Chart was the highest annual tally since Engelbert Humperdinck amassed 96 weeks during 1967.

That figure is even more impressive considering the band only released three new tracks as singles during the year – and the first did not appear until May, when 'Stand & Deliver!' made The Ants only the eighth act in UK chart history to have a single go straight to number one (the others being Elvis Presley – twice, Cliff Richard & The Shadows, The Beatles with Billy Preston, Slade – three times, Gary Glitter, The Jam and The Police) and only the second act, after The Jam, to do so with their first chart-topper.

Londoner Stuart Goddard formed Adam & The Ants in 1977, but despite building a loyal live following, was unable to achieve major success until a change of image to the 'glam pirate' look, unveiled in 1980, saw the band's new line-up firmly tagged as part of the emerging New Romantic movement, attracting a new audience.

Had it not been for the tragic death of John Lennon at the end of 1980, the band might have claimed four official number one hits in a nine-month period, 'Antmusic' being held at number two in January '81 as Lennon's 'Imagine' completed its own journey to one million sales, then a reissue of the band's number 48 hit from the previous year, 'Kings Of The Wild Frontier', was denied top billing in March by Roxy Music's Lennon tribute, 'Jealous Guy'.

Contributing one-third of the band's singles chart total for 1981 were releases from Decca and Do It Records, who were keen to capitalise on the 'antmusic' phenomenon by issuing old recordings from the act's pre-CBS days, with 1978 single 'Young Parisians' becoming a Top 10 hit.

Although released in November 1980, *Kings Of The Wild Frontier* emerged as the top album of 1981. After an initial two-week spell at number one in January 1981, growing colonies of Ant fans provided a majestic return to the albums top spot in March for 10 consecutive weeks, the longest run of any Official Albums Chart number one (excluding hits compilations and soundtracks) since Simon & Garfunkel's *Bridge Over Troubled Water* in 1970, and not beaten until Adele's *21* completed 11 consecutive weeks at the top in April 2011.

Their next album, *Prince Charming*, produced both 'Stand & Deliver!' and 'Prince Charming'. Both singles demonstrated how Adam & The Ants – perhaps more than any of their contemporaries – fully utilised the new opportunities to project an image through promo videos. The video for 'Deliver!' featured their flamboyant, face-painted frontman as the 'dandy highwayman', whose weapon of choice was a mirror, forcing others to consider the lack of imagination in their own appearance.

The official follow-up, 'Prince Charming' (with a video starring British actress Diana Dors as Ant's fairy godmother), also went to number one for four weeks from September 1981. In the process, it deposed the only single to outsell both of the band's chart-toppers by year-end, Soft Cell's 'Tainted Love'.

The *Prince Charming* album peaked at number two, having spent its first three weeks on the Official Albums Chart in the runner-up spot behind Queen's *Greatest Hits* (the UK's all-time bestseller) following its release in November 1981. Extraordinarily, given the level of their success in 1981, Adam disbanded his Ants in March 1982.

Going solo, with former Ant Marco Pirroni by his side, Adam Ant's solo career started with a number one ('Goody Two Shoes') but faded soon after that. Though Adam never recaptured the magic of 1981, recent years have seen him back on the road and attracting headlines.

SOFT CELL 1981
TAINTED LOVE

WRITER: Ed Cobb

PRODUCER: Mike Thorne

ALBUM: Non-Stop Erotic Cabaret

PEAK POSITION: Number 1 (2 weeks)

WEEKS ON CHART: 44 weeks (1981, 30; 1985, 6; 1991, 8)

SALES: 1.27m

In 1981, Soft Cell was a little-known synth-pop duo, and 'Tainted Love' was an obscure Northern soul tune, but together they created a timeless Eighties classic which topped charts around the world.

The achievement is all the greater as the duo had looked in danger of being dropped by their label at the time 'Tainted Love' emerged.

Born in Southport, England (but a frequent teenage visitor to London's Soho), Marc Almond formed Soft Cell with Blackpool-born David Ball while they were both studying at Leeds Polytechnic in 1978. Early live shows and a self-produced EP drew the interest of a handful of independent labels, including Mute and Some Bizzare, the group eventually signing with the latter, while some of their initial recordings were produced by the founder of the former (Daniel Miller).

But after the act's first single, 'Memorabilia', failed to trouble the singles chart, doubts had set in. The pressure was certainly on for the duo to break out of the underground and justify their deal.

Soft Cell offered a compelling combination of Ball's clinical synth sounds with Almond's soaring torch song vocals, backed by a sleazy aesthetic borrowed from the grimy backstreets of London's Soho. 'Tainted Love', with its lyrical theme of forbidden love, was a perfect match.

The relatively obscure Northern soul tune was written by US

songwriter Ed Cobb, formerly of male vocal quartet The Four Preps, for American soul/gospel singer Gloria Jones, who would later become best known in the UK as the partner of Marc Bolan. Jones recorded the single in 1965, as the B-side to 'My Bad Boy's Comin' Home', a comprehensive flop – until the track was picked up by the UK's northern soul clubs.

Soft Cell took the song apart and reconstructed it to create a timeless electronic anthem, coupled with a similarly transformed new version of The Supremes' 1964 hit 'Where Did Our Love Go?'. For the seven-inch single, the two tracks were A- and B-side, but they were mixed together for the 12-inch.

However, 'Tainted Love' was definitely the lead track. Climbing to number one on the UK Official Singles Chart in September 1981, it stayed there for two weeks, also topping the chart in more than a dozen other countries and reaching number eight on the *Billboard* Hot 100. It was named single of the year at 1982's BRIT Awards and the song (in Dave Ball's arrangement) has gone on to be covered by a long list of artists, including Marilyn Manson and the Pussycat Dolls.

Soft Cell continued for four albums, three of them recorded in New York City. The first, *Non-Stop Erotic Cabaret* (1981), was easily the most successful, peaking at number 22 in the US and at number five in the UK. At that time, the duo were spending more of their time in NYC, working on remix album *Non-Stop Ecstatic Dancing* – but, drawn into the city's drugs scene, the act slowly began disintegrating in the spotlight. The duo had already split by the time fourth album *The Last Night In Sodom* appeared, leaving a legacy of five Official Top 10 singles.

Their solo careers had already started before their split and continued, with Ball founding electronic dance group The Grid, while Almond became a chart star in his own right. Recasting himself as a bona fide 'torch singer', he scored a UK number one duetting with veteran Sixties pop singer Gene Pitney on 'Something's Gotten Hold Of My Heart' in 1989 and reached number four with 'The Days Of Pearly Spencer' in 1992 (taken from Almond's *Tenement Symphony* album).

Three decades later, 'Tainted Love' continues to be Almond's (and Soft Cell's) signature tune. It re-charted at number five in the UK in 1991, while the duo themselves reunited in 2001 for a series of live dates followed by the 2002 album *Cruelty Without Beauty*.

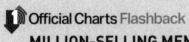

MILLION-SELLING MEMORIES
MARC ALMOND (SOFT CELL)

'Tainted Love' is one of the UK's biggest-selling singles of all time – did you have any ambition or expectation that it would be as successful when you first recorded it in 1981?

When we first started putting 'Tainted Love' into Soft Cell's live set we were curious about the reaction it would get. Electronic music at that time was meant to be cold and emotionless and about alienation. We wanted to be an electronic band with emotion and soul so we chose a northern soul number to put into our set for our audience to dance to. We never imagined that it would become as popular as it did. Who would think that? It took Soft Cell from being an underground art school band into the mainstream and fame. The fact our version is still played and is so popular, I find thrilling and amazing.

How did you come to record the track?

Dave Ball and I were both fans of northern soul, Sixties soul. Dave particularly was a real authority on it and he introduced me to a lot of great songs. He played me 'Tainted Love' by Gloria Jones and by Ruth Swan, which our version is probably closer to. I, of course, knew of Gloria, being a Marc Bolan fan, and I loved the title, lyrics and simple riff so it became part of our repertoire, the only cover we did at the time. It was very nearly Frankie Valli's 'The Night', which wouldn't have had the impact, I think. When we signed to Phonogram, it was an obvious, safe choice for a single. The rest is history.

Of course, yours is now widely viewed as the definitive version of the song (in fact, many people think it is the original version). How does it feel for it to have had that impact?

Our version was an introduction for a lot of people to northern soul and the original versions, particularly Gloria's. The song had really only been known by northern soul aficionados and was pretty obscure before that. Anyone that has covered it since has done so because of Soft Cell's version.

When you listen to it now, what do you think of 'Tainted Love' and its legacy?

It had such a different yet simple and infectious sound. Even though I've done many other successful things over the years, I look on 'Tainted Love' as a theme song and still love the reaction it gets when I sing it. It's wonderful that it is still being played at clubs, pubs and parties every Saturday night and is still on the radio somewhere all the time. Such a simple two and a half minutes has been a part of people's lives and memories and has given such joy and, of course, made me very successful. It opened a lot of doors for me.

When you and Dave Ball first came together to found Soft Cell, electronic music was still in its infancy. What and who were your influences at the time?

Soft Cell had quite arty influences but I loved punk and glam rock – Bowie, Bolan – disco, as well as Jacques Brel. Dave loved Kraftwerk, old soul, Giorgio Moroder – it was a real strange mixture of influences, but out of it came something original.

What music moves you now? How have your tastes evolved over time?

My tastes in music are very far ranging and eclectic; I'm very retro at the moment, rediscovering music I grew up with – I'm listening to lots of old school electronic music, late Seventies, very early Eighties, John Foxx, Giorgio Moroder, etc.

What was the first single you bought?

My first few singles were 'The Green Manalishi' by Fleetwood Mac, 'All Right Now' by Free, 'Ride A White Swan' by T. Rex and 'Sweet Dream' by Jethro Tull. I can't remember which one was the exact first.

THE HUMAN LEAGUE 1981

DON'T YOU WANT ME

WRITERS: Philip Oakey, Jo Callis, Philip Adrian Wright

PRODUCER: Martin Rushent

ALBUM: Dare

PEAK POSITION: Number 1 (5 weeks)

WEEKS ON CHART: 13

SALES: 1.54m

The Human League became the poster band for New Romantic pop when their signature tune 'Don't You Want Me' held the number one spot in the Official Singles Chart for five weeks in late 1981 and early 1982.

But, while the stylish image owed more to that newly emerged genre, the act's roots were embedded in Sheffield's industrial/electronic scene of the late Seventies; in reality, they were the first British band to take avant-garde electronica to the pop charts – albeit in a highly polished, slick style.

The Human League went through several incarnations, first emerging as The Dead Daughters and then The Future in 1977. Founded by keyboard players Martyn Ware and Ian Craig Marsh, The Future invited flamboyant hospital porter Phil Oakey to join them as vocalist – and renamed themselves The Human League, adding a non-playing member in Adrian Wright, whose slideshows and stage lighting were a key part of the band's visuals.

The first single, 'Being Boiled', was released through independent label Fast Product in summer 1978 and within a year the band signed to Virgin Records. But after two albums through the label – *Reproduction* and *Travelogue* – failed to find a commercial audience, Virgin began to lose faith.

In late 1980, the band were forced to choose which route to follow – creative or commercial. Ultimately, Oakey's desire to take a more commercial approach won out. Ware and Marsh jointly founded the British Electric Foundation and Heaven 17, leaving Oakey and Wright – now playing keyboards – to steer The Human League towards the commercial high ground.

Oakey recruited keyboards man Ian Burden, along with singers Susanne Sulley and Joanne Catherall (teenagers spotted dancing in a Sheffield nightclub), while ex-Rezillos guitarist Jo Callis joined in spring 1981. The resultant album, *Dare*, completed over a seven-month period with producer Martin Rushent, was a pop masterpiece which remains as fresh and vibrant today as it did on its release.

Despite *Dare* being criticised by the Musician's Union for threatening to rob musicians of work through its dependence on electronics, it was critically and commercially lauded. Quickly hitting number one in the UK's Official Albums Chart, it became one of the biggest hits of the year – so successful that Virgin chief Simon Draper insisted on another single being extracted before the end of the year.

Accompanied by a dramatic, polished promotional video, filmed in Slough by director Steve Barron, 'Don't You Want Me' had been relegated to final place on the album by Oakey, who believed it to be the poorest track. But it exploded, helping The Human League to claim both the official number one single and album of Christmas 1981. 'Don't' became a number one on the *Billboard* Hot 100, as well as across much of Europe and in New Zealand. In the UK, BRIT Awards for Best Producer and Best Newcomer went to Rushent and the band in 1982.

In just a few short months, The Human League had become the UK's biggest pop band. In summer 1982, a remix album, *Love And Dancing*, was released (under the name The League Unlimited Orchestra), and after a number of false starts and a falling out with Martin Rushent (replaced as producer by Hugh Padgham and Chris Thomas), the *Hysteria* album followed in May 1984.

The band's long delay between albums (then unusual, especially for a pop act) drew derision from journalists and contemporaries alike and, when *Hysteria* arrived, it failed to live up to expectations, peaking at three in the Official Albums Chart and quickly falling away.

The group returned in 1986 with *Crash* (which also failed to spark fans' imaginations) and, stripped to a core of Oakey, Sulley and Catherall, have recorded four albums since. While they continue to serve on the live circuit, their enduring legacy will be the record which lit up Christmas 1981.

TIGHT FIT 1982

THE LION SLEEPS TONIGHT

WRITERS: Solomon Linda, Hugo Peretti, Luigi Creatore, George David Weiss, Albert Stanton (Al Brackman)

PRODUCER: Tim Friese-Greene

ALBUM: Tight Fit

PEAK POSITION: Number 1 (3 weeks)

WEEKS ON CHART: 15

SALES: 1.01m

The fascinating, yet controversial, history of 'The Lion Sleeps Tonight' dates back to pre-apartheid South Africa and Zulu musician Solomon Ntsele, aka Solomon Linda, whose multi-monikered composition would grace the Official Singles Chart on four separate occasions – most notably when Tight Fit hit the summit in March 1982.

'Mbube' (a Zulu word variously translated as meaning 'wake up' or 'stay away', and an abbreviation of the word for 'lion'), also known as 'Wimoweh', was penned by Linda for his band, Solomon Linda & The Evening Birds, while working as a packer at the Gallo Record Company. Marketed to the black population, Gallo released the song in 1939 on a 78rpm shellac disc and Linda (1909-62) soon became a household name in South Africa. By 1948, Mbube had sold an estimated 100,000 copies and was instrumental in popularising a style of a cappella music called 'isicathamiya'.

'Mbube' began its journey on the world stage in 1949 when Decca Records' Alan Lomax introduced Linda's recording to folk singer Pete Seeger, resulting in a Top 10 hit in the US for his group The Weavers. Their version was called 'Wimoweh' after a word in the original chorus, 'uyimbube' (meaning 'you are a lion' in Zulu), was misheard by Seeger.

The song has been recorded by more than 60 acts since the 1950s, with The Tokens (number 11 in January 1962), Karl Denver (number four in March 1962) and Dave Newman (number 34 in May 1972) all charting in the UK. The Tokens' version, with new English lyrics by George David Weiss, reached number one on the *Billboard* Hot 100.

Tight Fit's first two UK Official Singles Top Five entries, 'Back To The 60's' and 'The Lion Sleeps Tonight', were recorded by session singers, with Roy Ward (formerly of late Seventies UK hit-makers City Boy) singing lead on the latter. However, when 'Lion' clawed its way to the top, a short-lived trio of singer/dancer/model Steve Grant and female vocalists Denise Gyngell (who married record producer Pete Waterman in 1991) and Julie Harris was formed by producer Tim Friese-Greene to appear on *Top Of The Pops*.

In March 1982, 'Lion' hit the top spot and remained there for three weeks. One particularly memorable mimed *Top Of The Pops* performance saw attractive girls sashaying around the 6'3" frame of a string-vested Grant, backed by drummers in traditional Zulu costume and with guest appearances from a human-size lion and gorilla.

When it emerged that the TV performers did not feature on the single, headlines such as 'It's A Fit Up' (*Smash Hits*) quickly followed. But fans were undeterred, pointing out that they did sing on the rest of the album, which included another three singles, 'Fantasy Island', 'Secret Heart' [later recorded by The Monkees] and 'I'm Undecided'.

Gyngell and Harris quit the act when the trio's eponymously titled album was released in September 1982 in a dispute over unpaid royalties, something that also bedevilled Linda in his lifetime (and his estate after his death), despite Seeger's attempts to ship money over to him after his recording with The Weavers. The album itself performed disappointingly, stalling at number 87.

In addition to numerous subsequent cover versions, 'Lion' featured in the 1992 Jim Carrey movie *Ace Ventura: Pet Detective*, but it was the song's use under licence to the Walt Disney Company in *The Lion King* (1994) that triggered a £900,000 lawsuit from Linda's family. In a 2006 legal settlement, they were granted "payment for past uses of 'The Lion Sleeps Tonight' and an entitlement to future royalties from its worldwide use".

While Linda's family can look forward to a financially secure future, the composer himself died with just £10 in his bank account and his impoverished widow was unable to buy a stone for her husband's grave.

DEXYS MIDNIGHT RUNNERS 1982
COME ON EILEEN

WRITERS: Kevin Rowland, Jim Paterson [sic], Billy Adams

PRODUCERS: Clive Langer, Alan Winstanley

ALBUM: Too-Rye-Ay

PEAK POSITION: Number 1 (4 weeks)

WEEKS ON CHART: 17

SALES: 1.31m

'Come On Eileen' is one of the most idiosyncratic million sellers of the Eighties, an enduring, much-loved folk-rock jig-and-party favourite created by one of the decade's most compelling frontmen.

The son of Irish parents, Wolverhampton-born Kevin Rowland's Dexys Midnight Runners were already a known force in British music when they re-emerged as a band transformed in 1982 with 'Come On Eileen' (and parent album *Too-Rye-Aye*).

In 1980, the Rowland-fronted Dexys (strictly no apostrophe) had arrived as a 10-piece, wearing donkey jackets or leather jackets and woolly hats. Their initial incarnation gave the band a UK number one single that March with 'Geno' (a tribute to British Sixties soul artist Geno Washington), from their album *Searching For The Young Soul Rebels*, which peaked at six in the UK chart in summer of that year. But Rowland was never keen to abide by musical rules and, as the album project progressed, he fell out with everyone – journalists (who he labelled "dishonest and hippy" in press ads), various band members over creative differences (with only trombonist 'Big' Jim Paterson left as Rowland prepared a follow-up album) and the band's label, EMI, from whom he withheld master tapes in an effort to secure a better deal.

When Rowland came back in 1982, he and his new 14-piece band were almost unrecognisable – barring his own highly distinctive, soulful vocals and ear for a catchy chorus. The 'Italian docker' look had been replaced by dungarees, leather waistcoats, neck-scarves and a general gypsy vibe. Dexys had been rebuilt almost from scratch and, supplemented by fiddler Helen Bevington (renamed Helen O'Hara) with her three-piece string section The Emerald Express, they were signed to a new deal with Mercury Records.

The second single from *Too-Rye-Ay*, following a minor hit with the new line-up's manifesto, The Celtic Soul Brothers, was 'Come On Eileen'. The standout track on an album which combined their new look with an unfashionable strain of Irish folk soul, it was released in June 1982. The lyrics of 'Eileen' gave the parent album its title and a clear hint of its musical style – combining fiddles, flute, banjo and saxophone with guitar, drums and bass, the album stood out dramatically in a musical era spanning pop and electronic acts such as Madness, Duran Duran, Kid Creole, Japan, Soft Cell and The Human League.

The inspiration for the song, 'Eileen' was nobody in particular, said Rowland – "probably a composite of a couple of people, from those teenage years, second generation Irish Catholic". But whoever she was, she inspired the UK's biggest-selling single of 1982 – which was also the 10th biggest seller of the Eighties, a number one in the UK's Official Singles Chart, as well as the US *Billboard* rundown and Australia's Aria Chart, plus the winner of Best British Single at the 1983 BRIT Awards.

Too-Rye-Ay went on to spawn three more Top 20 hits in the UK (a cover of Van Morrison's 'Jackie Wilson Said', 'Let's Get This Straight' and a reissued 'Celtic Soul Brothers') and helped cement Dexys' position in early Eighties British pop. While the success demonstrated Rowland and his band could strike twice, a third return proved beyond them when, three years after 'Come On Eileen', Rowland essayed another reinvention.

The Dexys unveiled on 1985's *Don't Stand Me Down* sported smart suits on the cover of an album that seemed almost deliberately inaccessible. Although now often cited as a lost classic, at the time it received a mixed critical response and a bemused commercial one. Two years later, Rowland opted to launch a solo career.

Seemingly deliberately wilful, Rowland had taken Dexys to the pinnacle of international stardom and back again. Dexys returned again in the Nineties, the Noughties and then in 2012 with a critically acclaimed new album – but 'Come On Eileen' remains the band's popular peak.

IRENE CARA 1982

FAME

WRITERS: Michael Gore, Dean Pitchford

PRODUCER: Michael Gore

ALBUM: Fame (soundtrack)

PEAK POSITION: Number 1 (3 weeks)

WEEKS ON CHART: 16

SALES: 1.05m

Twenty years before *Glee* hit television screens and music charts, *Fame* helped transfer a cast of performing students into the Top 10 of the Official Singles Chart.

In 1980, the soundtrack to the movie *Fame* hit the US Top 10, selling over one million copies, while its title song, performed by cast member Irene Cara (who played Coco Hernandez), reached the Top Five on the *Billboard* Hot 100. However, in the UK, the single failed to chart and the album peaked at number 21.

And yet, in 1982, on the back of the popularity of the film's spin-off TV series, which also spilled over into the Official Singles Chart, the original two-year-old soundtrack and its title song simultaneously topped the UK charts.

The film, which followed the progress of various talented teenagers at the New York High School Of Performing Arts, was nominated for six Oscars and won for Best Original Musical Score and Best Original Song for 'Fame' (a feat repeated at the Golden Globe Awards). For the first time, two songs from the same film were nominated for the Best Song Oscar, the other nominee being 'Out Here On My Own' – also performed by Cara.

Such was Cara's impact that she was nominated for Grammy awards as Best New Female Artist and Best New Pop Artist, and for a Golden Globe as Best Actress in a Musical. In addition, US music trade papers *Billboard* and *Cashbox* named her Top New Singles Artist and Top Female Vocalist, respectively.

In real life, Cara had attended a similar school of performing arts and graduated at the Professional Children's School in Manhattan. Her early career included regular appearances on the PBS show *The Electric Company*, alongside Bill Cosby and Morgan Freeman, and several Broadway and Off Broadway shows including *Ain't Misbehavin'*, *The Me Nobody Knows* and *Maggie Flynn*. *Screen World* magazine named her one of the dozen Most Promising New Actors of 1976, the same year urban music magazine *Right On!* named her Top Actress.

Fame was conceived and produced by David De Silva and directed by Londoner Sir Alan Parker (known for his work on other musicals like *Bugsy Malone, Pink Floyd – The Wall, The Commitments* and *Evita*). In an interview with the *Daily Telegraph*, Parker said that David Bowie once told him that he thought *Fame* was named after his 1975 hit (co-written with John Lennon), and the filmmaker admitted he was probably right.

The film's musical score was penned by composer Michael Gore, with lyricist Dean Pitchford collaborating on 'Fame' – which Gore has admitted was influenced by Donna Summer's 'Hot Stuff'.

In the UK, 'Fame' entered the singles chart at number 51, made a spectacular jump to number four and, in July 1982, replaced another movie-linked song, Captain Sensible's 'Happy Talk' (written for the musical *South Pacific*), at the top. The following week, the soundtrack topped the Official Albums Chart. The single, which ruled the roost for three weeks, finally passed the one million sales mark thanks to downloads in 2010.

The film's soundtrack was knocked off the summit after two weeks by the first album from the TV show, *The Kids From Fame*, which clocked up 12 weeks at number one. 'Fame' was also used as the title song for the TV series (sung by Erica Gimpel, who now played Coco Hernandez).

The Kids From Fame TV concept was hugely popular in the UK and had a deeper impact on the official chart, with four albums and three singles inspired by the show reaching the Top 20. For a few months, Leroy, Coco, Bruno and Doris were among the UK's biggest pop stars – although none of them went on to greater things.

Fame also spawned a 2009 film remake and the successful stage show *Fame – The Musical*, which between 1995 and 2006 grossed £56 million in the UK and was nominated for three Laurence Olivier Awards.

MILLION-SELLING MEMORIES

KEVIN ROWLAND (DEXYS MIDNIGHT RUNNERS)

'Come On Eileen' was such a huge hit for you, how do you feel about it today?

I almost feel like it was someone else now, not me. I don't really relate to it anymore. It is a good song and I understand that people want to hear it. And we have a way of doing it now live which works for us, that we can relate to. We've extended it, we've put a new section in. The only thing that has been difficult is that it got bigger than us. I suppose I do get tired of talking about the past a bit, especially when I've just done an album that I've put my heart and soul into for years and someone wants to talk about what I did 30 years ago. But it's okay.

When 'Come On Eileen' went to number one, what did that mean to you?

It was massive. Going to *Top Of The Pops* was always a great thing for me, I watched it since I was a kid – I loved it. I never took it for granted. I couldn't believe my luck.

Things could have gone very differently for me; I could've ended up in prison or anything like that. When 'Eileen' was going up the chart it was incredibly exciting because the record company had lost faith in us, our singles before hadn't been selling very well. So when that one started flying, we felt vindicated.

What do you think of it as a song?

I think we got it right. We have a system for the way we work – we write one line at a time, we make sure the melody, or rhythm, is really happening, that it all works together. And it can take five or six weeks to write a song. I felt slightly vindicated because people were half leaving the group over 'Eileen'; I got the band to play it in every key to see which worked best coming from the verse into the chorus. They were sick of it, but that's how we did it.

That sounds like an incredibly laborious way of putting a song together.

It's the only way I've ever done it. I think if you do things like that, you get that occasional gift that doesn't need a lot of work. But if I don't put that work in, I don't seem to get the gifts.

Where did the celtic folk musical style of the *Too-Rye-Ay* album come from?

I was very influenced by Kevin Archer [who had been in the band]. He played me a demo of one of his songs. We were using strings, but he was using them better. He told me about a fiddle player, Helen Bevington, now Helen O'Hara, and he said she would be great for you. So I got her involved.

I was influenced by his demo tape from a style perspective. He had a breakdown in one of his songs where it stopped and slowed down and then sped up. It wasn't the same rhythm, wasn't the same tempo. But I didn't take one note, one melody, one chord sequence, one lyric from his songs.

What about the image you used with *Too-Rye-Ay*?

We were trying to get a look together – we tried a few Dickensian things, but there was a band called Animal Nightlife who were doing that. And then Debbie Baxter [now Debbie Williams, married to Dexys' Pete Williams] was making clothes for us and she said why don't you try dungarees? So we went to this shop called Flip, which sold American clothes, and bought some. And we added things to them and messed around with it. But it was Debbie who came up with it.

SURVIVOR 1982
EYE OF THE TIGER

WRITERS: Frankie Sullivan, Jim Peterik

PRODUCERS: Frankie Sullivan, Jim Peterik

ALBUM: Eye Of The Tiger

PEAK POSITION: Number 1 (4 weeks)

WEEKS ON CHART: 19 (1982, 15; 2007, 4)

SALES: 1.41m

By the summer of 1982, the Official Singles Chart number ones of that year had not, in the main, really rocked, with novelty chart-toppers from acts including Captain Sensible, Tight Fit, Goombay Dance Band, Charlene, Eurovision winner Nicole and two from Bucks Fizz. But a heavyweight chart contender was about to enter the ring and knock out all competition in its fight to the top of the hit parade.

"The theme from *Rocky III*" was the single sleeve's boast, but Survivor were not the first choice of Sylvester Stallone – the film's writer/director and star. *Rocky* had grown from being a small budget film into a massive movie franchise and Stallone had become more hands-on with each sequel, to the point where the sleeve of the *Rocky III: Original Motion Picture Score* proudly states "all music on this album selected by Sylvester Stallone" – possibly explaining the inclusion of three songs by his younger brother Frank.

Legend has it that initial edits of the film's main fight sequence had featured Queen's 1980 hit 'Another One Bites The Dust', but Stallone had been unable to secure the publishing rights for the track's inclusion in the movie. So, having heard previous tracks from Survivor, he contacted them to ask for something that would have the same impact.

The band had formed in Chicago in 1978, but had scored just one US Top 40 hit before Stallone's movie brought their international breakthrough. For 'Eye Of The Tiger', the band's guitarist, Frankie

Sullivan, and keyboard player, Jim Peterik, duly delivered a hook with a thumping beat (courtesy of drummer Marc Droubay) and attacking guitar chords combining to create a riff that personified punches being thrown, along with a killer chorus and lyrics concerning the fight to achieve what you want, performed by vocalist Dave Bickler (the band's line-up was completed by bassist Stephan Ellis).

One week after the film's release, Survivor's theme song entered the US chart and went on to spend six weeks at number one. Although it ended up in a strong second place when the biggest US sellers of 1982 were calculated, behind Olivia Newton-John's 'Physical' (much like Stallone's Rocky in the film, initially losing to opponent 'Clubber' Lang), it refused to be beaten, eventually achieving sales of more than four million copies – leaving Newton-John out for the count in the long run.

The record spent four weeks at the UK summit in September and, by year-end, trailed only Dexys' 'Come On Eileen' and Irene Cara's 'Fame' in terms of total sales. The song's other achievements include being 1982's best-selling single in Australia and winning a Grammy Award for Best Rock Performance by a Duo or Group with Vocal. It was also nominated for an Academy Award and a Golden Globe for Best Original Song from a motion picture, but lost out to 'Up Where We Belong' from the Richard Gere film *An Officer And A Gentleman* in both cases.

Although recorded for *Rocky III*, the first long-player to feature the track was Survivor's own release, also called *Eye Of The Tiger*, which itself registered more than one million sales in the band's homeland but just missed a UK Top 10 placing.

The follow-up single, 'American Heartbeat', failed to chart in the UK, with Survivor's only other British success being 'Burning Heart', from *Rocky IV* (number five in 1986) – although the boundary between fantasy and reality became dangerously blurred in 1995 when Frank Bruno celebrated winning the WBC heavyweight title by releasing a Stock and Aitken-produced cover version of 'Eye Of The Tiger' and having a Top 30 hit with it.

Long after its initial release, 'Eye Of The Tiger' fell short of the million mark. But the arrival of digital downloads helped the track tip over the million sales threshold. The track's momentum also benefited from the change to chart regulations at the beginning of 2007, allowing songs to chart on sales of downloads alone.

NEW ORDER 1983
BLUE MONDAY

WRITERS: Gillian Gilbert, Peter Hook, Stephen Morris, Bernard Sumner

PRODUCERS: Gillian Gilbert, Peter Hook, Stephen Morris, Bernard Sumner

ALBUM: N/A

PEAK POSITION: Number 9 (original version)/ Number 3 (1988 remix)

WEEKS ON CHART: 54 (1983, 38; 1988, 11; 1995, 4; 2006, 1)

SALES: 1.16m

The biggest-selling 12-inch single in British musical history, 'Blue Monday' is arguably the closest thing to avant garde in the UK million sellers list.

'Blue Monday' was the creation of New Order, Manchester's defiantly alternative purveyors of post-punk electronic music – and a band that was reborn out of tragedy at the dawn of the Eighties.

Inspired by an early Sex Pistols' performance in Manchester, Bernard Sumner (aka Albrecht, born Dicken) and Peter Hook decided to form a band in 1977, recruiting their friends Ian Curtis on vocals and Stephen Morris on drums. Initially called Warsaw, the four-piece was renamed Joy Division (a reference to prostitutes operating in Nazi concentration camps) a year later and self-released a largely unnoticed EP in 1978 before signing to the Factory label set up by ambitious TV journalist Tony Wilson.

Their first album, *Unknown Pleasures*, received wide acclaim, as did the band's compelling live performances, with Curtis an extraordinary, unique frontman. But he was a tortured character, ridden with self-doubt and crippled by epilepsy and, in May 1980 he committed suicide. The following month, the band's best-known track, the haunting 'Love Will Tear Us Apart', was released, giving them a Top 20 hit in the Official Singles Chart. In July, second album *Closer* was released and reached the official albums Top 10, as did the live/rarities collection *Still* in October 1981.

That could have been it. But Sumner, Hook and Morris had other ideas. Recruiting keyboardist Gillian Gilbert, the band was recast – and renamed New Order (controversially seen as another Nazi reference).

Gilbert's keyboard work began pushing them in a new, more electronic direction and the new approach was developed on late 1981 single 'Everything's Gone Green' and album *Movement,* then honed on 1982 single 'Temptation'.

Then, in 1983, came 'Blue Monday', backed with an instrumental version, retitled 'The Beach'. An epic track, almost seven-and-a-half minutes long in its standard form, 'Monday' provided a critical mid-Eighties crossover point between experimental electronica, synth-pop and the emerging dance club scene. Famously, the release also embodied the almost anti-commerce approach of the band and their label Factory – initial units of the 12-inch came in a bespoke, die-cut sleeve from which the label lost 10p for every unit. Fortunately, as band members Sumner and Hook recall today, the issue was resolved for later runs.

The single also carried an air of mystery about it. Its Peter Saville-designed sleeve didn't feature the name of the band or track, instead using a colour pattern code that spelled out the relevant details – as was also employed on the subsequent album *Power, Corruption & Lies.* The only text was the catalogue number, 'FAC SEVENTY THREE'.

Peaking at number 12 in the Official Singles Chart when it was first released and then at nine later the same year, the single is the lowest charting million seller of all, but was the band's biggest chart hit at the time – and remained so until 'True Faith' reached number four in 1987. When released again in 1988 (a remix version helmed by Quincy Jones and John Potoker), 'Blue Monday' went one step further to peak at number three, but it remains one of only a handful of million sellers to peak short of the summit.

New Order eventually did get their chart-topper seven years later though – in the form of the 1990 England World Cup theme, 'World In Motion'. Since then, there have been three New Order albums – *Republic* (1993), *Get Ready* (2001) and *Waiting For The Sirens' Call* (2005), as well as a range of alternative projects from each member. In late 2011, a version of New Order returned to the stage without Peter Hook on bass.

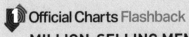

MILLION-SELLING MEMORIES

BERNARD SUMNER (JOY DIVISION, NEW ORDER)

'Blue Monday' is the biggest-selling 12-inch of all time. Did you ever really expect it to be such a successful and enduring track?

No, we never really felt that. We never really saw our involvement in music as a career. We were having a fine time, but the whole point of being a musician was to avoid having a career.

When it first came out I remember a few discouraging comments saying it's a different sound for New Order. I don't think they got it because it was such a distinct change of direction. When we wrote it, it was more a question of me and Stephen playing around with lots of new technology. Stephen had an Oberheim DMX drum machine and I had all these synths. We had been waiting for this drum machine to arrive, so we could link it up to the synth. 'BM' is pretty much totally electronic, apart from the odd bit of bass guitar here and there.

Do you still like it – or do you get fed up with a song like that, which becomes such a big part of your history?

If I'm honest, I'd say I enjoy 'Temptation' more; it's more of a spiritual song, it moves people. It gets them in the heart. But 'Blue Monday' gets people's feet moving. A few years ago, we went to a nightclub in Berlin and as soon as they put 'Blue Monday' on, everybody got up. It just makes you want to get up on your feet.

What were your influences at the time of 'Blue Monday'?

In the days of Joy Division, and even New Order, it was Lou Reed and Velvet Underground, Iggy Pop and Bowie. But through playing in America and going to Europe, and coming to London, we became exposed to lots of new forms of music. We had friends in America who would send over recordings of radio stations like Kiss FM.

There has been some talk that you were influenced by Donna Summer's 'I Feel Love'. Is that true?

[Producer] Giorgio Moroder's stuff was really important, of course. And Donna Summer. And 'I Feel Love' was a very important track. But we never actually got it out and listened to it in the studio at that time. We never got records out like that.

There is a story that 'Blue Monday' lost lots of money because of the sleeve design. Is there any truth in that?

I was busy producing a record for another band in a studio in Manchester. I remember Tony Wilson came in to see me. He said, "Do you want the good news or the bad news? 'Blue Monday' has got into the chart, it's doing really well. We are just losing money on every copy we sell." I just said, "Very funny, Tony. What are you going to do about it?"

It was because of the hole in the sleeve. We had this synthesizer called an Emulator 1. It used these large floppy discs with all these holes cut into them. [Designer] Peter Saville came into the studio, saw these and basically turned the sleeve into a huge floppy disc. I thought it was extremely funny. But then they changed the sleeve after a certain number were made.

Do you remember your other huge hit (and only number one), 1990's 'World In Motion', going to number one?

Yes, I was at my house in south Manchester and we were having a few drinks with friends. It was quite a brave thing for the FA to ask us to get involved. Up to that point, all of the songs were like 'Back Home' [the 1970 England World Cup song] and were all spectacularly awful. We felt like doing something new, although it was difficult to know how to approach it. I was friends with Keith Allen and we thought we would get him involved. We had never really worked with other people, so that broke the mould for us as well.

CULTURE CLUB 1983

KARMA CHAMELEON

| WRITERS: George O'Dowd (Boy George), Mikey Craig, Roy Hay, Jon Moss, Phil Pickett |
| PRODUCER: Steve Levine |
| ALBUM: Colour By Numbers |
| PEAK POSITION: Number 1 (6 weeks) |
| WEEKS ON CHART: 20 |
| SALES: 1.47m |

In 1983, Boy George became the best-known new face on the transatlantic music scene as, almost overnight, his group Culture Club established themselves as one of the most successful and most talked-about acts in pop music. They were the first act to reach the Top Five of the UK chart with their initial seven hits and their only UK million seller, 'Karma Chameleon', topped charts in 16 countries.

The name Culture Club came from the fact that the four group members came from different backgrounds: Irish (Boy George), Jewish (Jon Moss), Jamaican (Mikey Craig) and English (Roy Hay). Elements of reggae, soul, salsa, calypso and Latin American styles were woven into their pop sound, which O'Dowd has described as "a bridge between white rock and black soul".

The band clearly benefited from being part of the MTV generation, with their distinctive Sue Clowes-designed clothes, while O'Dowd's androgynous look of long, braided hair and heavy make-up drew huge media attention.

Born in Bexley, Kent, to Irish parents in 1961 – and a huge David Bowie fan as a teenager – Boy George first came to attention as a leading light on London's emerging New Romantic scene during the early 1980s, centred around London nightclub The Blitz. He briefly appeared in an early line-up of Malcolm McLaren-managed group Bow Wow Wow, before forming Culture Club and signing to Virgin Records, which released the band's debut single, 'White Boy', in May 1982.

After two low-selling singles, Culture Club's career took off that September when 'Do You Really Want To Hurt Me' reached number one in the Official Singles Chart. Hit after hit followed.

'Karma Chameleon' was the most successful of the band's nine Top 10 UK singles and nine Top 20 entries in the US. Featuring the harmonica playing of session musician Judd Lander, it topped the UK Singles Chart in September 1983, was Britain's best-selling single for the next six weeks and outsold every other record that year.

In the US, where 'Do You Really Want To Hurt Me' and 'Time (Clock Of The Heart)' had both peaked at number two, it was one of the biggest hits of what was called a second 'British invasion'. It topped the *Billboard* Hot 100 in February 1984, remaining there for three weeks. It was the only American chart-topper for the first act since The Beatles to score three Top 10 singles from their debut album.

'Karma Chameleon' featured on the group's second album, *Colour By Numbers*, which topped the UK chart for five weeks, while in the US it spent six weeks at number two (unable to displace Michael Jackson's *Thriller*). It spent over a year on both charts and reportedly sold in excess of 10 million copies internationally – four million of those in the US.

The group wrote 'Chameleon' with their occasional keyboard player Phil Pickett (who had first found fame in Seventies hit group Sailor), although similarities with Jimmy Jones' 1960 hit 'Handy Man' did draw a lawsuit from that song's writers. According to O'Dowd, the song had a deep meaning: "What we're saying is, if you aren't true, if you don't act like you feel, then you get Karma – justice. That's nature's way of paying you back."

The video for the single showed the group on an 1870s Mississippi river boat (named *The Chameleon*), crowded with colourful characters including gamblers and pickpockets – although it was actually filmed around Desborough Island, in the 'wild west' of Weybridge in suburban Surrey.

Among the trophies 'Karma Chameleon' garnered were BRIT Awards for Best Group and Best Single of 1983 (Steve Levine was named Best British Producer that year), while the band was voted Best New Artist at the Grammy Awards.

At the latter presentation ceremony, a playful George appeared via satellite, saying: "Thanks America, you've got style, you've got taste, and you know a good drag queen when you see one!"

MILLION-SELLING MEMORIES

BOY GEORGE (CULTURE CLUB)

You had your first number one with 'Do You Really Want To Hurt Me', after the impact of appearing on *Top Of The Pops*.

It was a weird one because we got on there by default. We were quite low in the chart, but back then records could bubble under for some time before climbing. Literally, the night before *TOTP* we got a call saying someone (it was either Elton John or Shakin' Stevens – Shakin' Stevens, I think) had pulled out. So we had to prepare ourselves to be on telly the next day. All the artists I had loved had been on *TOTP* – Bowie, Marc Bolan, Roxy Music.

And then this weird thing happened. Up until that point we had been doing promo, trying to get on TV and radio. But, after *TOTP* a whole lot of shows that had booked us tried to cancel us. Radio 1 called our plugger and said, "What the hell was that thing?" While the public loved us, the media didn't know what to think. That's the story of my career really. Whatever has happened, the public has always made up their own minds about us.

Do you remember where you were when you found out that it had become your first number one single?

I was actually on the verge of leaving the band. We had played at The Arches in Glasgow and I was losing my voice. I just wasn't used to playing as many shows. It was a hard time and me and Jon had had a massive fight. I really had decided to leave the band. And then we got up the next morning and heard that we were number one. We drove from Glasgow to Edinburgh and I literally got mobbed by people. Phil said to me, "That's it, everyone knows who you are now."

Then came 'Karma Chameleon' – which was an even bigger hit, and quickly became the second-biggest single of the Eighties...

Yes. 'Do You Really Want To Hurt Me' is a bit cooler. 'Karma Chameleon' is one of those songs nobody ever admits to buying. 'Hurt Me' was a really personal song, I didn't really understand why the label wanted to put it out. But I learned something massive from that – the more personal you were, the more intimate you could be, the more you connect with people. Even now, I try to write really personal songs. But when I sang 'Karma Chameleon' to the band for the first time, they just laughed at me. I wrote the melody pretty much all the way through in my head and I sang it to them back at Ray's flat and they laughed at me. Ray hated [it] [laughs].

What do you think about 'Karma Chameleon' looking back?

I have fallen in and out of love with it a number of times. There have been so many different styles of it – Mexican versions, choirs. Do I think it is the best song I've ever written? No. But I'm very proud of it. 'Il Adore' [from stage musical *Taboo*] is a beautiful song and makes me want to cry. I am very proud to be emotional about something I've written. But those songs are not necessarily the hits. I've met people over the years who have seemed to be able to write to order, but the best stuff I've ever written has been from the heart.

So what were your influences in those early days – and do you remember the first single you bought?

We were quite young and really thought we were cool. When you go into a band, you have four people influencing the sounds. Whatever I wanted us to be was very different to what we became (although what we became was brilliant). I was very into Bowie, of course, and Gladys Knight, T. Rex, Nico, *Cabaret* even, Marlene Dietrich and lots and lots of jazz. I was 17 and influenced by what was hip. My first single, I think, was 'Gypsys, Tramps & Thieves' – I was 11 in 1972, the year Marc Bolan and Bowie exploded. I saw Bowie in concert at the Lewisham Odeon, the night before the last Ziggy show. It was such a pivotal year.

BILLY JOEL 1983

UPTOWN GIRL

WRITER: Billy Joel

PRODUCER: Phil Ramone

ALBUM: An Innocent Man

PEAK POSITION: Number 1 (5 weeks)

WEEKS ON CHART: 17

SALES: 1.02m

Piano Man Billy Joel had been known in the US since that song gave him a minor hit in 1973 and already had three US million-selling singles under his belt by the time this tribute to The Four Seasons' sound was released. But he had yet to make an impact on the UK Official Singles Top 10.

All that changed for the Bronx-born ex-amateur boxer when, within three weeks of entering the UK Top 75, 'Uptown Girl' began its five-week run at the top of the Official Singles Chart. It would go on to be the second biggest-selling single of 1983, only outsold by the record it replaced at number one, 'Karma Chameleon' by Culture Club.

Although a transatlantic million seller, 'Uptown Girl' only reached number three in the US, where it stayed for five weeks – held off for four by the same two records that, in a transatlantic reversal of fortune, it would keep from the UK's official number one spot – Lionel Richie's 'All Night Long (All Night)' and 'Say Say Say' by Paul McCartney and Michael Jackson.

The same week in November 1983 that 'Uptown Girl' went to number one in the UK, its parent album, *An Innocent Man*, began a 47-week consecutive run in the Top 20 of the Official Albums Chart, but the album's campaign had not begun well.

The Motown tribute lead single, 'Tell Her About It' (a US chart-topper), had failed to chart in the UK. However, to capitalise on

'Uptown Girl''s success, the previous flop was promptly re-sleeved and re-promoted, becoming the second of five UK Top 30 hits from the album. For one week in December 1983, both tracks' paths crossed in the Top 10, making Joel the first US male to have simultaneous UK Top 10 solo hits since Jimmy Jones in July 1960 with 'Handy Man' and 'Good Timin''.

'Uptown Girl''s success turned around Joel's UK chart fortunes. On the week it entered the Official Singles Chart, it began a sequence which saw Joel claim at least one single in the UK Top 75 every week for a 10-month period.

The music video for Joel's breakthrough single featured the singer as the 'downtown man', working in a garage/gas station, who manages to lure the 'uptown girl' out of her chauffeured car to perform some basic dance steps with Joel and his colleagues before climbing onto the back of his motorbike and riding away with him. The girl was Joel's supermodel girlfriend Christie Brinkley, who became his second wife soon after, and his second ex-wife in 1994 – coincidentally, the last year he reached the UK Singles Chart with new material.

The high point of Joel's UK Albums Chart career came in June 1984 when, amid publicity surrounding a series of live concerts at Wembley Arena, *An Innocent Man* reached its peak of number two and was joined in the Top 100 by re-entries of five previous albums – *The Stranger*, *52nd Street*, *Glass Houses*, *The Nylon Curtain* and *Piano Man*. The only fly in the ointment was the refusal of Bob Marley & The Wailers' *Legend* compilation to budge from the top of the chart.

The son of a classical pianist, Joel's career began in local New York bands during the mid-Sixties and he recorded with groups The Hassles and Attila before making his first solo album in 1971. His fifth album, *The Stranger*, released in 1977, took him into the major leagues, peaking at number two in the US, and he would go on to become the first artist to have five albums each sell more than seven million copies Stateside.

'Uptown Girl' became the 24th song to be a UK number one for two different artists when Westlife released a cover version in 2001. It was the Irish boy band's biggest-selling single, shifting in excess of 750,000 copies in aid of Comic Relief.

Billy Joel has continued to tour and record, and in 2007 embarked on a parallel career as a classical composer and pianist. He has also toured extensively with Elton John.

FRANKIE GOES TO HOLLYWOOD 1983

RELAX

WRITERS: Peter Gill, Holly Johnson, Mark O'Toole

PRODUCER: Trevor Horn

ALBUM: Welcome To The Pleasuredome

PEAK POSITION: Number 1 (5 weeks)

WEEKS ON CHART: 59 (1983, 52; 1993, 7)

SALES: 2m

No one ever had a better start to their UK recording career than Frankie Goes To Hollywood (FGTH), whose first two singles both sold well over one million copies in 1983 and 1984. No previous act had reached the Top Five in the UK's Official Singles Chart with their first five singles either.

It was an extraordinary first 18 months for the five-piece from Merseyside. FGTH were fronted by singer Holly Johnson, who had briefly been in Liverpool band Big In Japan, a commercially unsuccessful cult outfit which contained several other members who became leading figures on the local punk/post-punk scene and beyond.

The rest of the band – whose name is said to be derived either from a Liverpool newspaper headline about Frankie Vaughan, or a picture caption relating to Frank Sinatra – comprised Peter Gill, Brian Nash, Mark O'Toole and Paul Rutherford.

Crucially, however, FGTH were produced by the man named Producer of the Year at the 1983 BRIT Awards, Trevor Horn. Horn, who had earlier given the world 'Video Killed The Radio Star', spotted FGTH performing an early version of 'Relax' on TV show *The Tube* and convinced them to sign to his label ZTT.

Horn felt 'Relax' had plenty of potential, but sounded more like a jingle than a song and set out to 'fix it'. With his stellar reputation, Horn was able to dictate matters easily – as Johnson admitted:

"Whatever he said, we went along with."

While Horn initially allowed the group themselves to play on the track, he subsequently drafted in Ian Dury's band The Blockheads, as well as a team of session musicians including Andy Richards and J.J. Jeczalik (of Horn's next hit act, Art Of Noise). On the final recording, although Johnson was the only band member to be heard, Horn explained: "There was no actual playing by the band, but the whole feeling came from them." Horn had invested the then-substantial sum of £70,000 on the recording.

The music was just one part of the package. ZTT Records co-founder Paul Morley mapped out a marketing campaign for the act, described as a "strategic assault on pop". This successful campaign courted controversy by highlighting band members Johnson and Rutherford's open homosexuality. They were, arguably, the best-marketed band up until then, and promotional tools such as the 'Frankie Says Relax' T-shirts proved extremely popular.

The single initially climbed the bestsellers at a very 'relaxed' pace, only reaching the Top 40 seven weeks after its initial arrival in the Official Singles Top 75. However, after being seen on *Top Of The Pops*, 'Relax' rocketed up and reached the summit in January 1984.

Its last movement towards the top was probably helped by a much-publicised ban imposed by BBC Radio 1's breakfast show DJ Mike Read, in January 1984. The track quickly received an overall BBC ban, so went unheard on *TOTP* during its five-week run at the top. In total, 'Relax' spent 22 weeks in the Top 10, the longest stay since fellow Liverpudlians The Beatles' 1963 hit 'She Loves You'. The ban was, however, lifted in time for 'Relax' to be heard on the Christmas 1984 edition of *TOTP*.

During its stay at the top, 'Relax' halted the progress to the summit of two notable singles: 'Girls Just Want To Have Fun' by Cyndi Lauper and Queen's 'Radio Ga Ga'. 'Relax' was also a chart-topper abroad, although in the US, like the UK, it was a slow starter, the Grammy-nominated record only peaking at number 10 on March 16, 1985, 11 months after first entering the *Billboard* Hot 100.

In total, 'Relax' (which apart from the standard seven-inch vinyl single was available in several 12-inch mixes) notched up 48 consecutive chart weeks on its first run, added a further five in 1985, and in 1993 returned to the Top Five as a reissue and increased its total chart weeks to 59 – a record at the time for a chart-topper.

FRANKIE GOES TO HOLLYWOOD 1984

TWO TRIBES

WRITERS: Peter Gill, Holly Johnson, Mark O'Toole

PRODUCER: Trevor Horn

ALBUM: Welcome To The Pleasuredome

PEAK POSITION: Number 1 (9 weeks)

WEEKS ON CHART: 27 (1984, 21; 1994, 3; 2000, 3)

SALES: 1.58m

Frankie Goes To Hollywood (FGTH) might easily be as remembered for the controversies they stirred as the music they made. But that would be to overlook the extraordinary record-breaking popularity they enjoyed in 1983 and 1984.

FGTH were the first act to see their first three releases all reach number one on the Official Singles Chart since Gerry & The Pacemakers in 1963. The second of these, 'Two Tribes', spent longer at the top than any other record in the 1980s.

While their previous single (the fellow million seller 'Relax') took 10 weeks to reach number one, 'Two Tribes' entered the Official Singles Chart at its first attempt, pushing Wham!'s 'Wake Me Up Before You Go-Go' from the top spot. It then held the number one position for nine weeks, before Wham!'s George Michael reclaimed the summit with 'Careless Whisper'.

For a short two-week spell, the group held the nation's top two singles slots (with this single and 'Relax') – something only The Beatles and John Lennon had previously achieved.

Inspired by a line from *Mad Max 2: The Road Warrior* ("When two great warrior tribes go to war"), FGTH had performed an early version of 'Two Tribes' on the John Peel radio show in October 1982, and by then it had its signature bassline, percussion arrangement and idiosyncratic middle eight sections and intro.

As Holly Johnson pointed out, "There are two elements in the music – an American funk line and a Russian line." It was down to producer Trevor Horn to make the most of these different sounds, and he delivered a wide range of mixes, including 'We Don't Want To Die', 'Annihilation', 'Carnage' and 'Hibakusha'. The track returned, almost inevitably in remix form, to the UK Top 20 in both 1994 and 2000.

A highly dramatic single, with a similarly dramatic promo video, the track opens with the sounds of an air raid siren and includes actor Patrick Allen approximating his narrations from the UK government's Protect And Survive public information films. In turn, 12-inch mixes include Chris Barrie from TV sci-fi spoof *Red Dwarf* impersonating US President Ronald Reagan.

Playing on the media and public concern at the increasingly chilly Cold War, the award-winning 'Two Tribes' video (directed by ex-10cc members Kevin Godley and Lol Creme) featured a wrestling match between US President 'Reagan' and Russian Premier 'Chernenko'. Photos were circulated of the group wearing both American and Russian military uniforms, and the record's cover art showed images of Reagan, Lenin and Margaret Thatcher. 'Two Tribes' ensured that, post-'Relax', FGTH continued to be a highly controversial act.

In most other territories where 'Relax' had hit the heights, including all the biggest markets in Europe, 'Two Tribes' also sold extremely well, although it stalled outside the Top 40 in the US. Overall, FGTH spent more weeks on the UK chart in 1984 than any other act, bringing the band a BRIT Award for Best British Newcomer and a Grammy nomination for Best New Act.

'Relax' and 'Two Tribes' were the first two tracks to be taken from the group's debut album, *Welcome To The Pleasuredome* – a bold double-vinyl set which also included FGTH's unique takes on Springsteen's 'Born To Run', Gerry & The Pacemakers' 'Ferry Cross The Mersey' and the Bacharach & David classic 'Do You Know The Way To San Jose'. Also featuring the subsequent single 'The Power Of Love' and the title track, the album shipped an unprecedented 700,000 albums and 400,000 cassettes in its first week in the UK alone.

It would prove to be a high point which the band would never emulate with its follow-up, *Liverpool*, which peaked at five in the Official Albums Chart following its release in November 1986, the year before the band split amid turmoil and acrimony. Johson has enjoyed a moderately successful solo career and there have been a handful of brief FGTH reunions over the years.

GEORGE MICHAEL 1984

CARELESS WHISPER

WRITERS: George Michael, Andrew Ridgeley

PRODUCER: George Michael

ALBUM: Make It Big (Wham!)

PEAK POSITION: Number 1 (3 weeks)

WEEKS ON CHART: 17

SALES: 1.45m

One of the few individuals to have a million seller both in his own right and as a member of a group during his own lifetime, this was George Michael's debut solo single – perhaps ironic given that he proudly declared "I'm not planning on going solo" in the chorus of Wham!'s preceding hit, 'Wake Me Up Before You Go-Go'.

Hailing from Bushey, north-west of London, Michael's musical career had begun as a teenager in tandem with his Wham! partner and former school friend Andrew Ridgeley in a ska band. But, when the band folded, the pair opted for a far poppier direction with Wham!, eventually signing with Innervision Records, and then Epic Records.

A sequence of four top 10 singles in 1982 and 1983 preceded the act's first official number one with 'Go-Go'. Through this solo outing and the Wham! follow-up, 'Freedom', Michael wrote and performed on three of five chart-toppers between June and November 1984, only being kept from the top spot by Frankie Goes To Hollywood's 'Two Tribes' and Stevie Wonder's 'I Just Called To Say I Love You'. As the filling in that FGTH/Wonder sandwich, 'Careless Whisper' was the second in an unprecedented run of three consecutive UK official number ones which each sold one million copies.

Written over the course of a few months in 1981, with finishing touches from Ridgeley, the lyrics tell the story of a teenage, two-timing, guilt-ridden Michael. The melody for the saxophone hook, played on the hit version by Steve Gregory, came to Michael during a bus journey on his way to DJ at a restaurant. Michael honoured his parents on the sleeve of this release with the message: "This record is dedicated to my mother and father – five minutes in return for 21 years."

The original recording of the song, produced by Atlantic Records soul music legend Jerry Wexler, had not lived up to Michael's expectations, so never saw the light of day during Wham!'s time at Innervision. However, during the duo's attempt to sign with Epic Records for their second album, a bitter legal dispute broke out, during which Innervision threatened to release the Wexler recording, which they owned. As the track had not yet been released, the song's publisher – Morrison Leahy Music – was able to block it by invoking their right to refuse the licence for issuing the first recording of any song for which they owned the copyright. That left Michael free to produce his own version of the song, which became the first million seller for the duo's new label.

In 1985, 'Careless Whisper' received an Ivor Novello Award for the Most Performed Work of the Year and George Michael received the first of his three Ivors for Songwriter of the Year. The song also topped charts in 14 countries including America (where it was credited to Wham! featuring George Michael), reaching the summit in February 1985 and becoming the biggest single of the year with sales of more than two million. Although a solo release, the recording was included on Wham!'s 1985 *Make It Big* album, which itself topped both the US and UK charts.

A second Michael solo single, 'A Different Corner', also topped the UK Official Singles Chart in 1986 and, with the 1987 transatlantic chart-topping duet 'I Knew You Were Waiting (For Me)' credited to Aretha Franklin and George Michael, he began his solo career with three consecutive number one hits, joining an exclusive club with only Gerry & The Pacemakers and Frankie Goes To Hollywood at the time – although Jive Bunny & The Mastermixers, Robson & Jerome, the Spice Girls, Aqua, B★Witched, Westlife, Will Young and Gareth Gates have since also taken delivery of their membership cards.

Selling one million copies in the UK of this single as a solo artist and 'Last Christmas'/'Everything She Wants' as a member of a group (Wham!) is rare indeed. But add in his contribution to Band Aid, along with the fact that all three releases topped six figures in the same calendar year, and Michael's really is a unique achievement.

STEVIE WONDER 1984

I JUST CALLED TO SAY I LOVE YOU

WRITER: Stevie Wonder

PRODUCER: Stevie Wonder

ALBUM: The Woman In Red (soundtrack)

PEAK POSITION: Number 1 (6 weeks)

WEEKS ON CHART: 26

SALES: 1.83m

When 34-year-old Stevie Wonder staged his European tour in 1984, he broke off from his hits-filled set halfway through each show to unveil his brand new single. It would go on to become the biggest hit of his entire career – the commercial highlight, if not the creative one.

At this stage, Wonder was already a genuine living legend. It was an epithet earned over 23 years and 12 Grammy Awards (since expanded to a 24-Grammy career haul) accumulated in a hot streak that stands comparison with any other music act in history. Wonder's five-year explosion of creativity (1972–1976) was all the more incredible, coming as it did after he began his career as one of Berry Gordy's notoriously stage-managed Motown stable of artists.

Born in 1950 as Steveland Judkins, Wonder lost his sight when excess oxygen was pumped into his incubation unit as a baby. Through his early years he showed prodigious musical talent, across percussion, piano and harmonica. By eight he was writing his own music and by 11 the child prodigy had signed to Gordy's then still-nascent label, where Gordy renamed Judkins 'Little Stevie Wonder'.

'Fingertips (Part 2)' became Wonder's first hit single in the US in 1963 when he was still aged just 13. After establishing himself as one of Motown's most bankable stars, Wonder was only 21 when he renegotiated his deal and secured more creative freedom than any previous artist signed to the label. The results were extraordinary.

Wonder created a pioneering concoction of soul, R&B and funk, experimenting with electronic synthesized sounds, to begin a run which would elevate him to the level of undisputed musical genius – spanning the five albums from 1972's *Music Of My Mind* through to 1976's *Songs In The Key Of Life. Innervisions* made him the first black act to win the prestigious Album of the Year Grammy, a win he followed up with both *Fulfillingness' First Finale* and *Songs In The Key Of Life*. In that short period, he scooped 12 Grammys.

With 1980's *Hotter Than July*, Wonder melded the commercial and critical through tracks such as 'Masterblaster (Jammin')' and 'Lately', while also driving his campaign for the declaration of Martin Luther King's birthday as a US public holiday through the song 'Happy Birthday'.

At the time of that European tour, Wonder had achieved 24 Top 10 singles in the US (including seven number ones), with a further 13 Top 10 hits in the UK. A solo UK number one continued to elude him, however, his only chart-topper in the Official Singles Chart being the 1982 duet 'Ebony And Ivory' with Paul McCartney. 'I Just Called To Say I Love You' would end that run.

When Wonder launched into a rendition of the new song on that European tour, it was clear that this was from the mushier side of his repertoire, rather than the more progressive soul/funk of 'Superstition', 'Sir Duke' or 'Boogie On Reggae Woman'.

The track was the lead song from Wonder's soundtrack album for a rather unremarkable movie, *The Woman In Red*, starring Gene Wilder. Written and co-produced with Gary Olazabal, the album was Wonder's first wholly studio offering since *Hotter Than July*. A far cry from the critically acclaimed heights of the previous decade, the creative decline in Wonder's career could arguably be traced to this album.

However, there was no arguing with 'I Just Called To Say I Love You'. Rising to number one in the Official Singles Chart in September, it held the top spot for six weeks on its way to becoming the third biggest single of the Eighties in the UK.

Also a number one in the US, Australia, Austria, France, Germany, Ireland, Italy, the Netherlands, New Zealand, Norway, Sweden and Switzerland, 'Called' also gave Wonder his only Golden Globe and Oscar awards, for Best Original Song.

RAY PARKER, JR. 1984

GHOSTBUSTERS

WRITER: Ray Parker, Jr.

PRODUCER: Ray Parker, Jr.

ALBUM: Ghostbusters (soundtrack)

PEAK POSITION: Number 2 (3 weeks)

WEEKS ON CHART: 35 (1984, 31; 2007, 1; 2008, 1; 2009, 1; 2010, 1)

SALES: 1.09m

While not exactly a one-hit wonder, Ray Parker, Jr. is a US R&B star who would mean little to British music fans but for his one huge smash – 'Ghostbusters', which spent seven months on the Official Singles Chart in 1984–85 and peaked at number two.

Before first tasting fame as leader of Raydio, Detroit-born Parker worked in the backing bands of The (Detroit) Spinners, was a regular session guitarist with the Holland-Dozier-Holland production team and was a member of Barry White's Love Unlimited Orchestra. He also worked as a session guitarist/songwriter with acts like the Carpenters, Aretha Franklin, Tina Turner, Diana Ross, The Temptations, Gladys Knight and Chaka Khan. Additionally, he played on the road with Stevie Wonder's band and can be heard on Wonder's acclaimed albums *Talking Book* and *Innervisions*.

Parker first came to the public's attention as the 'Ray' in Raydio, the R&B group whose single 'Jack And Jill' climbed up the UK's Official Singles Chart in 1978. Raydio, who split in 1982, also included Vincent Bonham, Arnell and Darren Carmichael, Charles Fearing and Jerry Knight (later of Ollie & Jerry fame) and Larry Talbert.

In America, Parker had a long string of successful solo singles prior to 'Ghostbusters', including the Top 20 pop singles 'The Other Woman' and 'I Still Can't Get Over Loving You', and the Top 10 R&B hits 'Let Me Go' and 'Bad Boy'. However, in the UK it was the theme to the hugely successful Bill Murray, Dan Aykroyd and Harold Ramis movie that gave him his first solo hit.

Parker has said that he was approached to write the theme song by the film's producers, who told him that they'd already had about 60 songs submitted but did not like any of them. He was shown the film and told to write something happy and funny. After initially worrying about finding rhymes for 'Ghostbusters', he thought of the idea of treating it almost like an advertising jingle, and then came up with the "Who you gonna call?" line.

As Parker said: "I wanted to make a simple, easy song that people could sing along with and not have to think about." Two days later he had not only written but recorded the track that would go on to grab a Grammy and sell in its millions around the globe. Parker later had some legal problems with Huey Lewis (of The News), who felt that the record's predominant bass/guitar riff was borrowed from his own earlier hit 'I Want A New Drug', but the case was settled out of court.

The song's promo video starred US TV actress Cindy Harrell and contained cameo appearances from several famous movie faces including John Candy, Irene Cara, Chevy Chase, Danny DeVito, Peter Falk, Melissa Gilbert and Carly Simon, as well as the film's stars.

Parker's spirited rendition of the song entered the UK chart in August 1984, peaked in the runner-up slot a month later and vanished from the Top 40 in November. However, just before Christmas, 'Ghostbusters' returned from the dead and had a second chart run, reaching number six on January 5, 1985.

The record that stopped 'Ghostbusters' reaching the top in the UK was another million-selling 'call' song, 'I Just Called To Say I Love You' by Parker's old boss Stevie Wonder – which also beat Parker to the Oscar for Best Original Song in a film.

'Ghostbusters' is another of those tunes which fell just short of a million in its peak years but has passed the million sales threshold since the arrival of digital downloading, its most popular period of the year being around Halloween, for which it has become an annual anthem.

BAND AID 1984

DO THEY KNOW IT'S CHRISTMAS?

WRITERS: Bob Geldof, Midge Ure	
PRODUCER: Midge Ure	
ALBUM: N/A	
PEAK POSITION: Number 1 (6 weeks)	
WEEKS ON CHART: 57 (1984, 13; 1985, 7; 1989, 6; 2004, 10; 2005, 1; 2007, 4; 2008, 4; 2009, 4; 2010, 4; 2011, 4)	
SALES: 3.69m	

As 1984 edged towards a close, it looked like two new titans of pop music were about to carry their battle for supremacy in the British music scene into the Christmas season. The year's Official UK charts had been dominated by Wham! and Frankie Goes To Hollywood (FGTH), who had racked up eight Top 10 and four number one singles between them over the previous couple of years.

Just as the nation began unpacking their Christmas decorations, FGTH were cueing the first ballad of their career, 'The Power Of Love' – quite a risk for a band whose biggest singles had been a paean to gay sex and a representation of the Cold War. Meanwhile, Wham! were preparing to offer 'Last Christmas' (backed by a cheesy promo video, setting young love amid the ski slopes).

FGTH were surely the favourites, having already scored two million sellers that year, but the game had already changed, dramatically.

For several months, the North African nation of Ethiopia had been slipping inexorably towards disaster amid a famine that would kill millions and soon draw the attention of BBC TV news journalist Michael Burke. His October 24 news report was watched by Boomtown Rats frontman Bob Geldof, who, appalled at what he saw, sought the help of Ultravox's Midge Ure to pull together a charity record.

With Ure writing music to Geldof's lyrics, he then went into his home studio and laid down the backing tracks to his own melody, the result being an almost complete recording, which the various guest singers would be able to add their vocals to.

In the meantime, Geldof set out to use his powers of persuasion to enlist the contributions of a legion of British pop legends, past, present and future. On November 24, they entered London's Sarm Studios to record what would prove to be the biggest-selling single in history at the time, toppling Wings' 'Mull Of Kintyre' from the throne.

With only eight hours of studio time at their disposal, the first singers contributing at 11 a.m. and the curtain falling at 7 p.m., the recording was completed in a day with 38 contributors later credited. By morning, Geldof was announcing the release on presenter Mike Read's BBC Radio 1 breakfast show and the single was mastered, manufactured and packaged to be in stores the following Monday, November 29, issued on Polygram's Mercury label.

It was by far the fastest turnaround single of all time and, five days later, nothing was going to stop it entering the Official Singles Chart at number one. It became what was then the fastest million seller of all time and held the top spot for the rest of 1984, a full four weeks.

The release disrupted some well-laid plans for chart success. FGTH's label ZTT (whose co-founder, FGTH producer and Sarm owner Trevor Horn, mixed the 12-inch vinyl version of 'Christmas') had planned to usurp Wham!, staking their claim on the chart early with a release in the last week of November, but racked up a single week at number one by the time Band Aid swept in to topple them.

In contrast, Wham!'s label Epic was primed for an early December release, but by the time the act's single reached stores, it had no chance and was destined to become the biggest-selling single never to top the UK chart.

The success of the Band Aid single created a spiral of events, not least the huge Live Aid concert that took place at Wembley Stadium the following summer, on July 13, 1985, creating a brand new standard by which to judge charity concerts. It also spawned a string of follow-ups including Band Aid II, Band Aid 20 and the Live 8 concert. Up to the end of 2011, the charity effort kicked off by Band Aid had raised a total of $190 million (approximately £120 million).

MILLION-SELLING MEMORIES

MIDGE URE (ULTRAVOX, BAND AID)

'Do They Know It's Christmas?' is one of the best-known British singles of all time – with possibly one of the most unusual recording processes behind it. How did you and Bob bring the song together?

I initially recorded the melody on a little toy keyboard onto a cassette. It was a lot slower than on the record. I sent it to Bob and he came over a couple of days later. He had this idea. He came up with the majority of the lyrics and at the time I thought these two things were totally incompatible. We started with these lyrics, 'there won't be snow in Ethiopia this Christmas', which didn't quite work, so we changed 'Ethiopia' to 'Africa'. The really hard part was to have this quite ominous change of time and then finish with this almost positive sing-along part which would be so memorable.

And then you went into the studio to record it?

At first, Bob wanted Trevor Horn to produce the record, but he takes six weeks just to produce a single! We just didn't have that. So, I just said leave it with me. Because I had a studio at the house, I went down there for four days and knocked this thing into shape. Bob would pop in occasionally, but I carried on working on the music, putting it together, instrument by instrument. John Taylor [of Duran Duran] laid down a track, and Paul Weller did some guitar which we didn't actually use. But everything on that record is synthesised, except for Phil Collins' drums, plus I also nicked a drum sound from Tears For Fears' *The Hurting*.

A couple of people came down to my studio and did their vocal parts before the day itself – and then we had only 24 hours in [Sarm Studio]. I would like to think that we did make the best job of it. But we had no budget, the time constraints were huge, we had to grab whoever, whenever we could. As you can imagine, these people are all over the world and weren't all available when we wanted them.

What do you think of the single and the song, looking back on them now?

They are two separate things. You have to look at it as a song and as a record. What we made was a record and it did a brilliant job. It was quite nicely produced, it had lots of textures on it, lots of highs and lows – and you hear it coming out of the radio and it still does the job today.

As a song, if you take away the periphery, the artists, the money raised and the reason we made it, I think it's not that great. It's not the best thing I've been involved in. But as a record…

Did you expect it to be quite as huge as it became?

Absolutely not. On the day we made it, it was a real media circus because of all the characters, because a bunch of artists had never got together like that before. There was a specific aim to get to number one at Christmas, but that was it. But it is a Christmas song and people seem to like pulling it out every year. We were very focused on getting to number one. It wasn't until much much later that we realised what it meant.

And, of course, aside from Band Aid, Ultravox's 'Vienna' is rather well known for not getting to number one. How much of an issue was that for you at the time?

We were very very aware of it. It was the first big, successful record we ever had. It captured a lot of people's imaginations at the time. But people remember it now because it was kept off the top by a comedy record, by Joe Dolce. It wasn't even a very good comedy record…

WHAM! 1984

LAST CHRISTMAS/ EVERYTHING SHE WANTS

WRITER: George Michael

PRODUCER: George Michael

ALBUM: N/A ('Last Christmas')/Make It Big ('Everything She Wants')

PEAK POSITION: Number 2 (5 weeks)

WEEKS ON CHART: 46 (1984, 13; 1985, 7; 1986, 4; 2007, 5; 2008, 5; 2009, 4; 2010, 4; 2011, 4)

SALES: 1.6m

This double A-side remains the biggest-selling single in the UK never to hit number one in the Official Singles Chart – and will forever be known as only the second million seller not to do so, after Acker Bilk's 'Stranger On The Shore' in 1962.

'Last Christmas' was written by Michael upstairs at his parents' house, while his Wham! partner, Andrew Ridgeley, was watching the football highlights on *Match Of The Day*. And, as it was being prepped for release, the conditions could not have been better. The year 1984 had already been an extraordinary one for Wham!, who had had two successive UK number ones ('Wake Me Up Before You Go-Go' and 'Freedom') and were looking for their third.

Their plans to release their latest single for the Christmas market would have been fine had it not been for the huge media event which was Band Aid's Ethiopian famine relief record-breaker 'Do They Know It's Christmas?' (which also featured Michael). Band Aid inevitably ruled Christmas 1984 – although Wham! demonstrated how unconcerned they were by donating royalties from their release to the Band Aid charity too.

For all that, 'Last Christmas' does have several claims to fame. Its arrival on the chart represents the first time in chart history that the number one and number two hits both had been new entries and the only time that the top two singles in the official chart on December 25 both had the word 'Christmas' in their titles.

Also, Wham! and their label planned to maximise the single's potential, Band Aid or not. Knowing that 'Last Christmas' would be obsolete sales-wise from Boxing Day onwards, it was coupled with a B-side remix of 'Everything She Wants'. The aim was to use the track to maintain the single's momentum into the New Year, with the UK chart reversing the A-side credits from the first week of January 1985.

Band Aid maintained its strength into the New Year, never allowing its chart rival a look-in, the pair holding positions one and two for five weeks solid. By this strange quirk, this biggest-selling Wham! single and their only million seller was the broken link in what would otherwise have been five consecutive number ones for Michael.

'Last Christmas' continues to be Wham!'s most enduring hit (as many Christmas tunes are for the artists who created them). Reissued without the second A-side the following December, the track reached number six, and a second reissue in 1986 also charted. In the download era, the track has become a regular feature of the festive charts, re-entering every year since 2007, when it achieved a Top 20 placing for the third time.

In the US, 'Last Christmas' never achieved anything greater than minor airplay. However, 'Everything She Wants', released from the start in its remixed form, topped the *Billboard* Hot 100 in May 1985, selling over one million copies and becoming one of three Wham! tracks in America's Top 30 singles of the year.

Although 'Everything' featured on the duo's 1984 transatlantic chart-topping *Make It Big* album, which shifted in excess of six million copies in the US alone, 'Last Christmas' did not appear on a Wham! album until 1986 when career retrospective *The Final* reached number two on the Official Albums Chart, while the related, but much abbreviated, album release *Music From The Edge Of Heaven* sold one million Stateside.

This release remains one of an elite group of singles that did not reach pole position in the UK chart but went on to sell one million copies.

JENNIFER RUSH 1985

THE POWER OF LOVE

WRITERS: Candy de Rouge (Wolfgang Detmann), Gunther Mende, Jennifer Rush, Mary Susan Applegate

PRODUCERS: Gunther Mende, Candy de Rouge

ALBUM: Jennifer Rush

PEAK POSITION: Number 1 (5 weeks)

WEEKS ON CHART: 36

SALES: 1.39m

Following the historic twinned famine relief concerts in London and Philadelphia on Saturday July 13, 1985, 'the Live Aid effect' helped a succession of number one singles from artists who had taken part in either event – Madonna, UB40 featuring Chrissie Hynde (she performed with The Pretenders), David Bowie & Mick Jagger, plus Band Aid co-founder Midge Ure (who led Ultravox).

However, the single that ended that sequence had been on the Official Singles Chart since two weeks before Live Aid – and still holds the record for the slowest climb to number one in the official chart by any single during a continuous chart run.

In stark contrast to the megastars who had experienced huge sales spikes after being broadcast to a global TV audience of almost two million people, its performer had no previous UK track record but ended up claiming the first million-selling single by a woman and the best-selling single by a female solo act in the first 40 years of the UK Official Singles Chart.

After the very first UK singles chart was published in 1952, 32 years and more than 10,000 hits had passed without a single one being called 'The Power Of Love'; then, suddenly, between December 1984 and October 1985 three Top 20 entries arrived with that title – two of which topped the chart.

Born Heidi Stern on September 28, 1960 in New York, Jennifer

Rush was a classically trained singer who lived and recorded in Germany at the time she co-composed and released this powerful love song.

The single's first 12 weeks on the chart were all spent pottering around between positions 41 and 75, during which time it slipped backwards down the chart on three separate occasions before recovering again, making it the first number one single to experience a triple dip. But it wasn't until CBS Records deleted the initial seven-inch pressing of the single (clocking in at six minutes long), and replaced it with a four-minute-20-second 'remix' by UK engineer Walter Samuel, that, in week 13, Rush finally had a Top 40 hit on her hands.

Powered by spectacular sales in Scotland and Northern Ireland, Rush suddenly found herself joining Huey Lewis & The News' hit of the same name in the Top 20, and in mid-October 1985, on its 16th chart appearance, 'The Power Of Love' completed its climb to the summit, less than a year after Frankie Goes To Hollywood had topped the chart in December 1984 with a song bearing the same title.

In setting a new record for sloth, the single beat Dead Or Alive's previous record-breaking 15-week slow-motion journey to number one with 'You Spin Me Round (Like A Record)', which had been established only seven months earlier.

After all that hard work getting there, Rush rested at the peak for five weeks, the longest run at the top by a female soloist since Freda Payne's six-week chart-topper 'Band Of Gold' in 1970.

'The Power Of Love' was the only single to shift one million units during 1985, Rush heading an all-female Top Three of bestsellers of the year, followed by Elaine Paige and Barbara Dickson's 'I Know Him So Well' and Madonna's 'Into The Groove'.

Although a Top 10 hit around the globe (topping the charts in Australia, Ireland, New Zealand, Norway and Spain [re-recorded as 'Si Tu Eres Mi Hombre Y Yo Tu Mujer']), Rush's recording failed to replicate its success in her homeland. Despite other attempts in the late Eighties, it was not until 1994, courtesy of Celine Dion, that 'The Power Of Love' became a US number one.

Dion's recording reached number four in the UK in February 1994 and, a year later, she would be the artist to equal Rush's 16-week climb to the UK number one spot when her own million seller, 'Think Twice', also took the scenic route to the top.

In 2010 Jennifer Rush released her first new album in 13 years.

BLACK BOX 1989
RIDE ON TIME

WRITERS: Dan Hartman, Daniele Davoli, Mirko Limoni, Valerio Semplici

PRODUCERS: Mirko Limoni, Valerio Semplici

ALBUM: Dreamland

PEAK POSITION: Number 1 (6 weeks)

WEEKS ON CHART: 30 (1989, 22; 1991, 8)

SALES: 1.05m

Italy has always been known as a land of song, which over the years has given the world many beautiful ballads and acclaimed operatic arias. But in the late Eighties it began to establish itself as an unlikely powerhouse for house music – with 'Ride On Time' as one of its biggest exports.

DJ/production trio Black Box's club classic 'Ride On Time' became the first Italian record to top the Official Singles Chart – and the first record by an Italian act to sell over one million copies in Britain, and was a hit in many other markets besides.

It is unlikely that when dance production duo Mirko Limoni and Valerio Semplici recorded the track for their Groove Groove Melody production house that they envisaged it becoming a worldwide hit. If they had, they would probably have recorded a new vocal contribution, rather than sampling from Loleatta Holloway's 1980 'Love Sensation', which had topped *Billboard*'s US Dance/Club Play chart that year.

Hailing from the town of House, Chicago, Holloway had sung in various gospel groups before releasing her debut album in 1973. She scored several disco hits in the US, before her best-known song 'Love Sensation' appeared in 1980.

Among the vocal lines appropriated from 'Love Sensation' for the Black Box recording was "Coz you're right on time" – which the Italians misinterpreted as 'ride on time', providing the title of their track. When the record took off, the producers recruited French model Katrin Quinol to front the record and mime to Holloway's vocals on video and TV.

As it turned out, Quinol was a better looker than a lip-syncher and it soon became apparent she was not the actual singer. Adams and 'Love Sensation' composer Dan Hartman (whose own Seventies hits included 'Instant Replay') reached a financial agreement with Black Box, who then also re-vocalled the track for remixed versions by both Heather Small (of M People) and Martha Wash (of The Weather Girls).

Wash later helped set a precedent for payments and credits for sampling when she sued Black Box for not mentioning her by name on this and other records.

Even though this record meant very little in Italy at the time, it entered the UK's Official Singles Chart on August 12, 1989, and had ridden to the top by September 9, a position it held for six weeks – and it ended up being the top-selling single of the year. Among the singles that stalled at number two behind it were Richard Marx's third successive US chart-topper, the appropriately titled 'Right Here Waiting', and fellow European house hit 'Pump Up The Jam', by Belgium's Technotronic featuring Felly, as well as Jason Donovan and Jive Bunny And The Mastermixers.

This was not the only UK hit that Limoni, Semplici and DJ Lelewel (as Daniele Davoli was known) enjoyed at the time. In the week that 'Ride On Time' hit number one, their single 'Numero Uno', released under the name Starlight, peaked at number nine and their million seller was replaced in the Top 10 by Davoli's 'Grand Piano', released under the name Mixmaster.

'Ride On Time' was also a major hit in many other countries, as was the album it appeared on, *Dreamland*, which topped the Australian chart for two months and went Gold in both the UK (the first album by an Italian act to reach the Official Albums Chart Top 20) and the US.

In the UK, Black Box recorded a run of six successive Top 20 entries, while in the US, where house music was less popular, 'Ride On Time' sold relatively few copies. However, the act later had a couple of Top 10 hits in the homeland of house music with 'Everybody, Everybody' and 'Strike It Up'.

Dan Hartman, a former member of The Edgar Winter Group, enjoyed a successful career as a songwriter and producer. He died in 1994.

BRYAN ADAMS 1991

(EVERYTHING I DO) I DO IT FOR YOU

WRITERS: Bryan Adams, Michael Kamen, Robert John 'Mutt' Lange

PRODUCER: Robert John 'Mutt' Lange

ALBUM: Waking Up The Neighbours/Robin Hood: Prince Of Thieves (soundtrack)

PEAK POSITION: Number 1 (16 weeks)

WEEKS ON CHART: 25

SALES: 1.72m

To say Bryan Adams' '(Everything I Do) I Do It For You' was the soundtrack to the summer of 1991 is an understatement – it was number one on the Official Singles Chart *all* summer.

Released on June 17 to coincide with the launch of the Kevin Costner film *Robin Hood: Prince Of Thieves* (the song was from the soundtrack) the previous weekend, it made its Top 10 debut at number eight the following Sunday. A week later, it climbed up the chart to number two, before knocking Jason Donovan's 'Any Dream Will Do' off number one on July 7, 1991. And there it would stay for the foreseeable future.

'(Everything I Do) I Do It For You' was penned during Adams' sessions for his sixth album, *Waking Up The Neighbours*, with British producer Robert John 'Mutt' Lange. In his homeland, Adams was a massive star; a guitar prodigy signed at the age of 18, his blue-collar anthems had made him the Canadian equivalent of Bruce Springsteen and, by this point in his career, he had clocked up over 12 Top 40 hits and three Top 10 albums both in Canada and the US. While a massive star in North America, Adams had yet to become a true international name. His highest charting track in the UK to date had been his debut single, 'Run To You', which reached number 11 six years before, in January 1985.

Adams' record company, A&M, decided to pair him with Lange, who had helmed both AC/DC's classic albums, 1979's *Highway To Hell* – the last to feature late vocalist Bon Scott – and their 1980 comeback album, *Back In Black*, which is widely regarded as the third-biggest-selling album of all time worldwide. Lange had also been instrumental in transforming Sheffield's Def Leppard into a chart-topping, arena rock behemoth. Arguably, he rewrote the anthemic pop rock rulebook (a template he would use to turn his future wife, Shania Twain, into an international megastar four years later), taking Adams into the mainstream.

The starting point for the track was a piece of orchestration from the late composer Michael Kamen's *Robin Hood: Prince Of Thieves* score. In an interview with www.songwriteruniverse.com, Adams revealed that he and Lange had the entire song nailed, from start to finish, in approximately three quarters of an hour. "It was a moment that I've only felt a few times," recalled the singer.

But a hit it definitely was. '(Everything I Do) I Do It For You' was number one on the Official Singles Chart for 16 consecutive weeks, from early July to late October 1991. During its reign at number one, the track would see off many pretenders to the throne: Heavy D & The Boyz' 'Now That We've Found Love', Extreme's 'More Than Words', Right Said Fred's 'I'm Too Sexy', Salt-N-Pepa's 'Let's Talk About Sex', Scorpions' 'Wind Of Change' and 2 Unlimited's 'Get Ready For This' would all try to topple it, but for the summer of 1991 the track reigned supreme.

'(Everything I Do) I Do It For You''s run at the top of the chart had to eventually come to an end – so at the end of October 1991, 'The Fly', the lead single from U2's then hotly-anticipated seventh studio album, *Achtung Baby*, took its crown. Nevertheless, during its time in pole position, it set a new official chart record – the longest unbroken run at number one in the history of the UK's Official Singles Chart.

That is a record the track still holds today. Wet Wet Wet's cover of The Troggs' 'Love Is All Around' – another soundtrack song, taken from *Four Weddings And A Funeral* – came close in 1994, spending 15 weeks at number one, but Whigfield's Europop anthem 'Saturday Night' replaced it to ensure Adams' title remained intact.

WHITNEY HOUSTON 1992

I WILL ALWAYS LOVE YOU

WRITER: Dolly Parton

PRODUCER: David Foster

ALBUM: The Bodyguard: Original Soundtrack

PEAK POSITION: Number 1 (10 weeks)

WEEKS ON CHART: 31 (1992, 23; 1993, 6; 2012, 2)

SALES: 1.53m

The late Whitney Houston honed her pop princess credentials with a string of Eighties hit singles, including three chart-toppers in the UK and a record seven consecutive number ones in the US. But few would dispute that her pure, powerful vocals were showcased most beautifully on this 1992 million-selling movie monster, a recording which will always remind listeners why they loved the lady from Newark, New Jersey.

'I Will Always Love You' was not written for Houston, being a Dolly Parton original, although the inevitable comparisons between the two are futile. Parton's plaintive, vulnerable composition, a 1974 *Billboard* Hot Country Songs number one in the US, was the sure-fire pop hit that never was, on either side of the Atlantic.

A cousin of Dionne Warwick, Houston's "towering pop-gospel assertion of lasting devotion to a departing lover" (in the words of the *New York Times*) played to her vocal strengths and was unashamedly designed for mass-market consumption in *The Bodyguard*, the film in which Houston made her acting debut as the Oscar-nominated singer/actress Rachel Marron.

What indelibly links the two versions is their record-breaking success. Parton's original, written in tribute to her mentor Porter Wagoner and featured in the film *The Best Little Whorehouse In Texas*, was the first song to return to number one on *Billboard*'s country chart, doing so after its composer re-recorded it in 1982.

In Houston's hands, the track set a string of chart records, including most consecutive weeks at number one on the Official Singles Chart by a female (a record shared with Rihanna's 'Umbrella') – 10 weeks from December 5, 1992 – and most consecutive weeks at number one on the US *Billboard* Hot 100 by a solo female – 14 weeks from November 28, 1992.

Dolly Parton later confirmed, "I will always be grateful and in awe of the wonderful performance she did on my song." Parton has undoubtedly amassed a sizeable fortune through millions of *Bodyguard*-inspired radio spins in the 1990s and beyond, which makes her decision not to sign away half the publishing rights to Elvis Presley's team in the mid-Seventies, when 'The King' showed an interest in recording the song, all the more significant.

Following Houston's untimely death on February 11, 2012, the song became the first by a female artist (and the second ever, after Chubby Checker's 'The Twist') to grace the Top Three of the *Billboard* Hot 100 on two separate occasions. At number 14, it was also the highest-placed of the record (for a female artist) 12 re-entries that flooded the UK chart on February 25, 2012.

The *Bodyguard* album, which features five other Houston performances, spent 20 weeks at number one Stateside and is the world's biggest-selling film soundtrack of all time, selling more than 44 million copies to date.

It could all have been so different had Houston gone with the filmmakers' original choice of song, 'What Becomes Of The Broken Hearted'. According to pop legend, *Bodyguard* co-star Kevin Costner was responsible for the inclusion of 'I Will Always Love You' in the film after he brought Linda Ronstadt's rendition, from her 1975 album *Prisoner In Disguise*, to Houston's attention. Another cover of the song, by US punk/Americana musician John Doe, also crops up in the film on a jukebox during a Houston/Costner dancing scene.

Houston's exceptional talent, first recognised as a member of the New Hope Baptist Junior Choir at the age of 11, saw her rack up worldwide record sales in excess of 150 million units, and between October 1985 and April 1988 she achieved an unprecedented run of seven successive US number one singles. Her back catalogue of ballads remains painfully difficult to listen to, given her early death.

WET WET WET 1994
LOVE IS ALL AROUND

WRITER: Reg Presley

PRODUCERS: Graeme Clark, Graeme Duffin, Marti Pellow, Tommy Cunningham, Neil Mitchell

ALBUM: Picture This/Four Weddings And A Funeral (soundtrack)

PEAK POSITION: Number 1 (15 weeks)

WEEKS ON CHART: 37

SALES: 1.85m

At around 6.55 p.m. on BBC Radio 1's *Official Chart Show*, for 15 consecutive weeks in the summer of 1994, the words "I feel it in my fingers, I feel it in my toes", sung by honey-voiced heartthrob Marti Pellow, greeted chart followers after the number one record was announced.

The indefatigable 'Love Is All Around' left a trail of destruction at number two during its record-breaking run on the Official Singles Chart, with 'Come On You Reds' by the Manchester United Football Squad (one week), Big Mountain's 'Baby I Love Your Way' (three weeks), 'I Swear' by All-4-One (a record-equalling seven weeks), 'Let Loose's Crazy For You' (two weeks), 'Compliments On Your Kiss' by Red Dragon with Brian and Tony Gold (one week) and Kylie Minogue's 'Confide In Me' (one week) all held off by its vice-like grip on the top rung of the chart. 'Saturday Night' by Denmark's Whigfield – the first artist from outside the UK or the US to debut at number one in the Official Singles Chart – eventually toppled 'Love' from its lofty perch.

"We did everybody's head in, in the summer of 1994," admitted frontman Pellow during an interview some years later, "[but] I still think it's a brilliant record. Any band would give their eye teeth to have a hit record like that. I'm very proud of it."

Back in October 1967, when Reginald Ball, aka Reg Presley, made the Top Five with his composition as frontman with The Troggs, little did he know he'd written what would become a chart behemoth some 17 years on – a song reportedly inspired by 'Love That's All Around' by Salvation Army pop group The Joy Strings.

Wet Wet Wet were a Glasgow-based band consisting of Pellow (Mark McLoughlin), Tommy Cunningham, Neil Mitchell, Graeme Clark and Graeme Duffin (although the latter was not an 'official' band member). All five received production credits on 'Love Is All Around', their seventh Top 10 entry and third number one. The first two were a cover of The Beatles' 'With A Little Help From My Friends' and the sumptuously melodic 'Goodnight Girl'.

Although the band were voted Best British Newcomers at the 1988 BRIT Awards, they would not add to their tally of three UK number ones which was completed by 'Love Is All Around'. Another six Top 10 hits followed, including the much-covered Beatles classic 'Yesterday' in 1997.

'Love Is All Around' received nationwide exposure in the British blockbuster *Four Weddings And A Funeral*, written by Richard Curtis and starring Hugh Grant and Andie MacDowell, which opened in cinemas three weeks before 'Love' first crowned the singles chart on June 4, 1994. It was the highest-grossing British film in history at that time and so it followed that the soundtrack would find favour with the record-buying public.

Not appearing on a Wets' album until the release of *Picture This*, 11 months after the single's release, 'Love Is All Around' holds the record for the most consecutive and cumulative weeks at number one by a group and has sold just shy of 1.8 million copies in the UK.

'Love' might even have spent longer at number one (challenging Bryan Adams for the most consecutive weeks at the top – 16 – or even Frankie Laine's record 18 cumulative weeks at the top with 'I Believe') had Pellow and co. not grown tired of its success and instructed their record label to delete the recording – in other words, to stop pressing copies and supplying them to retailers. Still, 15 weeks at number one and 37 weeks on the chart was a spectacular return for the BRIT Award-winning Glaswegians.

One thing is for sure: Reg Presley can happily live off the royalty cheques that come his way. Indeed, the Troggs vocalist is on record as saying that some of the proceeds have been spent on crop circle research – in the words of an earlier Wet Wet Wet hit, his very own 'Sweet Little Mystery'.

WHIGFIELD 1994

SATURDAY NIGHT

WRITERS: Larry Pignagnoli, Davide Riva

PRODUCER: Larry Pignagnoli

ALBUM: Whigfield

PEAK POSITION: Number 1 (4 weeks)

WEEKS ON CHART: 18

SALES: 1.14m

A simple, naggingly infectious slice of pop-dance made a Danish-born model and singer the first artist to enter the Official Singles Chart at number one with their debut single.

Whigfield's 'Saturday Night' was a pan-European smash in 1994, after an initial breakthrough in Spain at Christmas 1993. It topped the Spanish chart for 11 weeks, leading the artist to be signed in Britain by London Records subsidiary Systematic.

Though Whigfield joined the label in February 1994, Systematic head Christian Tattersfield cannily delayed releasing 'Saturday Night' as a single, reasoning that it would be a perfect release for the end of summer, targeting holidaymakers who were returning from their Continental breaks. The tactic paid off – after selling as an import for several weeks, its official UK release on September 5, 1994 would take it to number one for a month.

Born in the Danish town of Skælskør in 1970, Whigfield began life as Sannie Carlson but adopted a professional nickname in tribute to her childhood piano teacher, one Mr Whigfield. In 1992, by then based in Italy, she teamed up with producer Larry Pignagnoli, who had form with international Europop – most successfully, he had co-written and produced Spanish singer Spagna's 'Call Me', a UK number two hit in 1987.

With a memorable dance routine that vast numbers of fans seemed to want to emulate, 'Saturday Night' stylishly ended a 15-week run at number one for Wet Wet Wet's 'Love Is All Around'. In its second week on sale, it sold 220,000 copies, the highest seven-day sale of any single for nearly 10 years, and in little over a month it would sell 800,000 units. Whigfield herself was only the second female artist (after Mariah Carey just six months earlier) to enter the chart at the very top and the first act that was neither British nor American to do so.

Though 'Saturday Night' repeated its chart-topping performance in Germany, Italy and Switzerland, it failed to progress higher than second place in Whitfield's Danish homeland. Its infectious tune would trigger two claims of plagiarism in the months after its release, citing very different sources: 'Rub A Dub Dub' by Eddy Grant's Sixties pop/reggae band The Equals, and Newcastle folkies Lindisfarne's 1971 theme song 'Fog On The Tyne'. Both claims were dismissed.

On October 9, 1994, after four weeks, 'Saturday Night' was dislodged from the top by Take That's 'Sure', but four more Whigfield hits would reach the Top 40. The last was a cover version of Wham!'s million-selling 'Last Christmas', which peaked at number 21 over the festive period of 1995. That same year, she also supported then up-and-coming Irish boy band Boyzone on a handful of UK dates.

Although Whigfield has continued to write and record, and was still reaching the Danish Top 10 as recently as 2011, 'Saturday Night' remains her signature tune. It was Britain's second biggest seller of 1994 and the highest-selling debut single since Jennifer Rush's 'The Power of Love' in 1985.

CELINE DION 1994
THINK TWICE

WRITERS: Andy Hill, Peter Sinfield

PRODUCERS: Christopher Neil, Aldo Nova

ALBUM: The Colour Of My Love

PEAK POSITION: Number 1 (7 weeks)

WEEKS ON CHART: 31

SALES: 1.3m

Even the most vociferous Celine Dion fan might have to 'Think Twice' before naming both of her UK million-selling singles.

It seems odd that a song that spent seven weeks at number one on the Official Singles Chart in February and March 1995 and 31 weeks on the countdown in total (figures that would sink 'My Heart Will Go On' in a game of pop Top Trumps) could dip so spectacularly below the radar. Yet this soft rock monster was 'classic Celine' – combining powerhouse vocals (with a hint of anger on this occasion), a drop-dead gorgeous melody and, as befits her career to date, an ability to wring every ounce of heart-wrenching emotion out of the lyrics.

'Think Twice' was penned by Andy Hill, who co-wrote and produced Bucks Fizz's Eurovision Song Contest-winning 'Making Your Mind Up', with Peter Sinfield, co-founder of prog rockers King Crimson and lyricist for Emerson, Lake & Palmer.

Sinfield's involvement is one plausible explanation for the presence of a guitar solo – courtesy of co-producer Aldo Nova – on this track, which scooped an Ivor Novello Award for Song of the Year in 1995.

'Think Twice' was a slow-burner on the UK chart, debuting at number 30 in November 1994. It took a further four weeks to reach the Top 10 and another eight weeks to reach the summit. In its 13th chart week, in a new calendar year and after three weeks waiting patiently behind the Rednex romp 'Cotton Eye Joe', Dion chalked up her first UK number one single.

N-Trance ('Set You Free'), Annie Lennox ('No More "I Love You's"'), MN8 ('I've Got A Little Something For You') and Alex Party ('Don't Give Me Your Life') were the unfortunates stalled at number two during the seven-week chart-topping tenure of 'Think Twice', which made way for the multi-artist charity single 'Love Can Build A Bridge' in March 1995.

The CD versions of the single provided fans of early Dion with a handy career retrospective, featuring the blink-and-you'll-miss-it hit 'If You Asked Me To' (1992) on one CD and 'The Power Of Love' (1994) and 'Where Does My Heart Beat Now' (1993) on the other, as well as the first UK CD sighting of one of Dion's famed French language songs on the former ('Le Monde Est Stone').

Born in Quebec, Canada, on March 30, 1968, Dion first courted the European market when she won the Eurovision Song Contest in 1988, representing Switzerland. Her UK chart career began in 1992 with 'Beauty And The Beast', which sold one million copies in the US, and the aforementioned 'The Power Of Love', a US number one, introduced her to the Top Five in the UK – and British fans to the album that featured 'Think Twice', *The Colour Of My Love*. That 1994 album was the first of two Dion albums to rack up more than 100 weeks on the Official Albums Chart (the other being 1996's *Falling Into You*).

This would not be the last time Dion would join the millionaire's club. Four years later she would embark on a titanic journey to the singles chart summit.

168

OASIS 1995

WONDERWALL

WRITER: Noel Gallagher

PRODUCERS: Owen Morris, Noel Gallagher

ALBUM: (What's The Story) Morning Glory?

PEAK POSITION: Number 2 (1 week)

WEEKS ON CHART: 34

SALES: 1.26m

Manchester's rock sensations of the mid-to-late 1990s, Oasis achieved their only million-selling single with a track which was not one of their eight official number one singles in the UK.

Even with first-week sales of 163,000, 'Wonderwall' had to settle for a number two peak in the Official Singles Chart thanks to Robson & Jerome's 'I Believe'/'Up On The Roof'. Nevertheless, it was perhaps the key track on *(What's The Story) Morning Glory?*, Oasis's second long-player, which became the best-selling album of the 1990s in Britain.

The origin of the song's title lies in a George Harrison soundtrack album, *Wonderwall Music*, recorded for a little-seen 1968 film by director Joe Massot. The song's lyrical inspiration is less clear-cut; although its author, Noel Gallagher, reportedly said it was a tribute to his then-girlfriend Meg Mathews, he would later insist (after the couple's 2001 split) that it was a paean to an imaginary friend "who's gonna come and save you from yourself".

Born in 1967, guitarist Noel became the songwriting linchpin of Oasis when he joined younger brother Liam's group The Rain in 1991. Swiftly signed to Creation Records after its boss, Alan McGee, witnessed their set at a Glasgow venue in May 1993, the first of 26 British hits (23 of them Top 10) came with 'Supersonic' in April 1994. Their debut album, *Definitely Maybe*, released four months later, reached number one with almost comical ease, achieving the highest first-week sales of any album since Michael Jackson's *Bad* in 1987.

In May 1995, the same month 'Some Might Say' became Oasis's first Official Singles Chart number one, 'Wonderwall' was recorded at Welsh studios Rockfield during sessions for the group's second album. Although Noel Gallagher gave an impromptu performance of the song during Channel 4's TV coverage of the Glastonbury festival the following month, this more wistful, reflective addition to the group's repertoire was not yet part of its live set.

Losing a much-publicised battle for singles chart supremacy with Blur later that summer – when 'Roll With It' was beaten to number one by Blur's 'Country House' – Oasis looked as if they might suffer another setback when relatively lukewarm reviews for their second album appeared. But when *Morning Glory?* was released in the first week of October, 'Wonderwall' became an immediate airplay favourite. By the time the single was released on October 30, BBC Radio 1 was playing it 25 times a week and in the lead-up to Christmas 1995, the group's previous seven singles re-entered the lower reaches of the Official Singles Chart.

Many artists have covered 'Wonderwall' since, including Ryan Adams and Jay-Z, but the version that briefly received most publicity was a knowing easy-listening pastiche of the song, originally recorded for BBC Radio 1 DJs Chris Evans and Kevin Greening. Culprits The Mike Flowers Pops, who playfully pretended that Oasis had covered 'their' song from the 1960s, not only equalled Oasis's number two peak with their version, but also probably helped the original stay in the Top 10 over Christmas and into the New Year.

'Wonderwall' marked Oasis's international breakthrough and zenith: number eight in the US, number one in Australia and New Zealand, plus Top 10 showings everywhere from the Netherlands to Zimbabwe.

Its appeal in Britain has also been particularly enduring. The 10th best-selling single of 1995, it was voted the year's best single by *New Musical Express* readers and the all-time number one song by BBC Radio 1 listeners at Christmas 1996. It is undoubtedly one of the reasons why Oasis received a BRIT Award for Outstanding Contribution to Music in 2007.

Even after the group imploded in 2009, *(What's the Story) Morning Glory?* was given a special BRIT Award as the Best Album of the Past 30 Years – with 'Wonderwall' perhaps its best-loved track.

TAKE THAT 1995

BACK FOR GOOD

WRITER: Gary Barlow

PRODUCERS: Chris Porter, Gary Barlow

ALBUM: Nobody Else

PEAK POSITION: Number 1 (4 weeks)

WEEKS ON CHART: 13

SALES: 1.07m

The annals of pop indicate that Gary Barlow, Robbie Williams, Mark Owen, Jason Orange and Howard Donald were not, in fact, 'back for good' in April 1995 – but then 'back for the next 12 months before calling it quits and then mounting the greatest comeback in pop music history' would be less of a catchy title.

As it was, they settled for three words that would give headline-writers across the land a field day, both when the words "Take That are no more" were spoken at a press conference on February 13, 1996, and upon their triumphant return in May 2006.

Barlow's poignant love ballad is arguably the group's finest four minutes, setting a post-break-up/accepting the inevitable mood with the lyric: "Gotta leave it, gotta leave it all behind now."

Barlow, the group's songwriter-in-chief and an accomplished pianist and producer, was born in Frodsham, Cheshire, on January 20, 1971. He scored his first number one as a songwriter with Take That's 1993 single 'Pray' and has since racked up five Ivor Novello Awards for his compositions. And, in 2011 and 2012, he reinvented himself as head judge on TV's *The X-Factor* (alongside Louis Walsh, Kelly Rowland and Tulisa Contostavlos) before organising Queen Elizabeth II's Diamond Jubilee concert and travelling the Commonwealth to compose jubilee theme 'Sing'.

By today's standards, 13 weeks on the Official Singles Chart and fewer than five million YouTube views might be considered disappointing, but Take That's sixth number one, and what would turn out to be the second in a string of six ('Sure', 'Back For Good', 'Never Forget', 'How Deep Is Your Love', 'Patience' and 'Shine') from consecutive singles, excelled in all other areas – spending four weeks at number one and topping charts in more than 30 countries worldwide.

'Back For Good' debuted at number one with sales approaching 350,000 in April 1995, knocking The Outhere Brothers' 'Don't Stop (Wiggle Wiggle)' off its perch. The single came complete with a moody monochrome video which found the boys dancing around a car and getting drenched in the process.

The song was unveiled at the 1995 BRIT Awards on February 20, and 12 months on, Take That – now a quartet following Williams' departure in July 1995 (although he'd be back, but not for good) – were once again centre-stage on British music's biggest annual night out when they collected the prize for Best British Single, putting the 'Battle of Britpop' singles 'Country House' (Blur) and 'Roll With It' (Oasis) and Pulp's 'Disco 2000' firmly in their place.

The Ivor Novello Award-winning track, which was tipped over the one million threshold in 2010 thanks to digital sales, also became Take That's only US success, peaking at number seven in November 1995.

After two more singles – 'Never Forget' in August 1995 and 'How Deep Is Your Love' in March 1996 – and almost 20 million combined singles and album sales, Take That were "no more". Barlow, Williams and Owen all courted the Top Three, notably Barlow, who kicked off his solo career with two number ones, although it was Williams' enduring popularity that largely kept the group in fans' minds during the first half of the 2000s before they reunited, initially Robbie-less, in 2006.

Three number one singles and albums – including Williams' return on the 2010 *Progress* album – and a record-breaking tour later, and it's like Take That have never been away.

ROBSON GREEN & JEROME FLYNN 1995

UNCHAINED MELODY/THE WHITE CLIFFS OF DOVER

WRITERS: 'Unchained Melody' – Alex North (music), Hy Zaret (lyrics)/'(There'll Be Bluebirds Over) The White Cliffs Of Dover' – Walter Kent (music), Nat Burton (lyrics)

PRODUCERS: Mike Stock, Matt Aitken

ALBUM: Robson & Jerome

PEAK POSITION: Number 1 (7 weeks)

WEEKS ON CHART: 17

SALES: 1.86m

'Unchained Melody' was the first song to enjoy three chart-topping runs by three different acts and is the only track to have been a UK million seller on three separate occasions – courtesy of The Righteous Brothers in 1990, Gareth Gates in 2002 and this popular cover of the timeless ballad, which further cemented the link between TV and hit-making.

The Oscar-nominated song, which first topped the UK's Official Singles Chart (sung by Jimmy Young) in 1955, returned to the summit for a third time in 1995 after fans of ITV drama *Soldier Soldier* were treated to a rendition by actors Robson Green (Fusilier Dave Tucker) and Jerome Flynn (Sergeant Paddy Garvey), described by one critic as "nice lads [with] firm jaws, soft eyes, clean shirts, and reassuring imperfections".

On the show, the song was performed bashfully by the duo after a hired band failed to appear for a friend's wedding, and within a matter of weeks fans had all but forgotten about Patrick Swayze and Demi Moore's wandering, clay-covered hands in *Ghost* and were able to lay their own hands on a copy of Green and Flynn's double A-side.

The actors were, however, reluctant chart stars, and according to pop legend they had to be persuaded to record and release 'Unchained Melody' by RCA executive Simon Cowell (some years before his current *X-Factor* incarnation). It was a decision that paid off handsomely.

The fastest-selling debut single in UK chart history at that time, with 314,000 copies sold in the first week, it entered at number one in May 1995 and remained in pole position for seven weeks. Produced by Mike Stock and Matt Aitken, the track went on to sell 1.9 million copies and remains among the Top 10 biggest-selling singles ever in the UK.

The timing of the release, on VE Day, undoubtedly contributed to its success, and the nostalgic theme was further driven home by an accompanying video that included clips from the classic 1940s movie *Brief Encounter*. BBC Radio 1 ignored the single, but it made little difference.

The success of the single came at a moment when the nation was still swooning over Take That and just weeks away from witnessing the mightiest Britpop battle of them all (Blur vs. Oasis). Nevertheless, it launched a brief but profitable 18 months for Green and Flynn.

This was the first of their three official number one singles (from just three single releases) and they also bagged two official number one albums, the first an eponymously titled set featuring both 'Unchained Melody' and Walter Kent and Nat Burton's 'Cliffs Of Dover', a song first made famous by Dame Vera Lynn during World War II and also a hit, in 1966, for The Righteous Brothers. Sadly, Kent passed away in 1994 and was unable to enjoy his song's chart-topping success.

One-time shipyard worker Green (*Casualty*, *Waterloo Road*, *Extreme Fishing With Robson Green*) and Flynn (*London's Burning*, *Between The Lines*, the film *Best*), a direct descendent of Oliver Cromwell, have added several career strings to their bows, but arguably nothing has come close to matching the instantaneous success of 'Unchained Melody'/'(There'll Be Bluebirds Over) The White Cliffs Of Dover'.

'Unchained Melody' has now become one of the most recorded songs of the 20th Century, with over 500 versions in many different languages.

COOLIO FEAT. L.V. 1995

GANGSTA'S PARADISE

| WRITERS: Coolio, Larry Sanders, Stevie Wonder, Doug Rasheed |
| PRODUCER: Doug Rasheed |
| ALBUM: Gangsta's Paradise |
| PEAK POSITION: Number 1 (2 weeks) |
| WEEKS ON CHART: 24 (1995, 20; 2009, 3; 2011, 1) |
| SALES: 1.41m |

The first rap single to shift one million copies in the UK marked the first Official Singles Chart Top 40 entry for Californian rapper Coolio.

An adaptation of a Stevie Wonder song, 'Gangsta's Paradise''s international profile was boosted when it featured on the soundtrack to the movie *Dangerous Minds*. The film, starring Michelle Pfeiffer, was based on a true story in which a US marine named LouAnne Johnson swapped military life for teaching a class of difficult teenagers.

Born Artis Leon Ivey Jr. in 1963, Coolio made his recording debut as a solo artist in the late Eighties, before joining the ranks of the rap group WC & The Maad Circle in 1991. As a solo act, he was signed to Tommy Boy Records in 1994, the same year his single 'Fantastic Voyage' reached number three on the *Billboard* Hot 100.

For his biggest hit, Coolio reinvented 'Pastime Paradise', a standout track on Stevie Wonder's landmark 1976 album *Songs In The Key Of Life*. Like that album's 'Isn't She Lovely' (a 1977 UK hit for David Parton), 'Pastime Paradise' had never been issued as a Wonder single. In fact, it was far from being one of the performer's best-known tunes.

Coolio took a sample of Wonder's main rhythm and built his song around the original's structure, adding his own lyrics to contemporise it. The track featured as its guest vocalist L.V. (Large Variety), aka 37-year-old Larry Sanders, who had previously performed with rap group the South Central Cartel.

'Gangsta's Paradise' was released as a single in the UK in October 1995. It received little support from clubs and, with many radio stations still nervous about playing gangsta rap, initial airplay was almost exclusively confined to BBC Radio 1. Nevertheless, aided by press promotion and TV spots, it sold more than 250,000 during its first fortnight on sale, enough copies to prevent long-awaited comeback singles from Meat Loaf ('I'd Lie For You [And That's The Truth]') and Queen ('Heaven For Everyone') from reaching the top of the Official Singles Chart.

Even though it was outsold in week three by both Robson & Jerome's 'I Believe'/'Up On The Roof' and Oasis's 'Wonderwall', it stayed in the Top 10 for three months. The song continued to sell in vast numbers up until Christmas, by which time it had become Britain's second biggest-selling single of the year. Only Robson & Jerome's 'Unchained Melody'/'(There'll Be Bluebirds Over) The White Cliffs Of Dover' had sold more copies.

It also ruled the roost abroad, heading the *Billboard* Hot 100 in the US for three weeks and winning a Grammy Award for Best Rap Solo Performance in 1996. By then, it had become an international phenomenon, hitting number one in Sweden, Norway, France and Australia.

As is often the case, the monster success of 'Gangsta's Paradise' proved impossible for Coolio to repeat. He would never even come close to repeating this success, the nearest efforts being notably 'Too Hot' (number nine in early 1996) and 1997's 'C U When U Get There', which climbed to number three. He also briefly reappeared in the lower reaches of the chart in 2006 with 'Gangsta Walk', featuring another rap icon, Snoop Dogg.

In the UK, he returned to the limelight briefly in early 2009 by appearing in *Celebrity Big Brother*, in which he came third. However, he remains most memorable for 'Gangsta's Paradise', the first rap single to enter the UK's Official Singles Chart at the summit.

ROBSON & JEROME 1995

I BELIEVE/UP ON
THE ROOF

WRITERS: 'I Believe' – Ervin Drake, Irvin Graham,
Jimmy Shirl, Al Stillman/'Up On The Roof' –
Gerry Goffin, Carole King

PRODUCER: Mike Stock, Matt Aitken

ALBUM: Robson & Jerome

PEAK POSITION: Number 1 (4 weeks)

WEEKS ON CHART: 14

SALES: 1.11m

Just four months after their first single and
million seller dropped from the UK number
one spot, Robson & Jerome returned again
in November 1995 to prove that lightning
can strike twice.

Popular actors yet seemingly reluctant chart stars, Robson Green
and Jerome Flynn had topped the Official Singles Chart in summer
1995 with the exhaustively titled 'Unchained Melody'/'(There'll
Be Bluebirds Over) The White Cliffs Of Dover', so it only seemed
right that the *Soldier Soldier* duo should follow up one million-selling
double A-side featuring covers of much-loved musical standards
with another of almost equally gargantuan proportions.

The duo's second assault on the bestsellers survey combined
the Drake/Graham/Shirl/Stillman favourite 'I Believe', the song
which still holds the record for the longest stay at the summit by one
single (18 non-consecutive weeks in 1953 for Frankie Laine), plus
Gerry Goffin and Carole King's 'Up On The Roof', most famously
interpreted by The Drifters but a UK Top 10 hit for Kenny Lynch
at the tail-end of 1962 and also a minor hit for Julie Grant right at
the start of the following year.

Another entry for the bulging discographies of super-producers

Mike Stock and Matt Aitken, Robson and Jerome's 'I Believe'/'Up On The Roof' was extracted from the biggest-selling album of 1995, *Robson & Jerome*, which also featured covers of 'Daydream Believer', 'The Sun Ain't Gonna Shine Anymore' and Lennon and McCartney's 'This Boy'.

Like its predecessor, 'Believe' debuted at number one, in November 1995, dethroning Coolio's 'Gangsta's Paradise' (itself a million seller), but any hopes the single had of becoming the Christmas number one were extinguished when Michael Jackson's epic 'Earth Song' took hold of the number one position from early December. No matter: by that time, Robson & Jerome had amassed an impressive 11 chart-topping weeks in one calendar year, and they did claim the festive number one on the Official Albums Chart before making way for the return of *(What's The Story) Morning Glory?*

Precisely 12 months on, the duo were still unable to return to their day jobs. In November 1996, the 'triple A-side' 'What Becomes Of The Brokenhearted'/'Saturday Night At The Movies'/'You'll Never Walk Alone' gave them a third number one single from three releases, while its sister album, *Take Two*, crowned the albums chart in the same month.

In fact, the pair's only releases not to reach number one were a 1997 'best of' compilation entitled *Happy Days* and *The Love Songs*, an album that failed to make it into the Top 75 in 1999. Green's 2002 solo album, *Moment In Time*, fared little better, stalling at number 54.

Almost 20 years later, Robson Green and Jerome Flynn are back acting. Green was spotted in 2012 playing a werewolf called McNair in the BBC's supernatural drama *Being Human* and had a recurring role in the long-running *Waterloo Road*, while Flynn starred the same year in season two of the American medieval fantasy series *Game Of Thrones*, playing a character called Bronn.

Although a chart comeback probably couldn't be further from either's mind, for 18 months Green and Flynn embodied something that's always been fascinating about the UK's pop scene – enjoying successful careers which evaporated as quickly as they had begun.

Although many others appeared in *Soldier Soldier*, when Robson and Jerome left the series in 1995 viewing figures declined and the series was cancelled two years later.

MICHAEL JACKSON 1995

EARTH SONG

WRITER: Michael Jackson	
PRODUCERS: Michael Jackson, David Foster, Bill Bottrell	
ALBUM: HIStory - Past, Present And Future: Book 1	
PEAK POSITION: Number 1 (6 weeks)	
WEEKS ON CHART: 22 (1995, 17; 2006, 1; 2009, 4)	
SALES: 1.16m	

At the time of his premature death, this record-breaking artist was established as the most popular performer of his generation, even though his most recent records had not been huge hits.

Since Michael Jackson's death in June 2009, millions more of his albums have been sold, many of his past hit singles have returned to the Official Singles Chart and hundreds of impersonators have sprung up. It is a record which raises memories of an earlier entertainer.

However, one of the most surprising things about the man they called 'The King' is that only one of Elvis Presley's singles sold over one million copies in the UK – the same applies to the artist often called the 'King of Pop' (who in 1994 married Presley's daughter, only for the couple to divorce 18 months later).

Millions of pop fans grew up with Jackson, who from the age of 11 was breaking records by having his first four hit singles (singing lead with his brothers in The Jackson 5) going to the top of the US chart. Elsewhere in a career of highlights, *Thriller* remains the biggest-selling album ever worldwide and only Cliff Richard and Presley have had more UK Official Top 40 Singles.

Like his earlier hit compositions, 'We Are The World' (the 1985 US For Africa charity single co-written with Lionel Richie) and 'Heal The World' (1991), 'Earth Song' had socially conscious aspirations. Jackson said he wanted to compose a song that was "lyrically deep yet melodically simple" – nothing less than an anthemic and powerful plea to God that the whole world, including his non-English-speaking fans, could easily sing along to.

The track featured such noted session musicians as David Paich (keyboards), Steve Porcaro (synths), the London Philharmonic Orchestra and award-winning US gospel act the Andraé Crouch Singers, who joined Jackson on the song's dramatic call-and-response finale.

The song's co-producers were multi-Grammy Award-winner David Foster (Michael Bublé, Mariah Carey, Celine Dion, Whitney Houston, Madonna) and Bill Bottrell, who had worked on chart-topping Jackson albums *Bad* and *Dangerous*.

'Earth Song', the third single released from Jackson's *HIStory* album, entered the Official Singles Chart in December 1995 at number one. During its six weeks at the summit, this Christmas number one stopped The Beatles from scoring their first chart-topper for 26 years with 'Free As A Bird', as well as Boyzone from having their first number one with 'Father And Son'.

It was Jackson's follow-up to the chart-topping 'You Are Not Alone' (the first single ever to enter the US *Billboard* Hot 100 at number one) and was the only time that he had enjoyed official UK number ones with successive singles. Despite being over five minutes long, 'Earth Song' was also a huge hit right across Europe, selling over one million copies in Germany. However, in the US, it was only available on *HIStory*, a transatlantic chart-topper that shipped a record-breaking 2.3 million copies in the US (going on to sell over seven million copies), and sold a record 100,000 on its first day in the UK.

British nature photographer Nick Brandt directed the spectacular video for 'Earth Song', which showed the destruction and then rebirth of the Earth and was set in four locations: the Amazon rainforest, a war zone in Croatia, the jungles of Tanzania and a forest in Warwick, New York. The video ended with a plea for donations to Jackson's Heal The World Foundation charity, which he had founded in 1992.

In February 1996, when Jackson came to the BRIT Awards to collect a one-off Artist Of A Generation award, he performed 'Earth Song', although the headlines generated by his performance were largely down to Jarvis Cocker. Pulp's singer found the imagery in Jackson's Christ-like presentation offensive, so famously walked on stage mid-song and wiggled his backside at the audience.

BABYLON ZOO 1996
SPACEMAN

WRITER: Jas Mann

PRODUCERS: Jas Mann, Steve Power

ALBUM: The Boy With The X-Ray Eyes

PEAK POSITION: Number 1 (5 weeks)

WEEKS ON CHART: 14

SALES: 1.14m

January is traditionally a quiet month for record sales, but in early 1996 this futuristic-styled rock song fleetingly made Babylon Zoo Britain's most talked-about group.

Shifting over 400,000 copies in its week of release, 'Spaceman' dislodged George Michael from the official number one spot, outsold the rest of the Top 10 combined, and accounted for nearly 30 per cent of all singles sold that week. It is now commonplace for *X-Factor* winners to achieve such spectacular sales feats, but at the time only two acts – Whigfield and Robson & Jerome – had debuted at number one in the Official Singles Chart with their first release.

It clearly helped that sections of 'Spaceman' were already known to millions prior to release. It was featured in a TV and cinema advertisement for Levi's jeans, in which teenaged Russian model Kristina Semenovskaia portrayed an alien girl wandering through a town in the American Midwest at nightfall.

Premiered in November 1995, the commercial (titled 'Planet') was designed to launch Levi's new 501 range for women. 'Spaceman' was added to the mix when a Levi's marketing man happened to hear the track being played on a Manchester radio station. The version of 'Spaceman' used in the campaign concentrated on the varispeed vocals at the song's start and end (taken from a remixed version by Arthur Baker) rather than its rockier core.

"No one has made me tingle more since 1976" was how EMI

A&R supremo Clive Black then described Babylon Zoo, and specifically its creative nerve-centre, Jas Mann. Part Asian and part Native American, Mann was constantly trying to write about the experience of being a person from another planet. Born in the West Midlands town of Dudley in April 1971, he began sending demo tapes to record companies from the age of 15.

A stint as lead singer with Wolverhampton group The Sandkings in the late Eighties and early Nineties included support slots with Happy Mondays and The Stone Roses, but it was Mann's demo tape sent to Black in the spring of 1993 that led him, intrigued, to attend a band rehearsal. He recalls seeing a group of robot-style creatures housing backing tapes, and was so mesmerised by their vision that he signed the act.

Mann was compared by some to David Bowie, Marc Bolan, Prince or Nine Inch Nails' Trent Reznor, although more cautious observers wondered if Babylon Zoo would merely emulate Scottish rock act Stiltskin, which achieved only one massive hit ('Inside') after exposure on a Levi's commercial two years before.

The doubters were proved right. Although Babylon Zoo's debut album, *The Boy With The X-Ray Eyes*, reached the Official Top 10, the next single only just scraped into the Official Top 20, and the group's fifth and final hit, 'All The Money's Gone', appeared in 1999.

Mann went on to write the theme music for channel 4's *Speedway Grand Prix,* release songs under the name Mariachi Static and work for an aid agency in India. Though described by NME as a 'fluke', if only for a brief moment, Babylon Zoo made a massive impact. Levi's advertisements had spawned number one hits before – for reissues of Ben E. King's 'Stand By Me', the Steve Miller Band's 'The Joker' and The Clash's 'Should I Stay Or Should I Go?' – but never on quite such a stupendous scale.

Before topping charts around Europe, 'Spaceman' stayed at number one for five weeks on the Official Singles Chart and was 1996's third highest-selling single, outperformed only by the Fugees' 'Killing Me Softly' and 'Wannabe' by the Spice Girls.

Perhaps most impressively of all, its first week on sale in January 1996 was the biggest week for singles sales in the UK since December 1984, when Band Aid and Wham! (respectively) sold 750,000 and 500,000 copies of 'Do They Know It's Christmas?' and 'Last Christmas'/'Everything She Wants'.

BADDIEL & SKINNER & LIGHTNING SEEDS 1996
THREE LIONS

WRITERS: an Broudie, David Baddiel, Frank Skinner

PRODUCERS: Ian Broudie, Simon Rogers, Dave Bascombe

ALBUM: N/A

PEAK POSITION: Number 1 (2 weeks)

WEEKS ON CHART: 46 (1996, 15; 1998, 13; 2002, 6; 2006, 6; 2010, 6)

SALES: 1.53m

Over the years, scores of football songs have found a place in the Official Singles Chart, but only 'Three Lions' has netted UK sales in excess of one million.

Before first recording under the name The Lightning Seeds in 1989, Liverpool-born singer/songwriter/multi-instrumentalist/producer Ian Broudie had been a member of cult favourites Big In Japan, whose alumni also included Holly Johnson (Frankie Goes To Hollywood), Bill Drummond (The KLF) and Budgie (Siouxsie & The Banshees). He had also produced two of that city's top acts in the 1980s, Echo & The Bunnymen and The Icicle Works.

The Lightning Seeds may not have been regular chart-toppers, but they were regular chart visitors, and in the year before 'Three Lions' was such a roaring success they had three singles in the Top 20 – 'Perfect', 'Lucky You' and 'Ready Or Not'.

In 1996, the Football Association approached Broudie to write the official song for that year's European Championships. He agreed, on the understanding that the lyrics could be provided by comedians David Baddiel and Frank Skinner, who at the time hosted popular cutting-edge TV football programme *Fantasy Football League*.

Most football songs simply boasted about how great such-and-such a team were and how they were going to win. 'Three Lions' was different; the song bemoaned the fact that England had not won any football competition since 1966.

The song took its title from the badge on the England national team's shirt. Its catchy sing-along chorus optimistically looked forward to the Euro '96 tournament, announcing "football's coming home" – referring to the fact that the tournament would be held in England, which claimed to have invented the world's most popular game.

The song's lyrics name-checked England's 1966 World Cup winners Bobby Moore, Bobby Charlton and Nobby Stiles, and more recent hero Gary Lineker – although Broudie admitted that the supporters heard at the beginning of the track were actually fans of the Danish club team Brondby, whom he had recorded at a Liverpool match.

England failed once more to be crowned kings of European football in 1996, although they did reach the semi-finals of the competition, losing a penalty shoot-out to Germany (this official English team record was, intriguingly, also a German chart hit at the time). However, 'Three Lions' did become the king of the pop jungle when it entered the chart at number one in June 1996 before being dethroned by the Fugees' 'Killing Me Softly' – swapping the number one spot with that group for just one week some five weeks later.

In 1998, it was re-recorded and released as an unofficial anthem for England's World Cup campaign, now including mentions of then-current stars Alan Shearer, Paul Ince, Stuart Pearce and Paul Gascoigne (although neither Pearce nor Gascoigne were actually selected for England's World Cup Squad).

'Three Lions '98' sold 232,000 copies in its first week and entered at number one in June 1998, a position it held for three weeks (denying fellow football song 'Vindaloo' by Fat Les top spot), making it the only record to top the chart twice with different lyrics. England's performance didn't match the song's, however; the team failed to make the quarter-finals after being knocked out by Argentina.

'Three Lions' also returned to the Top 20 of the Official Singles Chart at World Cup time in 2002, 2006 and 2010. In 2010, the original actually out-performed another re-recording by Baddiel, Skinner and Broudie, with the addition of Robbie Williams, comedian Russell Brand and John Motson (under the name The Squad), which narrowly missed the Top 20.

The last word goes to legendary football commentator Motson: "As football songs go, 'Three Lions' is certainly the best."

MILLION-SELLING MEMORIES

DAVID BADDIEL

So, how did 'Three Lions' come about?

Well, at the time, Frank Skinner and I were doing this show [*Fantasy Football League*] that spoke to football fans. Ian Broudie [of Lightning Seeds] was asked to do the official single. He *had* done 'Life Of Riley', which had been used constantly on *Match Of The Day* so was in that world. And he asked if we wanted to have a go at writing the lyrics. We sort of felt that if we are going to do this, we should front it as well.

And it has now sold more than 1.5 million copies and is the 27th biggest-selling single of all time. When you first wrote it, did you really expect it to be as big as it was?

No, not at all, but I wasn't expecting to hear that even now. I knew it had sold a lot but not quite that much. People say did you know it was going to be as successful as it was, but that's not the way you approach anything like that. When you write jokes, or books or anything else, you write it the way it is, to be funny and do your best.

We were trying to do something that had never been done before. We decided to try and write it from the view of what it was like to be an England fan. Previous songs were about triumph. That is, aside from 'World In Motion', which wasn't really a football song at all. Also we were very fortunate that Ian Broudie wrote this great music.

As a football fan, it must have been amazing to be at Wembley hearing all those England fans singing that song, especially after the 4-1 Holland victory...

It was. But the absolute moment was against Scotland. When we played them, there was still a general feeling of despair. We had just drawn against Switzerland and had had a bad run up until then. Then we beat Scotland, and at the end of the match they played 'Three Lions' in the stadium and the entire crowd started singing along. That remains the most extraordinary moment of my life, publicly.

The thing it has done is killed off the England squad song. This year I don't think they bothered at all. People often ask if we are going to do another one, but I think we are not going to write a better one – we are in an ongoing moment, it's 46 years of hurt now...

What do you remember about that time?

There was a very definite difference between when it came out, before the tournament, and when the tournament got going. I was in the Seychelles when I got the message that we had gone to number one. We knocked Gina G off the top, I think. But the week after, the Fugees went to number one. We weren't allowed on *Top Of The Pops* at first; they hated it. Quite a lot of people didn't like it because they thought it was too laddish, I think.

Do you still get lots of appreciation for it?

Yes. Lots of people still say to me on Twitter how much they love 'Three Lions' and use it to get into the mood before a match. I remember even Gazza saying he used to play it on the coach to get the atmosphere going. When we first played it to the England team it wasn't quite like that though. I remember Terry Venables tapping his keys and saying, "It is a real key tapper" [laughs].

And finally, what was the first single you bought?

It was either 'Devil Woman' or 'Bohemian Rhapsody', I'm not sure. I wasn't a big fan of Queen, but I was about 11 at the time and I must have saved up to buy it. It seemed to be on all the time. I will say that one, then it doesn't have to be 'Devil Woman' [laughs].

FUGEES 1996

KILLING ME SOFTLY

WRITERS: Norman Gimbel, Charles Fox
PRODUCERS: A Tribe Called Quest, Fugees
ALBUM: The Score
PEAK POSITION: Number 1 (5 weeks)
WEEKS ON CHART: 20
SALES: 1.36m

Perhaps surprisingly, the top-selling single of 1996 was not by the all-conquering Spice Girls, but the first of two official number one hits that year for New Jersey rap trio the Fugees.

The Fugees formed in South Orange, New Jersey, in 1992. US-born singer Lauryn Hill also acted, with screen credits including a supporting role in the Whoopi Goldberg film comedy *Sister Act II: Back In The Habit* in 1993. Musician/producer Wyclef Jean and rapper Pras Michel were Haiti-born cousins who both relocated during their childhood to the US.

The three formed a group called the Refugee Camp, but the name had contracted by the release of their 1994 debut album, *Blunted On Reality*. It won warm reviews and fair sales, but the reception awarded to its follow-up, *The Score*, was little short of ecstatic. After its first single, 'Fu-Gee-La', hit number 21 on the UK Official Singles Chart in April 1996, the follow-up was released in late May to great excitement.

As UK record stores ran out of copies, Sony Music had to fly in extra stock from the Netherlands to meet demand. 'Killing Me Softly' began five (non-consecutive) weeks at number one from June 2 – it replaced 'Three Lions' to score its first week at number one, held the top spot for four weeks, relinquished to 'Three Lions' for a week, only to regain the summit for its fifth week. It repeated its chart-topping success in several other territories (including nine weeks in

Germany) but narrowly failed to do the same in the US, where it reached number two.

The trio's adaptation of 'Softly' wove sampled recordings together with a cover version of a famous song. It borrowed its distinctive sitar hook from A Tribe Called Quest's 1990 album track 'Bonita Applebum', but that motif in fact originated from 1967's 'Memory Band' by Chicago psychedelic soul group Rotary Connection, whose personnel included a young Minnie Riperton (of 'Lovin' You' fame).

'Killing Me Softly With His Song', to give it its full title, had previously been recorded by The Jackson 5, Carole King and Luther Vandross, but the definitive version came from Roberta Flack, who topped the US chart for five weeks in early 1973 and peaked at number six in the UK Official Singles Chart.

However, Flack's reading was not the original. Two years earlier, singer/songwriter Lori Lieberman had been inspired to record the song after seeing a live rendition by Don McLean of his composition 'Empty Chairs'. It has sometimes been reported that Charles Fox and lyricist Norman Gimbel wrote the song in direct response to McLean's performance, but 'Softly' was in fact already written when Lieberman attended the concert.

Flack's version collected several plaudits, including a Grammy Award for her vocal performance. The Fugees also scooped Best R&B Vocal Performance by a Duo or Group at the 1997 Grammys, where they additionally won Best Rap Album for *The Score*. Yet it marked the end of the group, with all three members embarking on noteworthy solo careers.

Pras Michel scored an international hit with 'Ghetto Superstar', while Wyclef Jean has been busy both releasing his own material (he has 10 solo albums to his name) and threatening to stand for election as President of Haiti (before being ruled ineligible). But Lauryn Hill has been the most critically lauded, landing five Grammies for her album *The Miseducation Of Lauryn Hill*, which was released in 1998.

Most recently, the band came back together for live shows which received a mixed reaction – and appeared to strike out any chance of a more permanent comeback.

At the time of their split, *The Score* had spawned four Official Top Five singles in the UK, including a second number one hit, 'Ready Or Not', but 'Killing Me Softly' was 1996's unbeatable single, reaching its millionth sale in a mere eight weeks.

SPICE GIRLS 1996

WANNABE

WRITERS: Matthew Rowbottom, Richard Stannard, Spice Girls

PRODUCERS: Matthew Rowbottom, Richard Stannard

ALBUM: Spice

PEAK POSITION: Number 1 (7 weeks)

WEEKS ON CHART: 26

SALES: 1.32m

A five-piece girl band that rewrote the rulebook for internationally ambitious pop acts in the late Nineties, the Spice Girls became a worldwide phenomenon – and 'Wannabe' was the single that started it all.

Observing the proliferation of boy bands in the early Nineties, father and son Bob and Chris Herbert spotted a gap for a feisty female pop outfit. An extended search during the first half of 1994 saw the pair audition and eventually select Victoria Adams, Melanie Brown, Emma Bunton, Melanie Chisholm and Geri Halliwell.

Within a year the quintet had parted company with the Herberts to work with producer/songwriter Eliot Kennedy, who introduced them to established manager Simon Fuller. They signed to Virgin Records in September 1995 and, after a name-change from Touch to Spice then the Spice Girls, they began preparing for their launch into an unsuspecting world.

Their debut 'Wannabe' was written with the band and produced by Matt Rowe and Richard Stannard, and completed in little more than half an hour. It broke many of pop's conventions, with each member of the group sharing the vocal responsibilities, but Virgin had their doubts, insisting it was not punchy enough. After several mixes, the final 'Wannabe' cut was agreed.

'Wannabe''s video also broke new ground, receiving mass rotation on music TV. Filmed inside the then-derelict St Pancras Hotel in north

London, it was shot as if it were one continuous take and features the band leading the viewer through the building, and then into a waiting taxi.

The overall impression was of a tight unit of savvy young girls (then aged 20, 21, 22, 22 and 24), with a feisty attitude and a vaguely politicised 'Girl Power' agenda, with each member labelled to appeal to target audiences – as Posh, Baby, Scary, Sporty and Ginger.

When the single was unleashed in June 1996, the media was undecided about its merits, but everyone was interested. In the UK, the much-publicised 'Wannabe' entered the Official Singles Chart at three and was number one a week later, a position it held for seven weeks. The single went to number one in the *Billboard* Hot 100 for four weeks and ultimately sold an estimated six million copies worldwide, as well as winning a BRIT Award for Best Single and Best British-Composed Single at the Ivor Novello Awards.

Its significance as the single that ushered in Spicemania should not be overlooked. In the UK, 'Wannabe' kicked off a run of six straight official number one singles, the beginning of a UK career which spanned just 11 singles, of which nine were official chart-toppers. It was a key track on their first album, *Spice,* which is estimated to have sold 28 million copies worldwide; second album *Spiceworld* chipped in with another 20 million – making them the globe's biggest albums of 1997 and 1998 respectively. But in May 1998, with the group still on top of the world, Geri 'Ginger Spice' Halliwell announced her decision to leave the band – just two years after 'Wannabe' had set the juggernaut moving.

After a break for personal and professional reasons, the remaining quartet came back with the album *Forever* in November 2000. But the magic had gone. Its sole single 'Holler'/'Let Love Lead The Way' was the band's ninth number one single, but the album peaked at two and internationally barely sold five million copies – perfectly respectable for any other act, but not by Spice standards.

In December 2006, the original five Spice Girls announced plans to reform. Their new single, 'Headline (Friendship Never Ends)', in aid of Children In Need, stalled at 11 in the Official Singles Chart in late 2007 and a world tour set to run from December 2007 until March 2008 ended prematurely, with the band citing personal commitments.

They would never again hit the peak of Spicemania, but with 'Wannabe' they created not just one of the iconic songs of the Nineties, but the biggest-selling single of all time by a female group.

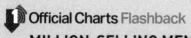

MILLION-SELLING MEMORIES

MELANIE CHISHOLM (SPICE GIRLS)

'Wannabe' is a member of the select list of million-selling singles. Congratulations!

Thank you, I'm just really floored by that! Everything I did with the Spice Girls was so… insane! It was incredible and I'm just really, really proud that we did it. We did it for the girls, and we did it for the country on a global scale.

'Wannabe' was your first single and first number one on the Official Singles Chart. What do you remember about that week? How did you feel when you heard the news?

We had very high hopes for 'Wannabe', we were very ambitious; our midweek was number six and on the weekend it went up to number three. We were absolutely over the moon – we couldn't believe that we were going to have a Top Five hit in the official chart! We were so, so excited. We thought we were just superstars, in just one week. And then we went over to Japan because we were starting to have really great success over there. The second week we were in Japan, 'Wannabe' climbed to number one. It was amazing. But we couldn't believe we weren't in the UK the week of our first single going to number one. Luckily though, it stayed there for *seven* weeks, so we were able to come back and perform it on *Top Of The Pops*.

Did you listen to the Official Charts while growing up?

Being a music lover, I listened to the chart show every Sunday without fail. There was something about putting the radio on and taping your favourite songs. I know that's probably piracy, but I was just so excited finding out where people were and who was number one. In those days, you didn't know what was going to be number one until it was announced at seven o'clock on a Sunday night. I've got great, great memories about that.

With the Spice Girls and the Britpop movement, the late Nineties were seen as a bit of a heyday for British music. Do you still think British music can compete on a global scale?

I think that British music is really thriving right now. We have so many great genres, and we have cross-genres and great artists collaborating with each other. We do everything good; we do indie good, we do rock good, we do urban good, we do pop good, of course, we just do everything good. I'm a big fan of so many British artists at the moment: Jessie J, Adele, Ellie Goulding, The Prodigy, Coldplay, Muse. The list is endless! We do music great.

And finally, is there any number one single that you secretly wish you'd written?

It wasn't a number one, but it's by a great British artist that we have now, and I believe for a long time to come. I'm talking about Adele of course. Her song 'Rolling In The Deep' is such an incredible track, I really, really wish it was mine!

SPICE GIRLS 1996

2 BECOME 1

WRITERS: Spice Girls, Richard Stannard, Matt Rowe (Matthew Rowbottom)

PRODUCERS: Richard Stannard, Matt Rowe (Matthew Rowbottom), Andy Bradfield

ALBUM: Spice

PEAK POSITION: Number 1 (3 weeks)

WEEKS ON CHART: 23

SALES: 1.11m

The first act to have Official Singles Chart number ones with each of their first six releases, the Spice Girls' third single in that sequence (and second million seller) proved that girl power also had its mellow side.

'2 Become 1' was the first of the Girls' three consecutive UK Christmas chart-toppers, emulating The Beatles from 1963-65. With this release, the band achieved cumulative sales of more than three million singles in their first six months on the UK chart, an opening total which no other act has matched.

The Spice Girls had arrived with 'Wannabe' (another million seller) in July 1996 and been embraced as an antidote to both Britpop and boy bands. They had already spent nine weeks at the top of the chart by the time they turned on the Christmas lights in London's Oxford Street and world domination seemed to be on the cards.

Although lyrically an overture to sexual liaison, '2 Become 1' continued the female empowerment theme of the band's previous hits, with the lyrics leaving the listener in no doubt that the night's proceedings were being orchestrated by a woman in charge. Similarly, the Girls towed the safe sex line, pointing out that men needed to take responsibility for this too with the line "Put it on, put it on."

The single's release date had been delayed by a week in order to allow Dunblane's 'Throw These Guns Away'/'Knockin' On Heaven's

Door' a week at number one, avoiding any negative publicity that might have been generated by preventing a single raising money for children's charities (in memory of the March 1996 massacre at Dunblane Primary School in Scotland) from getting to the top of the chart.

Released just in time for the Christmas chart, '2 Become 1' sold 429,000 copies in its week of release and took the Christmas number one slot in the Official Singles Chart, selling in sufficient quantities during its first two weeks on sale to join the band's first two chart-toppers, 'Wannabe' and 'Say You'll Be There', in the Top 10 best-selling singles of 1996. All three were on the album *Spice*, which itself topped the Official Albums Chart for a total of 15 weeks between November 1996 and May 1997, shifting enough copies to be in the Top Three albums of the year for two years running.

For the three weeks that '2 Become 1' was the nation's number one single, *Spice* was also the top album. The only other acts to have topped both charts at Christmas are The Beatles (three times – 1963, 1964 and 1965), Queen (1975 and 1991), Cliff Richard (1988) and, subsequently, Robbie Williams (2001). Also, being the group's second million seller (after 'Wannabe'), this single made them eligible to join The Beatles, Boney M. and Frankie Goes To Hollywood in the elite club of groups with more than one British million seller.

An even more exclusive list to feature the band is that of artists who have strung together six consecutive UK number ones. Only The Beatles had done so previously with an uninterrupted series of seven, but the Spice Girls were the first act to do so with their first six releases – a record some would argue still stands due to Westlife's sixth chart-topper in their opening run of seven being a collaboration with Mariah Carey, whereas all the Girls' singles were undiluted Spice.

In total, the group had nine UK Official Singles Chart number ones from 10 releases in just over four years, with the only exception being 'Stop', which was kept from the top spot by Run-D.M.C. vs. Jason Nevins' 'It's Like That' in March 1998.

PUFF DADDY FEAT. FAITH EVANS AND 112 1997

I'LL BE MISSING YOU

WRITERS: Sting, Todd Gaither, Faith Evans

PRODUCERS: Sean 'Puff Daddy' Combs, Stevie J

ALBUM: No Way Out

PEAK POSITION: Number 1 (6 weeks)

WEEKS ON CHART: 25 (1997, 21; 2007, 2; 2009, 2)

SALES: 1.56m

A number of the UK's million sellers captured the imagination of the British public as heartfelt tributes following an untimely death – 'Candle In The Wind 1997' in memory of Princess Diana, 'Imagine' in 1980 following the murder of John Lennon and 'Bohemian Rhapsody' in 1991 after Queens frontman Freddie Mercury's death from AIDS.

'I'll Be Missing You' has that in common, although it is a rare case of a song that was written and recorded specifically as a tribute, in this case following the gang-related murder of Christopher Wallace (aka The Notorious B.I.G., aka Biggie Smalls).

In the mid-1990s, as the popularity of gangster rap grew, so did a bitter feud between the scene's biggest players. But the war of words between California's Death Row Records and New York's Bad Boy Entertainment would quickly escalate into all-out war, leading to the deaths of two of the genre's most promising young stars – Tupac Shakur and The Notorious B.I.G., who were their respective labels' biggest-selling artists.

On September 7, 1996, Death Row rapper Shakur was gunned down in Las Vegas. Six months later, on March 9, 1997, Christopher Wallace, who was signed to Bad Boy, was shot and killed in Los Angeles.

While both murders remain unsolved today, there has been much speculation that they were somehow connected because of remarkable similarities between the circumstances surrounding the two incidents

– both rappers were shot multiple times while sitting in the front passenger seat of their respective vehicles, both incidents took place on crowded streets following major public engagements and both rappers had their record company's CEOs (Death Row's Suge Knight and Bad Boy's Sean 'Puff Daddy' Combs) in tow.

Shakur's family and friends ensured that his fifth album, *The Don Killuminati: The 7 Day Theory*, was completed and released (several more posthumous releases have followed), while Combs, together with Wallace's widow, R&B singer Faith Evans (who was also signed to Bad Boy), released the tribute song 'I'll Be Missing You'.

In hip-hop and R&B's grand tradition of sampling, the track, which also featured the talents of Atlanta R&B quartet 112, comprises a re-recorded extract from American composer Samuel Barber's 1936 classical piece, 'Adagio For Strings', while the chorus is a reworking of The Police's 1983 hit 'Every Breath You Take'. It was released in the US in May 1997 and debuted on *Billboard*'s Hot 100 chart at number one the following week (where it would remain for 11 weeks), making it the first hip-hop single to reach the top of the US chart in its first week on sale.

The UK release followed in June and, in a move that echoed its US chart performance, the single also debuted at number one on the Official Singles Chart, knocking American boy band Hanson's 'MMMBop' off the top spot.

The track's success could have been incredibly short-lived, however, as neither Bad Boy nor its then parent company Arista Records had sought clearance to use the Police sample. Thankfully for them, an out-of-court settlement was quickly reached with Police frontman Sting (the song's composer) being given sole ownership of 'I'll Be Missing You's publishing.

While Sting appreciated the sentiment behind the track, he was surprised at the use of his original – a song about "jealousy and surveillance and ownership", as he told *NME*. But he subsequently became firm friends with Combs, joining him on stage at the MTV Video Music Awards, where the tribute track won the Best R&B Video award. The following year, it would also win a prestigious Grammy Award for Best Rap Performance by a Duo or Group.

As tribute songs go, 'I'll Be Missing You' is up there with the best – a fact which is underlined by its return to the Official UK Top 40 in July 2007, the 10th anniversary of Christopher Wallace's death.

ELTON JOHN 1997

SOMETHING ABOUT THE WAY YOU LOOK TONIGHT/CANDLE IN THE WIND 1997

WRITERS: Elton John, Bernie Taupin

PRODUCER: George Martin

ALBUM: The Big Picture (Something About The Way You Look Tonight)

PEAK POSITION: Number 1 (5 weeks)

WEEKS ON CHART: 24

SALES: 4.9m

When Elton John and his label team were drawing up a shortlist for the lead single for John's 26th studio album *The Big Picture* in summer 1997, little were they to know that their choice would be part of the world's biggest-selling single since UK and US charts began in the 1950s.

In truth, despite getting top billing on the cover of the double A-side, the Rocket Man's gloriously uplifting ballad 'Something About The Way You Look Tonight' had to play second fiddle to the non-album track 'Candle In The Wind 1997', a reworked version of John and songwriting partner Bernie Taupin's 1974 tribute to the actress Marilyn Monroe.

In the aftermath of the death of Diana, Princess of Wales, amid an unprecedented outpouring of grief, 'Candle In The Wind 1997' shifted a staggering 33 million copies worldwide – with all artist/composer royalties and label profits benefiting the Diana, Princess Of Wales Memorial Fund. Only Bing Crosby's festive favourite 'White

Christmas', with estimated worldwide sales of 50 million since 1942, burns brighter than 'Candle' in terms of all-time global sales.

'Candle In The Wind' (a phrase Taupin had heard used in tribute to Janis Joplin) first featured on *Goodbye Yellow Brick Road*, John's number one album from 1973, and had twice before been a UK hit – originally in 1974, when it peaked at number 11, and again in 1988, when an in-concert version made the Top Five after appearing on the *Live In Australia With The Melbourne Symphony Orchestra* album.

However, it is the 1997 version, poignantly performed with amended lyrics at Diana's funeral to a TV audience that peaked at 32.8 million in the UK alone (many millions more watched worldwide), that will go down in history. After hearing of the death of Princess Diana – a close friend of Elton's and a fellow AIDS campaigner – the performer called Taupin and asked him to adjust the lyrics of the song. Taupin did just this, most notably replacing the opening "Goodbye Norma Jean" – Norma Jean Baker being the birth name of the song's original subject, Marilyn Monroe – with "Goodbye England's rose".

The double A-side did, of course, enter both the UK's Official Singles Chart and the US *Billboard* Hot 100 at number one in its first week. And it has, to date, sold 4.9 million copies in the UK, where it not only holds the record for the biggest-selling single of all time but also the fastest selling, with 1.55 million copies flying off the shelves in the first week and almost five million in six weeks. In the US, it has sold 11 million copies and is the only single in US chart history to be awarded a Diamond certificate (for sales of 10 million) by the Recording Industry Association of America.

Born in March 1947, Elton John has travelled a long, long way since first tinkling the ivories as three-year-old Reginald Dwight in a council house in Pinner, Middlesex. He first met up with Taupin when both responded to a Liberty Records talent ad in New Musical Express. The pair struck a long-lasting songwriting partnership that provided the platform for John to go on to become the biggest-selling pop act of the 1970s. To date, since his *Elton John* album in 1970, he has scored 28 Top 10 albums in the UK, including six number ones – as well as 32 Top 10 singles and seven number ones.

The multiple BRIT, Grammy and Ivor Novello Award-winner, who was inducted into the Rock and Roll Hall of Fame in 1994 and knighted in 1998 in recognition of his tireless charity work, has sold an estimated 250 million records worldwide... and he's still standing.

AQUA 1997
BARBIE GIRL

WRITERS: Claus Norreen, Søren Nystrøm Rasted

PRODUCERS: Søren Nystrøm Rasted, Claus Norreen, Johnny Jam, Delgado

ALBUM: Aquarium

PEAK POSITION: Number 1 (4 weeks)

WEEKS ON CHART: 26

SALES: 1.79m

Chart acts don't come much more colourful than Aqua, whose inimitable brand of bubblegum pop not only resulted in three consecutive official number one singles in the UK but also, in the case of 'Barbie Girl', a headline-grabbing lawsuit between their label MCA Records and toy company Mattel.

'Barbie Girl' was penned by the three-quarters Danish, one-quarter Norwegian quartet Aqua. The act included guitarist Claus Norreen and keyboardist Søren Nystrøm Rasted – arguably the less recognisable 50 per cent of the outfit after vocalist Lene Nystrøm and bald-headed singer/rapper and DJ René Dif.

The song was written and recorded in 1997, inspired by an exhibit on kitsch culture. The Google definition of 'kitsch', "Art, objects or design considered to be in poor taste because of excessive garishness or sentimentality, but appreciated in an ironic way", could have been written specifically for Aqua as the song became a guilty pleasure for countless millions of 'tweenagers' around the world – and a good few mums and dads too.

Norreen and Rasted's brief was a simple one: write a catchy song that didn't take itself too seriously, but little were Aqua to know that their well-intentioned lyrics would ultimately land them in hot water with Mattel.

In hindsight, given Aqua's target market, 'Barbie Girl''s lyric was risqué – even by 1997 standards. It was lines such as "You can brush my hair, undress me everywhere" that incurred the wrath of Mattel, who sued the band on the grounds that they had violated the Barbie trademark and turned their beloved, almost 40-year-old doll into a sex object.

In 2002, Aqua's assertion that Mattel had misconstrued the lyrics was vindicated when a judge ruled that the song was protected under free speech, throwing out a counter-claim for defamation by Aqua's record label, MCA, and advising both parties to 'chill'. Almost inevitably the lawsuit drew attention to the record and helped it become a success.

Aqua formed in 1989 as Joyspeed, but it was only after changing their name to Aqua and rescuing Nystrøm from a career as an entertainer on a Norway-Denmark ferry that the act made progress. In their homeland, 'Roses Are Red' and 'My Oh My' (the single that eventually got a UK release in 1998 but halted their run of three successive chart-toppers) were number one records in 1996 and 1997 respectively, but the UK's first taste of Aqua came on October 25, 1997, when 'Barbie Girl' crashed into the Official Singles Chart at number two in the week Elton John's 'Candle In The Wind 1997' was replaced at number one by 'Spice Up Your Life'.

'Barbie Girl' was a perfect antidote to the melancholy mood in the weeks that followed the death of Diana, Princess of Wales, and climbed to number one a week after its debut. For three of its four weeks at the summit, 'Barbie Girl' was also solely responsible for denying Natalie Imbruglia a chart-topping debut with her million-selling 'Torn'.

Despite its success, critics have regularly thrown the song into a heap of 'worst' lists ever since, including VH1's Most Awesomely Bad Songs... Ever and *Rolling Stone's* 20 Most Annoying Songs. *Blender* magazine observed: "Perhaps the gambit sounded acceptable in helium-huffing singer Lene Nystrøm's native Norwegian, but in English it's just plain wrong."

Aqua did become one of a select few acts who reached number one with their first three releases, however, with 'Doctor Jones' and 'Turn Back Time' (from the same *Aquarium* album as 'Barbie Girl') entering the chart at the top. But their follow-up album, the similarly titled *Aquarius*, failed to capture the same mood, either in the UK or internationally, and it wasn't long before the band split. The quartet came back with a reunion tour in 2008 and album in 2011, but made no impact on the UK.

NATALIE IMBRUGLIA 1997

TORN

| WRITERS: Scott Cutler, Anne Preven, Phil Thornalley |
| PRODUCERS: Phil Thornalley, Scott Cutler |
| ALBUM: Left Of The Middle |
| PEAK POSITION: Number 2 (3 weeks) |
| WEEKS ON CHART: 19 (1997, 17; 2007, 1; 2010, 1) |
| SALES: 1.11m |

Australian soap *Neighbours* has produced a number of pop stars who have scored success in the UK, not least Kylie Minogue, Jason Donovan and Craig McLachlan, among others. To that list, Natalie Imbruglia's name was added in 1997, with her rendition of 'Torn'.

Two years before the Australian actress/singer scored her very biggest hit, the song had altogether more humble beginnings as a non-charting single by Ednaswap, alternative rockers from Los Angeles.

'Torn''s history can be traced through the career of one man: Phil Thornalley – songwriter, one-time Cure bassist/Johnny Hates Jazz frontman and producer to the stars (Bryan Adams, Duran Duran, Sting and the Thompson Twins, to name but a few). Suffolk-born Thornalley had a hand in writing 'Torn' with Ednaswap's Scott Cutler and Anne Preven, and produced cover versions for a couple of Scandinavian singers (Denmark's Lis Sørensen – who emerged with the first recorded version of the song, then titled 'Burnt' – and Norway's Trine Rein) before teaming up with Imbruglia.

A singer/songwriter, part-time model and actress, Imbruglia was born in Sydney, Australia in February 1975, to an Anglo-Celtic Australian mother and a father of Italian descent. Her hopes for a career in dance were shelved when she drifted into acting via TV commercials for Coca-Cola and Twisties snacks.

Imbruglia's pop-oriented 'Torn' was a far cry from the track's history as a rock number, but it fitted more with her wholesome, girl-next-door image, developed for millions of TV viewers in Ramsay Street, the setting for the Australian soap opera *Neighbours*, where the actress made her name as Beth Brennan.

Like Kylie Minogue before her and several notable actresses-turned-singers since (Holly Valance, Delta Goodrem), Imbruglia – who has lived in London since 1994 – decided to quit the show (after becoming disillusioned with her scripts) and chase pop stardom. Impressing RCA label bosses with her rendition of 'Torn', she was soon signed up.

The opening track from her debut album *Left Of The Middle*, Imbruglia's 'Torn' (one of only two songs on that album that she didn't receive a co-writing credit for), had the misfortune to be up against Aqua's 'Barbie Girl' on the Official Singles Chart countdowns of November 1997. 'Torn''s three weeks at number two were entirely down to the Scandinavian group's tribute to Barbie. But Imbruglia was the real thing, winning the hearts of admirers wherever she went.

The single, featuring background vocals from Eurovision Song Contest winner Katrina Leskanich (Katrina & The Waves), with a video starring *Holby City* actor Jeremy Sheffield, remains one of the biggest-selling singles never to top the UK chart. A huge radio hit at the time, it remained in the chart for 17 weeks and returned fleetingly in 2007 and 2010 – by virtue of the song's appeal as a cover on UK TV's talent shows.

Imbruglia was also Grammy-nominated in the Best Female Pop Vocal Performance category for 'Torn', only to be sunk by Celine Dion's titanic 'My Heart Will Go On'.

'Torn' was followed-up with a second official number two hit, 'Big Mistake', and in 2005 her *Counting Down The Days* album reached number one in the UK's Official Albums Chart. But, despite those high points (and having all the necessary attributes – a decent voice, model looks, media profile and the opportunity to work with stars including Coldplay's Chris Martin), Imbruglia's career has never quite exploded as expected.

Most recently, she has balanced music-making with an acting career (notably in the Rowan Atkinson vehicle *Johnny English*), and spells judging on Australia's *X-Factor*. In 2003, Natalie married Silverhair frontman Daniel Johns, but they were divorced in 2008.

ALL SAINTS 1997
NEVER EVER

WRITERS: Rickidy Raw (Robert 'Esmail' Jazayeri, Sean 'Mystro' Mather), Shaznay Lewis

PRODUCERS: Cameron McVey, Magnus Fiennes, Rickidy Raw

ALBUM: All Saints

PEAK POSITION: Number 1 (1 week)

WEEKS ON CHART: 24

SALES: 1.31m

When the Official Singles Chart number one for the week ending January 17, 1998 was announced as 'Never Ever' by All Saints, a new record was set. The track had been on the chart since November the previous year and had already sold 770,000 copies before finally reaching the top spot – more than any previous single that went on to reach pole position.

All Saints comprised Londoners Melanie Blatt and Shaznay Lewis, plus Canadian sisters Nicole and Natalie Appleton. Their urban edge made them the coolest girl band on the block; the East 17 to the Spice Girls' Take That.

After several attempts at chart success, a line-up and name change and after being dropped by label ZTT, All Saints duly had a Top Five hit in September 1997 with the Steely Dan-sampling 'I Know Where It's At' – a slice of good-time R&B/pop. However, its follow-up, 'Never Ever', was a much darker affair, dealing with the feelings of desolation after a relationship break-up and the need to understand where it all went wrong.

Having entered the Official Singles Chart at number three, 'Never Ever' faltered at number five the following week, dropping to number six as the Christmas release schedule went into overdrive, bringing chart-toppers for the Various Artists Children in Need fundraiser 'Perfect Day' and 'Teletubbies Say "Eh-Oh!"' (also both million sellers), leaving the All Saints single looking like it would never ever get its turn – but finally, it reached the top.

Although climbing to the number one position so late was not unheard of in the first few decades of the Official Singles Chart, it became a much less common occurrence from the mid-1990s onwards, reaching the point where a single that did not enter at number one was unlikely ever to get there. The previous hit to spend longer on the chart before getting to number one was Celine Dion's 'Think Twice', which did so on its 16th consecutive chart week in February 1995, but the next track to take longer than All Saints to reach pole position during a continuous chart run didn't come until March 2009 when Lady Gaga's 'Poker Face' turned the trick in week 10.

During an impressive 15-week run in the Official Top 10, 'Never Ever' spent at least one week in each of the Top Seven positions in the chart – a rare feat indeed. It was the first in a run of three consecutive number ones by the Saints during 1998 (followed by 'Under The Bridge'/'Lady Marmalade' and 'Bootie Call').

The band had two further chart-toppers in 2000 with the William Orbit-produced 'Pure Shores' and 'Black Coffee'. In complete contrast to the nine weeks 'Never Ever' took to top the chart, all four of the group's other number ones debuted there.

All Saints performed 'Never Ever' at the 1998 BRIT Awards, when the track won both Best British Single and Best British Video. They were crowned Best New Act at the 1998 MTV Europe Music Awards after the track became a Top 10 hit all over Europe, and it was also a number one hit in Australia and New Zealand. It even reached number four in America, where the *All Saints* album eventually became a million seller (although it only peaked at number 40 on the *Billboard* 200).

Although the band's internal tensions never seemed far from the surface, after an initial split in 2001 they reformed for the 2006 album *Studio 1*, which produced a final Top Three hit, 'Rock Steady', before their second, permanent, break-up. In their time together, every one of the group's nine hits made the UK Top 10.

All of the Saints tasted Top 10 success in the years following their first split, but none have done so since their final parting of the ways, although Lewis did take part in the recording of Band Aid 20's 'Do They Know It's Christmas?'.

VARIOUS ARTISTS 1997
PERFECT DAY

WRITER: Lou Reed

PRODUCER: Simon Hanhart

ALBUM: N/A

PEAK POSITION: Number 1 (3 weeks)

WEEKS ON CHART: 22 (1997, 21; 2000, 1)

SALES: 1.55m

The only single credited to 'Various Artists' to reach number one on the Official Singles Chart, this multi-artist charity remake of a Lou Reed song became the fourth million seller of 1997.

The track began life as a four-minute promotional film, designed to reflect the breadth of musical genres awarded airtime by the BBC's television and radio services. A wide range of singers and musicians took part in the film, each singing a line or two of a song which, although 25 years old and very well known, had never been a hit for the man who wrote and first recorded it.

'Perfect Day' first appeared on New Yorker Reed's 1972 David Bowie/Mick Ronson-produced album *Transformer*, which also included his only solo Top 10 single to date, 'Walk On The Wild Side'. The song became a Top 40 hit for the first time in 1995 as a cover by Duran Duran, but Reed's original reached a new audience shortly afterwards, when it was featured in Danny Boyle's film *Trainspotting*, starring Ewan McGregor.

Since the song accompanied a scene in which McGregor's character was taking heroin (and Reed's earlier work, notably with pioneering New York rock band The Velvet Underground, had frequently referenced drug use), many have assumed that 'Perfect Day' was a tribute to drug-taking. Reed himself has always hotly denied the suggestion, maintaining that it is a sincere love song.

The brainchild of BBC marketing executive Jane Frost, the

promotional film for 'Perfect Day' took 10 months to prepare and complete. Director Gregory Rood, whose credits included an Eric Cantona short film promoting anti-racism, began approaching participants in October 1996.

With the unannounced broadcast shown on BBC Television for the first time on September 20, 1997, the response from viewers was enormous, many wanting to know if the track was available to buy. This surge of interest prompted the BBC to begin negotiations to iron out contractual issues and find a label to release it as a single.

After a month of TV and cinema showings, the film was withdrawn, but it reappeared in time for the single's eventual release on November 17. Proceeds from sales of the single were donated to the BBC's annual Children In Need appeal, which took place four days later. Two million pounds was raised from 'Perfect Day' alone, in a year that marked the 70th birthday of the first Children In Need radio broadcast in 1927.

Several of the 'Perfect Day' soloists had tasted number one success before, among them Tom Jones, Bono (from U2), Boyzone, Gabrielle, Elton John and David Bowie. But it also gave Lou Reed – who sang the opening and closing lines – a first UK official chart-topper. Others who sang on the record – M People's Heather Small, Shane MacGowan (of The Pogues), Suzanne Vega, Suede's Brett Anderson and Reed's partner Laurie Anderson – bettered their previous chart singles peak of number two.

Emphasising the BBC's support towards other musical genres outside pop, it brought hit-maker status to acts like operatic crossover soprano Lesley Garrett, tenor Thomas Allen, string ensemble the Brodsky Quartet, tenor horn player Sheona White, blues giant Dr John and the Visual Ministry Choir.

A charity single of unusually high quality, 'Perfect Day' sold a mammoth 385,000 copies during its first week in the shops. It was the 17th official number one single to have been made in aid of charitable causes since Band Aid had inaugurated the tradition in December 1984, and the third in 1997 alone.

Its initial stay at the top was confined to a fortnight because of another BBC tie-in (namely 'Teletubbies Say "Eh-Oh!"') but it returned for a further week early in January 1998. In Ireland, its chart domination was more impressive still: it was number one for seven consecutive weeks.

ROBBIE WILLIAMS 1997

ANGELS

WRITERS: Robbie Williams, Guy Chambers

PRODUCERS: Guy Chambers, Steve Power

ALBUM: Life Thru A Lens

PEAK POSITION: Number 4 (1 week)

WEEKS ON CHART: 27

SALES: 1.11m

Robbie Williams had already had higher charting singles before 'Angels', but it is this timeless ballad which really set his solo career aflame.

A consummate showman, Williams was born in Stoke-on-Trent in February 1974. Having enjoyed success with Take That, he exited the band in 1995 – announcing the launch of his new solo career at a press conference on the evening after England were famously beaten by Germany in the Euro '96 football championship semi-finals in London.

His first single was a cover of the Wham! song 'Freedom', which reached number two in the Official Singles Chart, a success which he followed up with 'Old Before I Die' the following spring. By then, his debut album was mostly recorded and finally hit the chart in September that year, albeit with something of a whimper.

Williams' return as a solo artist was big news in the music world, but initial signs were not good – the album debuted at 11 before quickly slipping out of the Official Albums Chart, his third single from the album ('South Of The Border') peaked outside of the Official Singles Top 10 at 14.

Then came 'Angels'. Charting at seven on its release in mid-December, the single immediately became one of radio's all-time favourite tracks, exposure which helped the song hold on to a Top 10 position in the Official Singles Chart for 12 weeks solid and 27 weeks in the Top 75. The effect on its parent album was just what his label ordered, pushing it to number one in the Official Albums Chart and helping it on its way to 123 weeks in the Top 75. In many ways, 'Angels' jump-started Williams' solo career.

The genesis of the song is slightly less clear, however. Irish musician/songwriter Raymond Heffernan has regularly insisted the "verse and verse melody" were his. Heffernan says he had met Williams by chance in a Dublin pub and took the singer back to his mother's house, where he played a song called 'Angels' (written as a tribute to the unborn baby he lost in 1996) on his acoustic guitar.

Heffernan, who reportedly earned a one-off payment to forsake his writing credit and renounce any claim to royalties, says Williams and his songwriting partner Guy Chambers added the "big chorus melody". For his part, Williams is on record as saying that the fourth single from his debut solo album, *Life Thru A Lens,* was written about his aunt and uncle and was completed in just 25 minutes with Chambers.

But, to add to the mystery, the single's sleeve carried the words: "Even Fallen Angels Laugh Last – Thanks to Raymond Hefferman." The Irishman apparently liked the finished version and did eventually get the credit (of sorts) he so craved – albeit with a spelling error.

Whatever the truth, 'Angels' is an undisputed modern classic – and a bigger seller even than Take That's biggest single, 'Back For Good' – even if it wasn't the biggest seller of 2007 or 2008 (the year it peaked), nor a number one (it peaked at four).

It holds an important place in the hearts of UK music fans, however. At the BRIT Awards' 25th anniversary event in 2005, it received the BRITS 25 Award as the best single from the previous 25 years – up against rivals including Queen ('We Are The Champions'), Joy Division '(Love Will Tear Us Apart'), Kate Bush ('Wuthering Heights') and Will Young ('Leave Right Now').

To date Williams has won more BRIT Awards (17) than any other artist, including Best British Single for 'Angels' in 1999 and five with Take That, the group he re-joined in July 2010 for their sixth studio album, *Progress.*

Solo, Williams has sold an estimated 70 million singles and albums worldwide and was voted the Greatest Artist of the 1990s by the currently dormant UK Music Hall of Fame.

In August 2010 Williams married his long-term girlfriend, Turkish American actress Ayda Field, and in May 2012 the couple announced they were expecting their first child.

TELETUBBIES SAY "EH-OH!"

WRITERS: Andrew McCrorie-Shand, Andrew Davenport

PRODUCER: Andrew McCrorie-Shand, Steve James

ALBUM: N/A

PEAK POSITION: Number 1 (2 weeks)

WEEKS ON CHART: 32

SALES: 1.11m

Simon Cowell, now an international TV superstar and possibly the most famous music industry executive of all-time (alongside Beatles A&R man/producer George Martin), has a connection with more than half a dozen million-selling singles. But it hasn't always been about Sunset Boulevard billboards and Christmas in Barbados.

After getting a taste for novelty Christmas number one singles in 1993 with Mr Blobby – the pink costumed character from TV/radio presenter Noel Edmonds' Saturday night variety show, *Noel's House Party* – Cowell (then a relatively humble A&R executive within the BMG Records group) aimed his sights on being number one in 1997's festive Official Singles Chart with the most unlikely pop stars of the day, the Teletubbies.

Teletubbies was a children's TV show produced by Ragdoll Productions, voiced by a string of established stars ranging from veteran comic actor Eric Sykes to Eighties new wave chart star Toyah Willcox, which aired on BBC 1 from March of that year until 2002. The programme followed the antics of four fictional alien babies with televisions in their tummies (Tinky Winky, Dipsy, Laa-Laa and Po) and their housekeeper Noo-Noo, a blue robotic vacuum cleaner.

All of them apparently lived in a futuristic 'eco-house' sited in the middle of the Warwickshire countryside.

The show's simplistic storylines, nonsensical speech, bright colours and slapstick comedy helped it become an instant hit with pre-school children worldwide – while the programme's psychedelic look and feel, plus a mid-morning UK transmission slot, also helped it gain a cult following among college students. The children's characters were a genuine phenomenon. Associated *Teletubbies* merchandise was in incredibly high demand, the spin-off cuddly toys winning the prestigious Toy of the Year award by the British Association of Toy Retailers and becoming *the* must-have Christmas present of the year, sparking fights outside stores among parents.

Simon Cowell had his own fight on his hands. "I heard another record label were about to sign the Teletubbies, so I got the BBC in my office," Cowell later told *The Sun*. "I told them I would give them £500,000 in advance. We knew a record like that would make over £2 million."

The first single from the 'band' was a version of the show's theme tune, 'Teletubbies Say "Eh-Oh!"'. Written by show co-creator Andrew Davenport with songwriter/musician Andrew McCrorie-Shand (who had previously had a hand in the themes to the kids' TV programmes *Rosie & Jim*, *Brum* and *Tots*), and produced by McCrorie-Shand with producer/engineer Steve James, the single was released on December 1, 1997. It shot straight to the top of the Official Singles Chart, selling over 317,000 in its first week on sale and 230,000 more in its second week.

A battle royal was set up with the ruling pop royalty of the time – the Spice Girls. The girl power outfit had scored five official number ones with their first five singles and were also targeting their second successive Christmas number one in the Official Singles Chart. But William Hill rated the *Teletubbies* as odds-on favourites, 8/13 versus the Spice Girls' 13/8.

For once, the bookmakers were proved wrong, however, and Baby, Ginger, Posh, Scary and Sporty toppled Tinky Winky, Dipsy, Laa-Laa and Po from the summit to take the 1997 Christmas prize. '...Say "Eh-Oh!"' would also go on to spend 29 weeks in the Official Top 75. With the Teletubbies never again releasing another single, '"Eh-Oh!"' would also earn the title of the biggest-selling one-hit wonder in British chart history.

CELINE DION 1998

MY HEART WILL GO ON

WRITERS: James Horner (music), Will Jennings (lyrics)	
PRODUCERS: Simon Franglen, James Horner, Walter Afanasieff	
ALBUM: Let's Talk About Love/Titanic: Music From The Motion Picture	
PEAK POSITION: Number 1 (2 weeks)	
WEEKS ON CHART: 20	
SALES: 1.48m	

In 1998, it seemed that nobody was immune to the charms of Celine Dion and 'My Heart Will Go On', the main theme to the biggest movie of the year which went on to become the highest-grossing movie of all time.

The *Titanic* movie, starring Kate Winslet and Leonardo DiCaprio, was an epic, fictionalised account of the demise of the RMS *Titanic*, released in December 1997. It was an immediate box office sensation (grossing an estimated $2 billion worldwide) and went on the following year to sweep the board at the Academy Awards, collecting a total of 14 awards, including best film.

'My Heart Will Go On' would proceed to become the world's biggest-selling single of 1998, from the world's biggest-selling orchestral film soundtrack of all time, but it wasn't always plain sailing. The song started out as an instrumental motif composed by James Horner which appeared in several *Titanic* scenes. Lyricist Will Jennings ('Tears In Heaven', 'Didn't We Almost Have It All', 'Up Where We Belong') came on board to breathe life into a composition that neither *Titanic* director James Cameron nor Dion initially wanted anything to do with.

Eschewing Cameron's concerns that 'My Heart Will Go On' would over-commercialise his film, the song was eventually given the green light to accompany the end credits and, as a result, sailed to the top of charts around the world – the UK, US and Australia among them.

Like Dion's earlier UK number one, 'Think Twice', 'Heart' went to the top of the Official Singles Chart after its parent album (*Let's Talk About Love*) had spent time in pole position on the Official Albums Chart – a situation that would usually dim the sales potential of a single for your average pop star. Yet 'Heart' achieved UK sales alone in excess of 1.31 million, buoyed by slightly different versions appearing on two albums and some radio stations airing a third version interspersed with dialogue from the box-office smash.

It was the Canadian vocalist's second official UK number one single to reach seven sales figures in the UK. Until the emergence of Rihanna, who, at the time of writing, has three UK million sellers to her credit, Celine Dion shared a spot at the head of the class as the female with the most UK million sellers, alongside Olivia Newton-John and All Saints' Shaznay Lewis (who had featured on the Band Aid 20 single). What sets Celine apart from all of the above-named stars, however, is the fact that both of her seven-figure-sellers have been solo singles.

1998 was a good year for ballads associated with film tragedies. Six months after the release of *Titanic*, Touchstone Pictures rolled out *Armageddon*, featuring Aerosmith on the Diane Warren-composed 'I Don't Want To Miss A Thing'. Both songs continued the Nineties' trend for mega-selling ballads from mega-grossing films – '(Everything I Do) I Do It For You', 'I Will Always Love You', 'Love Is All Around' and 'Gangsta's Paradise', to name but four.

In 2012, the 100th anniversary of the sinking of the RMS *Titanic* with the loss of 1,514 lives, there was a 3D reissue of the movie and its soundtrack was relaunched. There were also numerous TV documentaries about the disaster, and all this brought 'My Heart Will Go On' back to the forefront of many people's minds.

In a more macabre recent twist, survivors of the cruise ship *Costa Concordia*, which ran aground and partially sank off Isola del Giglio, Italy, in January 2012, reported hearing 'My Heart Will Go On' being played in a restaurant as the ship struck a rock. This single's tragic links will, it seems, go on and on.

RUN-D.M.C. VS. JASON NEVINS 1998

IT'S LIKE THAT

WRITERS: Darryl McDaniels, Joseph Simmons, Jason Mizell

PRODUCERS: Jam Master Jay, Russell Simmons, Larry Smith, Jason Nevins

ALBUM: Run-D.M.C. (original version)

PEAK POSITION: Number 1 (6 weeks)

WEEKS ON CHART: 16 (excluding 4 weeks on import)

SALES: 1.25m

With their 1986 reworking of Aerosmith's 'Walk This Way', Run-D.M.C. not only brought hip-hop into the mainstream, they also revived the then-flagging career of one of America's most celebrated rock bands. So it's perhaps appropriate that a decade later, when their own career was on the wane, it was a remix that gave the Queens, New York trio's music a whole new lease of life.

The early Nineties had not been kind to Run-D.M.C. The group – Joseph 'Run' Simmons, Darryl 'D.M.C.' McDaniels, and Jason 'Jam-Master Jay' Mizell – were struggling to cling onto the commercial success and critical acclaim they had received the previous decade. 1990's *Back From Hell* album, which saw the trio embrace the emerging New Jack Swing sound, was a disaster; panned by the press, it barely scraped the Top 100 of the US *Billboard* chart and failed to dent the UK's Official Albums Chart.

As a result, their lives took a darker turn; McDaniels spiralled into alcoholism, Simmons sank into depression while battling to clear his name following a rape allegation, and Mizell survived two gunshot wounds in what is thought to be a gang-related incident.

However, after a three-year hiatus and much soul searching – both Simmons and McDaniels found solace in Christianity – the trio decided to give music another chance. Returning to their earlier sound, albeit with a grittier edge, and pulling in favours from hip-hop's new breed – Pete Rock & CL Smooth, Q-Tip and Jermaine Dupri all guested on the record – 1993's *Down With The King* seemed, outwardly at least, a success.

It debuted on the *Billboard* Top 200 at number seven, and the Official Albums Chart at number 41. The title track even gave Run-D.M.C. another Top 20 hit in their homeland – it reached number 69 in the UK. But when its follow-up single, 'Ooh, Whatcha Gonna Do', failed to make a dent in the charts on either side of the Atlantic, the trio's confidence was once again shot. They continued to actively tour, but due to tensions between Simmons (who was now going by the moniker of Rev Run) and McDaniels (who had become hooked on prescription painkillers) no new music would emerge. Mizell, meanwhile, seemed content to apply his creative energies to his emerging record label, JMJ Records, while schooling fellow Queens rappers Onyx and a young 50 Cent.

Fast forward to the summer of 1997, and, unknown to the group, Jason Nevins, a 23-year-old New York club DJ, released a remix of their 1983 debut single, 'It's Like That', in Europe.

Nevins had been working on a track of his own when he stumbled across a Run-D.M.C. *Greatest Hits* compilation in his studio, deciding to splice 'It's Like That' with his own work. "It was a labour of love," Nevins later told US radio presenter Ron Slomowicz. "I had always said that I wanted to use something from [Run-D.M.C.'s] first album, so I basically took their record, put it on top of mine and merged the two records together".

The track became a massive club hit, before topping charts all across the continent the following year. Released in the UK in early March 1998, it went straight to number one, selling nearly a quarter of a million copies in the process.

'It's Like That' stayed at number one for a further five weeks, preventing 'Stop' from giving the Spice Girls an official charts record of seven consecutive number ones with their first seven singles.

Sadly, the resulting interest in Run-D.M.C. wouldn't last; continued tensions between McDaniels and Simmons forced the group to implode once more, and Simmons spectacularly walked out during the group's world tour with Aerosmith in 2001. Sadder still, before the trio could reconcile, in October 2002 Mizell was shot and killed outside his studio in Queens, New York. His murder has never been solved.

BOYZONE 1998

NO MATTER WHAT

WRITERS: Andrew Lloyd Webber (music),
Jim Steinman (lyrics)

PRODUCERS: Jim Steinman, Andrew Lloyd
Webber, Nigel Wright

ALBUM: Where We Belong

PEAK POSITION: Number 1 (3 weeks)

WEEKS ON CHART: 15

SALES: 1.13m

Boyzone had already reached the official singles Top Five with their first 11 singles (including three number ones) before this musical number helped them deliver their only million seller.

The single's success might almost have seemed guaranteed with industry veterans Andrew Lloyd Lloyd Webber and Jim Steinman on board. Composer Lloyd Webber had a dozen West End and Broadway musicals to his credit (*Jesus Christ Superstar, Evita, Starlight Express, The Phantom Of The Opera*) before embarking on *Whistle Down The Wind*, based on the 1961 film of the same name starring Hayley Mills, Bernard Lee and Alan Bates.

In turn, Steinman was the writer/producer who had transformed Meat Loaf from a dubious dinner-time treat into a global superstar with albums like *Bat Out Of Hell* and *Dead Ringer*, before standing by Welsh vocalist Bonnie Tyler's side during the most successful period of her career.

'No Matter What' was taken from the musical composed by Lloyd Webber and Steinman, based on the story told in the 1961 movie about a group of Lancashire children who find a fugitive in their barn and believe him to be Jesus, leading them to hide him from the police who are searching for him.

The single was released in August 1998, six weeks after *Whistle Down The Wind* had made its West End debut at the Aldwych Theatre on July 1 – with a children's cast during its original London run which included a pre-teen Jessica Cornish, now a million-selling recording artist in her own right as Jessie J.

Polydor certainly pulled out all the stops to maximise the single's potential. Sleeve images of all five Irish heartthrobs in reflective poses, on a garish yellow background, were just for starters. The single also promoted its link with the new musical, and was offered with a CD-ROM advertised as "secrets from the 'No Matter What' video shoot".

The single faced ferocious competition during its three-week run at number one – it dethroned the Spice Girls' 'Viva Forever' and held off no less than five new entries in the top seven positions, most notably Stardust's 'Music Sounds Better With You', to retain its crown.

Boyzone's fourth UK chart-topper and the 12th of what would become 17 consecutive Top Five hits (a record chart start tally beaten only by their fellow Irish, Louis Walsh-honed counterparts Westlife) cemented their place at the top of the boy band league. The band ably filled the void left by the then-defunct Take That in 1998, a year that witnessed pop rub shoulders with rap (Run-D.M.C.), R&B (Usher), rock (the Manic Street Preachers), swagger (Oasis), vocal enhancement (Cher) and even more years of hurt (Baddiel & Skinner & Lightning Seeds) at the summit of the Official Singles Chart.

'No Matter What' was included both on Boyzone's studio album *Where We Belong*, released two months ahead of the single, as well as the *Whistle Down The Wind* concept album. That set additionally featured Tom Jones, Donny Osmond and Tina Arena's title track, which made the Top 30 earlier in the summer; the aforementioned Steinman associates Meat Loaf and Tyler also put in an appearance, as well as The Everly Brothers and Boy George.

Boyzone were assembled by Irish impresario and future *X-Factor* judge Louis Walsh. They consisted of Ronan Keating, Stephen Gately, Keith Duffy, Mikey Graham and Shane Lynch, with Keating and Gately sharing lead vocals on this track and the other three contributing background harmonies.

The group called it a day in 2000 after selling almost 6.5 million singles in the UK alone, but reunited in 2007 for a mega-grossing tour and a fourth studio album, *Brother*. Notwithstanding the absence of Stephen Gately, the band founder who tragically died aged 33 in October 2009, a new 2012 album will precede a 2013 tour celebrating their 20th anniversary.

AEROSMITH 1998

I DON'T WANT TO MISS A THING

WRITER: Diane Warren	
PRODUCER: Matt Serletic	
ALBUM: Armageddon – The Album (soundtrack)	
PEAK POSITION: Number 4 (2 weeks)	
WEEKS ON CHART: 26 (1998, 20; 2008, 1; 2011, 3; 2012, 2)	
SALES: 1.03m	

It took nearly 30 years for US rock giants Aerosmith to reach the UK Top 10 in their own right, and they did so with a track that remains their Official Singles Chart peak and their only million-selling single.

Born Steven Tallarico in 1948, Steven Tyler formed Aerosmith in Boston in 1970. Over the following 40 years, they have become an iconic American rock act. Centring round a core line-up of Tyler, Joe Perry (lead guitar), Brad Whitford (rhythm guitar), Tom Hamilton (bass) and Joey Kramer (drums), they have sold over 150 million albums (including 65 million in the US).

But the UK market took a good 15 years to warm up to the US rock outfit and their US commercial success was not replicated in Britain until 1986, when the group finally broke their duck in the Official Singles Chart.

Rap outfit Run-D.M.C. teamed up with Aerosmith to recast their 1975 classic 'Walk This Way' as a truly genre-bending rock-rap hit – arguably one of music's earliest mash-ups – which became a smash in America, but also peaked at number eight in the UK. The track reinvented Aerosmith and brought them a whole new generation of fans.

It wasn't an immediate impact, however. Aerosmith's *Permanent*

Vacation the following year was their first album to hit the Top 40 – but only at 37. Then, in 1989, led off by Top 20 single 'Love In An Elevator', *Pump* reached number three and in 1993 *Get A Grip* went one better at number two on the Official Albums Chart.

But a Top 10 UK hit continued to elude the band – until 1998. 'I Don't Want To Miss A Thing' was the latest in a string of anthems pushed up charts all around the world thanks to an appearance in a blockbuster movie. In this case, it was the disaster epic *Armageddon*. Featuring an A-list cast including Bruce Willis, Ben Affleck, Billy Bob Thornton and Steven Tyler's own daughter Liv, the movie tells how NASA sends a team of drillers to save the world, when it becomes apparent that an asteroid is hurtling towards Earth.

Unusually for Aerosmith, 'I Don't Want To Miss A Thing' is one of the few hits in their repertoire which they didn't compose themselves – instead it was penned by California-born songwriter Diane Warren, who has since said she was inspired by a TV interview in which Barbra Streisand told how her husband James Brolin had said romantically, "I don't wanna fall asleep, because I'll miss you."

Whatever the inspiration, Warren is certainly one of the modern songwriting greats. After breaking through in the mid-Eighties with DeBarge's 'Rhythm Of The Night' (a transatlantic Top 10 hit in 1985), she would go on to write several other British number one hits and the illustrious and long list of artists to record her songs includes Celine Dion, Cher, Meat Loaf, Toni Braxton, Belinda Carlisle, Tina Turner and the Pet Shop Boys.

'I Don't Want To Miss A Thing' was released at the end of August 1998, the same week it entered the US chart at number one and remained there for a month. In the UK, the band were denied a chart-topper, the single climbing no higher than four on the Official Singles Chart. By the end of the year, it was still only 1998's 17th best-selling single.

The song has remained popular in the intervening years. Music royalty collectors PRS for Music said in 2009 that it was the second most popular choice among newlyweds for their 'first dance', while it has become an auditionees' favourite on TV talent shows. This has brought it back into the Official Top 75 in 2008, 2011 and 2012 and helped boost sales by 450,000 copies in the download era. Ironically, Tyler himself became a judge on US talent show *American Idol* in 2011.

CHER 1998

BELIEVE

WRITERS: Brian Higgins, Paul Barry, Steven Torch, Matthew Gray, Stuart McLennen, Timothy Powell

PRODUCERS: Mark Taylor, Brian Rawling

ALBUM: Believe

PEAK POSITION: Number 1 (7 weeks)

WEEKS ON CHART: 28

SALES: 1.74m

In one week at the end of October 1998, the UK's Official Singles Chart entered previously uncharted territory – for the first time, the entire Top Five were new entries. Heading the countdown was the oldest female soloist to top the Official Singles Chart – 52-year-old Cher – with a track that remains the biggest-selling single in the UK by a female.

California-born Cherilyn Sarkisian was by no means the only mature artist in the chart's upper echelons that week. Other established acts with high debuts were George Michael ('Outside'), U2 ('Sweetest Thing') and Culture Club ('I Just Wanna Be Loved'), resulting in the oldest recorded Top Four in chart history, with an average age of 39. The fifth new entry, 'Thank U', came from comparative spring chicken (at 24) Alanis Morissette.

Although 'Believe' was a number one debutant, the song's success had been far from overnight. It originally had just four composer credits, while various producers had been assigned, without success, to create a version worthy of release. Eventually, it was offered to London-based Metro Productions (Mark Taylor and Brian Rawling), who drafted in British songwriters Paul Barry and Steven Torch to rework the song, keeping the chorus but rewriting the rest.

During recording, Taylor and Rawling came up with the single's distinctive sound, running Cher's vocals through Auto-Tune on an extreme setting for deliberate creative effect, producing a smooth, robotic sound. While its use as a vocal effect in pop music has become common in recent years, 'Believe' was the first significant hit to employ the tool, with the single's sleeve proudly boasting "vocal effects in Metrovision".

The result was a seven-week residency at the top of the UK Official Singles Chart, during which time Cher conducted a one-woman campaign against boy bands – preventing East 17, 5ive and Boyzone from reaching number one.

The only female soloists to have spent longer than seven weeks with a single at number one in the UK are Doris Day (a total of nine weeks in 1954 with 'Secret Love') and Whitney Houston (10 consecutive weeks with 'I Will Always Love You' from December 1992). Both Olivia Newton-John and Rihanna also had longer runs, but in collaboration with John Travolta (nine weeks) and Jay-Z (10 weeks), respectively.

'Believe' became the UK's biggest-selling single of 1998 and topped charts in more than 20 other countries, including the US, where it reached number one in March 1999, just two weeks short of 25 years since Cher's previous *Billboard* Hot 100 chart-topper, 'Dark Lady', in 1974 – the longest gap between number one hits in US chart history – and went on to be the year's bestseller Stateside.

The single won three 1999 Ivor Novello awards, including Best Song Musically and Lyrically, and its parent album enjoyed global sales in excess of 11 million copies, producing three further UK Top 30 hits: 'Strong Enough', 'All Or Nothing' and 'Dov'è L'Amore'.

Part of an elite group of Academy Award-winning actors to top the UK chart (the others being Frank Sinatra, Lee Marvin, Barbra Streisand and, subsequently, Nicole Kidman), Cher already held the record for the longest wait for a solo number one by any female artist, with more than 25 years elapsing between her solo chart debut, 'All I Really Want To Do' in 1965 and her 1991 chart-topper 'The Shoop Shoop Song (It's In His Kiss)'.

However, taking into account the Sonny & Cher hits on which she duetted with her then husband Sonny Bono, the time from Cher's first week at number one with 'I Got You Babe' in late August 1965 to 'Believe' being replaced at the top on December 19, 1998 by B★Witched ('To You I Belong') gives her a number ones span of 33 years and 112 days – the longest for any credited female artist (and only exceeded by Elvis Presley and Cliff Richard).

STEPS 1998

HEARTBEAT/ TRAGEDY

WRITERS: 'Heartbeat' – Jackie James/'Tragedy' – Barry, Maurice and Robin Gibb

PRODUCER: Pete Waterman

ALBUM: Step One

PEAK POSITION: Number 1 (1 week)

WEEKS ON CHART: 30

SALES: 1.18m

For a group who were never meant to be anything more than one-hit wonders, scoring their first number one – and spawning a nation-wide dance craze – cemented Steps' position once and for all as one of the defining UK pop acts of the Nineties.

Formed in May 1997, Steps were created by artist manager Tim Byrne and songwriters Steve Crosby and Barry Upton for the sole purpose of getting '5, 6, 7, 8' – a track penned by the latter pair – to the top of the Official Singles Chart. Fusing the techno stylings of 2 Unlimited with American line-dance music, the track's writers hoped to cash in on the line-dancing craze that had swept in from the States. The single didn't, in fact, perform as well as hoped on the UK's Official Singles Chart (peaking at number 14 in November), but it was a consistent seller and spent 10 weeks in the Top 20.

It did, however, top the chart in Australia and went Top Five in New Zealand and Belgium – after which Byrne and label Jive Records quickly realised that the group – consisting of Claire Richards, Faye Tozer, Ian 'H' Watkins, Lee Latchford-Evans and Lisa Scott-Lee – really had potential.

The label recruited producer Pete Waterman – the man who, as part of the Stock Aitken Waterman production team, was responsible for launching the pop careers of Kylie Minogue, Jason Donovan and Rick Astley in the previous decade – who envisioned Steps as a pre-millennial re-imagining of ABBA.

The next was a cover of 'Last Thing On My Mind', a track Waterman and songwriting partner Mike Stock had penned for girl group Bananarama some six years previously. It faired considerably better than '5, 6, 7, 8', peaking at number six.

The follow-up, 'One For Sorrow', peaked at number two in August, paving the way for Steps' debut album, *Step One*, the following month. Despite impressive first-week sales, it also peaked at number two, held off the top of the chart by Welsh rockers Manic Street Preachers' *This Is My Truth Tell Me Yours*.

The group's planned bid for the 1998 Christmas number one also looked like being beyond their grasp when, having dominated the previous two years' Christmas charts, the Spice Girls announced the December 8 release of single 'Goodbye' – their first since the departure of band member Geri Halliwell. So Jive made a tactical decision to release Steps' next single – a double A-side of album track 'Heartbeat' and a new cover of the Bee Gees' 1979 classic, 'Tragedy' – in November.

The promotional video for 'Tragedy' – which saw Latchford-Evans and Watkins kidnap Richards, Tozer and Scott-Lee from their respective weddings and take them to a party where Pete Waterman was DJ-ing – proved to be a hit with music TV channels, with the routine the group performed during its big dance scene becoming a national craze. Initially, 'Heartbeat'/'Tragedy' stalled at number two behind Cher's 'Believe' (then in the middle of a seven-week stand at the top of the Official Singles Chart). Then, of course, came the Spice Girls for their already traditional Christmas number one.

However, 'Heartbeat'/'Tragedy' endured throughout the Christmas period and, after eight weeks in the Top 10, it knocked the Spice Girls off the top perch. It only stayed one week but became the first chart-topper of 1999 – just as the act's album, *Step One*, broke through the 600,000 sales barrier to be certified Double Platinum.

Steps' next album, 1999's *Steptacular*, hit number one in June that year, and they went on to have 11 more Top Five singles (including the number one, 'Stomp', in 2000) before disbanding in 2001.

The group officially reformed in 2011, and a greatest hits package, *The Ultimate Collection: Steps,* topped the Official Albums Chart in October of that year.

MILLION-SELLING MEMORIES

LISA SCOTT-LEE AND LEE LATCHFORD-EVANS (STEPS)

Over the course of your career you have clocked up two number one singles, 13 Top Five singles, two number one albums and, collectively, 4.5 million album sales. And that was all within your first four years.

LISA: It's just amazing when you hear that! That's not someone else's stats, they are ours and we played our part in that. We're very proud in what we achieved and it's lovely to hear that.

LEE: That's the key thing behind it all; it wasn't over 10 or 20 years, so that's quite cool. It's hard to believe. It was like living in a bubble and even when we were going through it, people were shouting our names out in the street and I'd be thinking, "I don't even know you! I don't get it!" It's the same with our chart stats; it's like another world. It's just… crazy!

Did you realise what you were achieving at the time?

LEE: I think it was after. We were so busy and it really was 16-hour days, seven days a week and we barely got breaks or days off. When you're that busy, all over the world, it's hard to take grasp of it.

LISA: I did really appreciate it at the time. I didn't need hindsight. I loved being in Steps and it was very much a dream come true for me. I had been singing and dancing from the age of four and that was where I was always hoping to end up. Looking back you do pinch yourself and think "Wow!"

LEE: We were so lucky living a life most people can only dream about. Not many people are realistically ever going to have that. I never thought I would have that in all honesty. It was a fantastic life.

LISA: It was wonderful. We like to say that we were together for five years and we genuinely were good friends and had amazing experiences. It was really only at the end when tension mounted.

It all started with '5, 6, 7, 8' and yet, incredibly, it was supposed to be a one-off wasn't it?

LISA: We had a one-single deal and it's incredible to think we went on to release four albums. We really did evolve as a line-dancing band. We started out with the help of Pete Waterman and the help of the public. The public really took to us and even though the media were negative at times, we kept proving them wrong!

The song ['5, 6, 7, 8'] reached number 14 and remains one of the best-selling singles to not make the Top 10.

LISA: That's really interesting! It wouldn't go away and it was over the Christmas party season, so that's why it did well and the record company took notice and thought, "Wow, quick sign them up!"

'Heartbeat'/'Tragedy' is a bona fide million seller and was the first Steps single to go to number one on the Official Singles Chart.

LISA: What was great is that we really appreciated it, because it didn't go straight in at number one. It took weeks to get to number one. We were away on holiday, but when we came back we all congratulated each other.

How was it working with pop producer extraordinaire Pete Waterman?

LEE: It was interesting and he's a big character. Pete's had a lot of success. It was phenomenal to be part of that PWL experience [Pete's production company that bore many pop hits of the Eighties, including Kylie Minogue, Sonia and Mel & Kim].

What do you think of music now and how it has changed?

LEE: It's cool. At the moment pop is creeping back in, with The Wanted and The Saturdays, for example. I think the likes of Lady Gaga and Katy Perry have a different take on pop and it's getting edgier.

BRITNEY SPEARS 1999
...BABY ONE MORE TIME

WRITER: Max Martin

PRODUCERS: Max Martin, Rami Yacoub, Denniz Pop

ALBUM: ...Baby One More Time

PEAK POSITION: Number 1 (2 weeks)

WEEKS ON CHART: 22

SALES: 1.51m

In a world dominated by manufactured boy bands, girl groups and angry young men wielding guitars, Britney Spears'...Baby One More Time' changed the musical landscape of the late Nineties and signalled the rebirth of 'The Pop Icon'.

A child star, Spears was singing in Off Broadway musicals aged nine and, by 11, was appearing as a Mouseketeer on Disney's 1990s revival of its 1950s TV show *The Mickey Mouse Club* (alongside future 'NSync singer Justin Timberlake, her future pop rival Christina Aguilera and Ryan Gosling, now an established Hollywood star).

During the summer of 1997, Spears' mother, Lynne, was in discussions with the Backstreet Boys and 'NSync's manager Lou Pearlman about her then 14-year-old daughter joining Innosense, a new girl group he was putting together. She asked family friend Larry Rudolph for his opinion on whether young Britney would stand a chance at the upcoming auditions for the group. However, Rudolph was so impressed by the young star's demo tape that he decided to manage her himself.

Rudolph immediately booked Spears studio time so he could shop her around a few record companies. Initial rejections followed the general consensus that the public wanted the next Spice Girls or TLC; the next Madonna or the next Debbie Gibson would only be in demand if she were in a group with other Madonnas or Debbie Gibsons. However, one label, the independent Jive Records, was particularly impressed by Spears' rendition of Whitney Houston's 'I Have Nothing' and signed her.

Jive put Spears to work with one of their producers, Eric Foster White (who had worked with Whitney Houston, Backstreet Boys and Samantha Fox). He set about shaping her individual vocal style to create a different product from the octave-hopping approach favoured by the likes of Mariah Carey.

Spears would begin recording her debut album the following spring, flying to Sweden in March 1998 to work with successful producers Max Martin, Denniz Pop and Rami Yacoub (Backstreet Boys, Ace Of Base). The trio played Spears a track entitled 'Hit Me Baby One More Time', which they had submitted for TLC's next album, 1999's *FanMail*, but which the US R&B group had rejected. While Spears thought the title glorified domestic violence and asked for it to be shortened to '...Baby One More Time', she was confident it was going to be a hit.

After Spears returned to the US in April 1998, she opened for 'NSync on their nationwide tour for the rest of the summer. Meanwhile Jive had decided '...Baby One More Time' would be Spears' first single. For its accompanying video, the label had liked the concept of an animated video, although Spears wanted something to showcase her dance moves. She reportedly proposed the idea of dressing up as a schoolgirl and singing the track while making her way through campus.

Released in October 1998, the single was slow to make an impact in her homeland; it took two and a half months to reach the top of the *Billboard* Hot 100, eventually hitting number one in January 1999. A month later '...Baby One More Time' debuted at number one on the Official Singles Chart in the UK – selling more than 463,000 copies in its first week, it made Spears the fastest-selling female artist in British chart history at the time (she would retain this record until *X-Factor* winner Leona Lewis' 'A Moment Like This' took the title in 2006).

'...Baby One More Time' would hold on to the top spot for a further week, selling over 231,000 during its second week on sale, before losing its place to Boyzone's cover of Billy Ocean's 'When The Going Gets Tough'. The track stayed in the Top 40 for a further 20 weeks.

EIFFEL 65 1999

BLUE (DA BA DEE)

WRITERS: Jeffrey Jey, Maurizio Lobina, Massimo Gabutti

PRODUCERS: Maurizio Lobina, Massimo Gabutti, Luciano Zucchet

ALBUM: Europop

PEAK POSITION: Number 1 (4 weeks)

WEEKS ON CHART: 21 (excluding 5 weeks on import)

SALES: 1.07m

The last single of the 20th century to sell one million copies in the UK was the sixth official number one of 1999 – and the third in a row to originate from continental Europe, following the success of Vengaboys and Lou Bega.

Eiffel 65 were three Italians, singer Jeffrey Jey (born Gianfranco Randone), keyboardist Maurizio Lobina and DJ/producer Gabriele Ponte. With 'Blue (Da Ba Dee)', they briefly became a worldwide phenomenon thanks to the song's catchy, seemingly nonsensical refrain, delivered in distorted vocals via a vocoder.

Surrounding the choruses was a lyric devised by Jey. He had constructed a character called Zoroti, and fleshed him out by imagining his lifestyle and tastes, from how he might buy a house to what girlfriend he might desire. "Then I came up with a colour," Jay later recalled, "a colour I thought described the way he saw things." The promotional video for 'Blue', which featured computer-generated 3D animation, depicted Jey being abducted by blue aliens during a concert.

The song was first issued as a single in April 1999, and by late summer was a smash all over Europe. Though not yet released on a UK record label, hunger for the track among British record buyers saw more expensive import copies snapped up, leading it to climb as high as number 39 on the Official Singles Chart.

Very few singles had reached the Top 40 purely on import sales – rare exceptions had included The Jam's 'That's Entertainment' (1981) and, only weeks earlier than 'Blue', Lou Bega's chart-topping 'Mambo No. 5 (A Little Bit Of...)'.

When Eiffel 65's British label, Eternal, finally granted Blue an official release in September 1999, it quickly knocked the Vengaboys' 'We're Going To Ibiza' off the top spot in the Official Singles Chart, towering over all competition for three weeks, after which it was displaced by Christina Aguilera's debut single 'Genie In A Bottle'.

It added more European flavour to what was already a very continental year in the UK, with number ones spanning seven weeks in the Official Singles Chart claimed already in 1999 by France's Mr. Oizo's 'Flat Beat' (two), Dutch outfit the Vengaboys' 'Boom, Boom, Boom, Boom!!' (one), German act ATB's '9pm (Till I Come)' (two), German singer Lou Bega's 'Mambo No. 5 (A Little Bit Of...)' (one) and the Vengaboys' 'We're Going To Ibiza' (one) – even aside from the Puerto Rican Ricky Martin's 'Livin' La Vida Loca' (three) and the eight Official number ones (spanning 11 weeks) by Irish acts B★Witched ('Blame It On The Weatherman'), Boyzone ('When The Going Gets Tough' and 'You Needed Me'), Westlife ('Swear It Again', 'If I Let You Go', 'Flying Without Wings' and 'I Have A Dream'/'Seasons In The Sun') and Ronan Keating ('When You Say Nothing At All').

It topped the singles charts in Australia, Austria, Canada, France, Germany, Switzerland and Sweden, peaking at number three in the trio's Italian homeland and even reaching a very respectable number six in the US.

Steve Allen, head of A&R for Eternal, had a theory about the Europop genre's specific global appeal at the close of the 1990s, referring to the increasing tendency for holidaying Brits to return home with a tune in their heads – a fact which inevitably impacted on the UK chart every summer/autumn.

Follow-ups to 'Blue' couldn't help but seem anti-climactic, though 'Move Your Body' did top charts in Austria, Italy and France and reached number three on the UK chart in February 2000.

When Ponte went solo in 2005, the remaining duo soldiered on under the name Bloom 06. While 'Blue' itself suffered the ignominy of being covered by Crazy Frog in 2006, Eiffel 65's original was only foiled as the UK's bestseller of 1999 by Britney Spears' '...Baby One More Time'.

BOB THE BUILDER 2000
CAN WE FIX IT?

WRITER: Paul K. Joyce

PRODUCER: Grant Mitchell

ALBUM: Bob The Builder

PEAK POSITION: Number 1 (3 weeks)

WEEKS ON CHART: 22

SALES: 1.02m

The race to become the Christmas number one is traditionally the biggest event in the Official Singles Chart's calendar. With December accounting for an uplift in sales of around 40 per cent, there is unquestionable prestige attached to scoring the festive chart-topper.

Since the Official Singles Chart's inception, there have been numerous attempts to elevate novelty records to the top in the week leading up to Christmas. These have ranged from the sublime ('There's No One Quite Like Grandma' by St Winifred's School Choir in 1980) to the ridiculous (Mr Blobby with his eponymous track in 1993), and occasionally the charity/political, such as 'Do They Know It's Christmas?' by the Band Aid project in 1984 and 1989. In 2000, however, it was Bob The Builder's time to shine.

Bob The Builder was a character on the children's BBC TV programme of the same name. In each episode Bob, along with black and white cat Pilchard and his mechanical friends Scoop (a digger), Muck (a bulldozer), Dizzy (a concrete mixer) and Lofty (a crane), attempt to renovate buildings in the fictional town of Bobsville. The show, aimed at pre-school children, has an underlying message of teamwork and co-operation summed up by the "Can we fix it? Yes we can!" refrain of its theme tune.

After scoring chart success in 1993 with BBC character Mr Blobby (who won the Christmas number one race that year) and again in 1997 with the Teletubbies (whose track 'Teletubbies Say "Eh-

Oh!'" was narrowly pipped at the post in that particular Christmas chart battle by the Spice Girls), the Corporation had established its own record company, designed to take on the established labels.

After launching the characters of another BBC children's show, the *Tweenies*, the previous month, when their track 'No.1' reached five in the Official Singles Chart, their next project was Bob. The target was to pitch a variation on *Bob The Builder*'s theme music and score the first Christmas number one of the new millennium.

'Can We Fix It?' was written by children's television composer Paul K. Joyce (who had previous credits for the themes to *Noddy* and the *Fimbles*) and sung by *Men Behaving Badly* star Neil Morrissey, who also voiced Bob in the show. It debuted in the Official Singles Chart at number two on December 17, one place behind US rapper Eminem's 'Stan', before climbing to the top spot the following week and thus claiming the Christmas number one. It held the position for a further two weeks and was later established as the biggest-selling single of that year – winning Joyce an Ivor Novello award for his songwriting.

'Bob The Builder' would go on to top the Official Singles Chart again in September 2001 with a cover of Lou Bega's 'Mambo No. 5'. A self-titled album that featured his two chart-toppers along with tracks from the show and a cover of Sir Elton John's 'Crocodile Rock' was released in October 2001 and reached number four on the Official Albums Chart. The 2008 follow-up, *Never Mind The Breeze Blocks*, however, barely scraped the Top 100, reaching number 87.

In 2008, the US Democratic Party's presidential hopeful, Barack Obama, adopted "Yes we can!" as his campaign slogan, which led to numerous comparisons – mostly by the British press – between him and Bob The Builder. The Obama campaign later revealed that the slogan was inspired by that of United Farm Workers Of America, and not actually Bob. Still, it made for some interesting internet memes and YouTube parody videos.

SHAGGY FEAT. RIKROK 2001
IT WASN'T ME

WRITERS: Shaggy, Ricardo 'RikRok' Ducent, Shaun Pizzonia, Braun Thompson

PRODUCER: Shaun Pizzonia

ALBUM: Hot Shot

PEAK POSITION: Number 1 (1 week)

WEEKS ON CHART: 20 (excluding 3 weeks on import)

SALES: 1.28m

The top-selling singles artist of 2001 – and the name behind the new millennium's first million seller – was a Jamaican-born reggae icon making a spectacular return after a lean period in the late 1990s.

Shaggy's 'It Wasn't Me' was inspired by the idea of a man asking a friend how to respond after his girlfriend caught him with another woman. The supposedly foolproof solution was to deny everything – a concept that saw a 1980s routine by stand-up comedian Eddie Murphy cited by some as an evident source of inspiration for this track. Though 'It Wasn't Me' lasts nearly four minutes, Shaggy's total contribution to the track lasts less than a minute, with far greater prominence given to featured vocalist RikRok.

Born Ricardo George Ducent in London in 1972, RikRok's Jamaican family returned to the Caribbean in his teens, and he went with them. There, he became a backing singer and a member of a vocal quartet called Lust, before being offered a songwriting deal by one Robert Livingston – who just happened to be the manager of another Jamaican artist.

That was Shaggy, who began life as Orville Richard Burrell in 1968 and moved from Jamaica to New York in his late teens. There, he joined the US Marine Corps and served in Operation Desert Storm during the Gulf War of 1991. Two number one hits in the UK followed:

'Oh Carolina' (1993) and 1995's 'Boombastic'. But by 1998 he had been dropped by his label, Virgin, after reportedly selling fewer than 3,000 copies of his album *Midnite Lover*.

Shaggy's remarkable comeback began when he was signed to MCA and released the 2000 album *Hot Shot*. 'It Wasn't Me' was not originally earmarked for single release and only became considered as such when a Hawaiian DJ called Pablo Sato downloaded the album and began playing the song on air as a potential smash hit. He later claimed that when he played it, "the phone lines lit up right away. Within a couple of days, it was our number one requested song."

The record-buying public's reaction mirrored that of Sato's listenership: in February 2001, the single replaced Destiny's Child at the top of the *Billboard* Hot 100.

Like Eiffel 65's 'Blue (Da Ba Dee)' in 1999, 'It Wasn't Me' sold impressively in Britain as an import, climbing as high as number 31 before its UK release propelled it to number one in the Official Singles Chart, ending a month-long reign at the top by Atomic Kitten's 'Whole Again'. It was itself demoted after just seven days, by Westlife's version of Billy Joel's million seller 'Uptown Girl' (a Comic Relief charity fundraiser), but hung on for a further five weeks at number two on the chart.

Shaggy's first hit of any substance in nearly four years, 'It Wasn't Me' proved to be no comeback fluke. The next single, 'Angel' (featuring Rayvon), again topped the charts on both sides of the Atlantic, with *Hot Shot* also heading the Albums Chart, by far his most successful long-player in the UK. Sizeable hits continued until 'Hey Sexy Lady' left the Top 10 at the end of 2002.

But there is little doubt that 2001 was Shaggy's year. He sold nearly two million singles in the UK alone, where he doubled his previous tally of two number one hits.

What's more, 'It Wasn't Me', the best-selling single of the year, sold 345,000 copies in its first week on sale, making it the fastest seller since Britney Spears' debut single ('...Baby One More Time') two years earlier.

HEAR'SAY 2001

PURE AND SIMPLE

WRITERS: Peter Kirtley, Tim Hawes, Alison Clarkson

PRODUCERS: Jiant (Peter Kirtley, Tim Hawes)

ALBUM: Popstars

PEAK POSITION: Number 1 (3 weeks)

WEEKS ON CHART: 25

SALES: 1.09m

It was the perfect start to a chart career: first-day single sales in excess of 160,000, a total for week one of 549,823 (a record, at that time, for a non-charity release) and the fastest-selling debut single by any group in British chart history. However, 18 months later, it would all be over.

The new phenomenon started with teasers during TV ad breaks with the words "Nigel, pick me" appearing briefly. These, it transpired, referred to TV producer Nigel Lythgoe who, along with music promoter Nicki Chapman and Polydor A&R man Paul Adam, was a judge on a new kind of TV talent search called *Popstars*. Rather than acts competing against each other for public approval, the aim was to form a new vocal group from thousands of hopefuls, allowing viewers full access to the audition process.

The series began in January 2001, with audiences of up to 12 million watching the contenders being whittled down by judges until the final five were revealed. Once chosen, group members Danny Foster, Myleene Klass, Kym Marsh, Suzanne Shaw and Noel Sullivan lived together, along with a camera crew, so viewers were privy to recorded footage of life in the group, which was named Hear'Say.

The final programme of the series was broadcast on Sunday March 18, 2001, bringing viewers right up to date, with the band's reaction to the unveiling of the position of their debut single in the Official Singles Chart being captured live on TV.

The song had been recorded originally by UK/Dutch girl band Girl Thing for an album that never got a UK release, but just before 7 p.m., BBC Radio 1's Mark Goodier announced 'Pure And Simple' by Hear'Say as the UK's official number one single.

The reality TV pop experiment had proved a success, with Hear'Say's first-week sales only being surpassed subsequently by solo graduates from the *X-Factor* and *Pop Idol* schools, excluding hits with a fundraising connection.

While the single continued at the top of the chart, Hear'Say's debut album *Popstars* also went straight to number one, smashing Oasis's record for the fastest-selling debut album in the UK (*Definitely Maybe* – 86,000 copies) by shifting 306,631 copies in its week of release. In recent years, only Arctic Monkeys, Leona Lewis and Susan Boyle have exceeded this figure in their first week on the Official Albums Chart. By holding the top spot in both the Official Singles and Albums Charts simultaneously with their debut releases, Hear'Say became the first British group to achieve this feat.

The *Popstars* album produced a further number one hit in the shape of 'The Way To Your Love' in July 2001, which was followed by *Hear'Say It's Saturday*, a TV series featuring the band in a variety of sketches and musical performances.

A second album, *Everybody*, was issued in time to capitalise on the Christmas market but failed to reach the Top 20, with its title track only climbing to number four on the Official Singles Chart.

Marsh left the band in January 2002 and was replaced by Johnny Shentall in further televised auditions. However, negative publicity followed the discovery that Shentall (formerly of UK pop act Boom!) was engaged to Steps vocalist Lisa Scott-Lee, resulting in accusations that the audition process had not been genuine and fair.

Although the new line-up displayed a more mature pop/R&B sound, the single 'Lovin' Is Easy' spent only one week in the Top 20 in August 2002 and the act announced its split two months later. The members went on to careers incorporating acting, presenting, musical theatre, modelling and other reality TV shows.

'Pure And Simple' received a BRIT nomination for Best British Single and made the final shortlist for the ITV-broadcast Record of the Year awards, losing out to S Club 7's 'Don't Stop Movin'' on both occasions. However, it did get an Ivor Novello award for Best-Selling UK Single of 2001.

KYLIE MINOGUE 2001

CAN'T GET YOU OUT OF MY HEAD

WRITERS: Cathy Dennis, Rob Davis

PRODUCERS: Cathy Dennis, Rob Davis

ALBUM: Fever

PEAK POSITION: Number 1 (4 weeks)

WEEKS ON CHART: 25

SALES: 1.15m

If Kylie Minogue had been told back in 1988, when her first UK single was released, that she would notch up 20 UK Top 10 entries in that century yet still have her biggest hit still ahead of her, she might well have retorted, "I should be so lucky".

Born in Melbourne in 1968, Minogue made her Australian TV debut when she was only 11. She first found fame in the UK as schoolgirl-cum-garage mechanic Charlene Mitchell in the Aussie soap *Neighbours*, a role that resulted in her being the youngest person ever named Most Popular TV Performer in her homeland. In 1987, her first Australian single, 'The Loco-Motion', was the biggest hit of the year Down Under.

After a slow start, *Neighbours* became a 'can't-miss' programme for millions of UK soap watchers, with Charlene one of its most popular characters. Her TV popularity and Australian record sales brought her to the attention of the UK's top pop production team, Stock Aitken Waterman, and in their five years working together they amassed four number one singles, six number twos and an unprecedented 13 successive Top 10 entries. When it comes to longevity on the Official Singles Chart, singer-turned-actor Madonna is the only female artist to have matched actor-turned-singer Minogue.

Her biggest hit, 'Can't Get You Out Of My Head', was the first single from her eighth studio album, *Fever* (2001). It had been written by ex-hit artists Rob Davis and Cathy Dennis, who also produced Minogue's cut of a song they reportedly originally offered to Sophie Ellis-Bextor. Davis, who had been in Seventies chart-toppers Mud, also played keyboards, guitar and drums on the track.

Dennis, who had been the most successful UK artist on the US Hot 100 in 1991, has written seven UK number ones, won more Ivor Novello awards than any other female and penned hits for fellow female superstars Britney Spears and Katy Perry.

The single was an instant hit in the UK, where, as certain club DJs refused to play 'unhip' tracks by Minogue, some advance promotional copies of the track had been sent out bearing the artist name Special K. On the first day of release, 77,000 copies were sold and by the end of the week the total was over 306,000.

The record entered the Official Singles Chart at number one in September 2001 and held the top slot for the next four weeks, stopping both Steps ('Chain Reaction'/'One For Sorrow') and Michael Jackson ('You Rock My World') from adding to their chart-topping tallies. It was the most played record of 2001, and at the Ivor Novello awards it picked up the trophies for Most Played Record, Best International Single and Best Dance Record.

An international chart-topper, the single sold more than four million copies globally, selling in excess of 500,000 in both France and Germany. In the US, it was Minogue's first Top 10 entry since 'The Loco-Motion' in 1988. Such was the success of the song that Minogue named her 2002 autobiography *La La La* after its opening lyric.

The singer could always be counted on for an eye-catching video and she surpassed herself with the multiple award-winning one for the track, set in a computer-generated, futurist metropolis with Minogue sporting a selection of provocative outfits.

The track's electro-pop parent album, *Fever*, sold over eight million copies worldwide. In the UK, it topped the Official Albums Chart, sold over 1.5 million copies, picked up the BRIT Award for Best International Album and helped Minogue secure the trophy for Best International Female Solo Artist. It also went Gold in the US, entering the *Billboard* 200 at number three.

WILL YOUNG 2002

ANYTHING IS POSSIBLE/EVERGREEN

WRITERS: 'Anything Is Possible' – Chris Braide, Cathy Dennis/'Evergreen' – Jörgen Elofsson, Per Magnusson, David Kreuger

PRODUCERS: Cathy Dennis, Oskar Paul/Per Magnusson, David Kreuger

ALBUM: From Now On

PEAK POSITION: Number 1 (3 weeks)

WEEKS ON CHART: 16

SALES: 1.79m

Will Young currently holds the record for the biggest-selling single of the 21st century with 'Anything Is Possible'/'Evergreen'. But it could all have been so different…

This double A-side, penned by Chris Braide and Cathy Dennis ('Possible') and Jörgen Elofsson, Per Magnusson and David Kreuger ('Evergreen', which had previously been recorded by Irish boy band Westlife), was the winner's single for the first series of the UK's *Pop Idol* in 2002. The reality TV singing contest's three finalists – Young, Gareth Gates and Darius Danesh – had recorded both tracks but only one version of each would ever see the light of day.

With Danesh having already been knocked out in the previous week's semi-final show, Young went head-to-head with bookies favourite Gates live on ITV on February 9, 2002 to determine who would be the nation's *Pop Idol*. His renditions of the future single's tracks, along with a cover of his choice (The Doors' 1967 classic 'Light My Fire'), won over the viewers of the show with a then 23-year-old Young taking the lion's share (4.6 million) of the 8.7 million votes.

This was much to the chagrin of judge Simon Cowell, the music impresario later claiming that he felt physically sick when hosts Ant and Dec declared Young to be the show's inaugural winner – Cowell favouring Gates and his boy band looks.

Young's versions of 'Anything Is Possible' and 'Evergreen' were released two weeks later on February 25, 2002. In a pre-digital age, this was the quickest that record label BMG could physically get the single pressed and into record stores. Nevertheless, the momentum Young had built up since winning the show seemed to stay with him through to release week and beyond.

The astonishing impact of Young's single was unheard of at the time – but then so was the success of the platform from which his career had launched. The brainchild of Spice Girls manager Simon Fuller, *Pop Idol* represented a new approach to TV talent shows, with as many people tuning in to hear judges Simon Cowell, Pete Waterman, Nicki Chapman and Neil Fox's critiques of the would-be pop stars as the performances of the contestants themselves. Unlike previous attempts at reality TV singing contests – ITV's *Popstars* and *Popstars: The Rivals*, and the BBC's short-lived series *Fame Academy* – it also gave the public an emotional connection to the contestants, one which transcended its Saturday night time slot.

The impact of this was illustrated by the opening sales of 'Anything Is Possible'/'Evergreen', which went straight to the top of the Official Singles Chart, selling a staggering 403,000 copies in its first day on sale and 1.1 million copies during its first week. That made it the fastest-selling single since Elton John's 'Something About The Way You Look Tonight'/'Candle In The Wind 1997'.

Young would continue to top the chart for a further two weeks before being knocked off the summit by… Gareth Gates himself. Gates had also been signed up by Cowell following his defeat on the show and his cover of 'Unchained Melody' (his choice for the *Pop Idol* final) also became a million seller.

The duo's rivalry was short-lived, however, with both Young and Gates teaming up for 2002's Children In Need charity single 'The Long And Winding Road'/'Suspicious Minds'.

During the ten years since Young won *Pop Idol*, his career has gone from strength to strength. He has clocked up 13 Top 40 singles, including four number ones, five Top 10 albums (three of which topped the Official Albums Chart), and won multiple awards.

However, one of his dreams remains unfulfilled. "Ten years ago I won *Pop Idol*," wrote Young on Twitter in 2012. "Since then I have still not achieved my dream of a Tupperware range. Life can be cruel…"

GARETH GATES 2002
UNCHAINED MELODY

WRITERS: Alex North (music), Hy Zaret (lyrics)

PRODUCER: Steve Mac

ALBUM: What My Heart Wants To Say

PEAK POSITION: Number 1 (4 weeks)

WEEKS ON CHART: 30

SALES: 1.34m

Gareth Gates was a spiky-haired 17-year-old with a cheeky glint in his eye when he first came to public attention on the inaugural series of *Pop Idol*. Even though enduring pop star Will Young squeaked past Bradford's finest in the final, attracting 53.1 per cent of the 8.7 million votes, a star had been born.

And what better way to launch his career than with a tried and tested ballad that had previously crowned the Official Singles Chart on three separate occasions. Gates' version of 'Unchained Melody' received its first *Pop Idol* airing on January 26, 2002, in a quarter-final also featuring Young and two singers who would flirt briefly with stardom after the show – Darius Danesh and Zoe Birkett.

'Unchained Melody' helped secure Gates' place in the semi-final, and the classic tearjerker was unashamedly reprised for the final on February 9, 2002. However, fans of the teenager had not bargained for the TV audience's unexpected fondness for The Doors' mid-Sixties psychedelic masterpiece 'Light My Fire' – which did the trick for Young and left Gates having to settle for the runner-up spot.

But his story didn't end there. As has become the tradition on the reality music shows that followed *Pop Idol*, notably *The X-Factor*, all manner of finalists can secure that all-important recording contract and so it proved for Gates. Within two months of the *Pop Idol* final, amid the deafening screams of hordes of 'tweenagers', Gates had replaced Young's 'Anything Is Possible'/'Evergreen' at the top of the chart and was the new kid on the block.

Suddenly, a year that had begun with back-to-back posthumous number ones for Aaliyah and George Harrison had come alive with incredible first-week sales for both finalists – 1,108,269 for Young and 850,535 for 'Unchained Melody'. With total sales of 1,330,000 copies, Gates' 'Melody' remains one of the 50 biggest-selling singles of all time in the UK – quite an achievement considering he hit his peak five years before digital music became an option for modern-day music-buyers.

Any far-flung notion that Gates was a one-hit wonder was soon dispelled – within five months he had three chart-toppers under his belt and was mirroring his *Pop Idol* conqueror's career every step of the way. 'Anyone Of Us (Stupid Mistake)' provided a second number one, and the finalists teamed up for a double A-side featuring Elvis' 'Suspicious Minds' and The Beatles' 'The Long And Winding Road'.

Gates returned to familiar territory almost exactly a year after his first visit to the summit when he covered 'Spirit In The Sky' – itself a previous chart-topper, twice – with a little help from TV comedy family The Kumars.

After the hits dried up in 2003 and he had been dropped by record company BMG, Gates attempted to revive his career with a new album, *Pictures Of The Other Side*, in 2007. When the album and its singles flopped, he branched out into musical theatre and was lauded for roles in *Joseph And The Amazing Technicolor Dreamcoat* and *Les Misérables*.

Gates is a now qualified speech coach (inspired by his own public fight against a stammer) and has been an active charity supporter, most notably in his role as patron of the HIV/Aids charity Body And Soul.

Gareth Gates was born in West Bowling, Bradford, on July 12, 1984, the eldest of four siblings. His first brush with fame was as head chorister of Bradford Cathedral, performing solo in front of Queen Elizabeth II in 1997, and he had secured a place at Manchester's Royal Northern College of Music before auditioning for *Pop Idol*.

Subsequently, he became the youngest British male solo artist to have an official number one single, a record Craig Douglas had held since September 1959 – for 'Only Sixteen', read 'only 17 years, eight months and 18 days'.

BAND AID 20 2004

DO THEY KNOW IT'S CHRISTMAS?

WRITERS: Bob Geldof, Midge Ure

PRODUCERS: Nigel Godrich (producer), Midge Ure (executive producer)

ALBUM: N/A

PEAK POSITION: Number 1 (4 weeks)

WEEKS ON CHART: 11 (2004, 10; 2005, 1)

SALES: 1.16m

There is no doubting Band Aid's huge impact both in generating funds and raising awareness. And 20 years after the original, 'Do They Know It's Christmas?' was re-recorded for the third time, prompted by another mounting human catastrophe in Africa.

Five years after Bob Geldof, Midge Ure and a cast of dozens created what was then the biggest-selling single in UK history, 1989 saw a collection of stars come together as Band Aid II. With the then imperious producers Stock, Aitken and Waterman at the helm, the group – including SAW protégées Kylie Minogue and Jason Donovan, as well as Wet Wet Wet, Bananarama and Lisa Stansfield, among others – scored another number one hit, which held the summit for three weeks, including the Christmas week of 1989.

But it was the third version, another 15 years later, that was to join the 1984 original on the million sellers list. This time the catalyst was a growing crisis in the Darfur region of Sudan, prompting a new group of stars to enter Air Studios in London on Sunday November 14, 2004, with Radiohead producer Nigel Godrich at the helm and Midge Ure as executive producer.

The opening line was sung by Coldplay singer Chris Martin, and artists including Will Young, Jamelia, Joss Stone, Fran Healy of Travis,

Beverley Knight, Tom Chaplin of Keane and Justin Hawkins of The Darkness followed. Dido and Robbie Williams contributed their vocals from Melbourne and Los Angeles respectively, while Dizzee Rascal offered a new lyrical element – a rap in the middle of the song.

And while Midge Ure provided all the instrumentation on the original, this time a 'super group' did the honours, comprising Sir Paul McCartney (bass), Radiohead's Thom Yorke and Jonny Greenwood (piano and guitar), The Darkness' Ed Graham and Justin Hawkins (drums and guitar) and Supergrass' Danny Goffey (guitar).

This time round the world was more prepared for the phenomenon. With the single broadcast for the first time on the Radio 1, Virgin and Capital breakfast shows on November 16, the video was then shown across a range of TV stations, including BBC1, BBC2, ITV, Channel 4 and Five, at teatime on November 18. It was also accompanied by an hour-long documentary on the making of the single, which went out on BBC1 and subsequently on MTV from early December, meaning the profile of the single was huge.

Released on November 29, it sold 72,000 copies on its first day, had topped 600,000 sales by the time it took the Christmas number one and surpassed one million sales two weeks later. For a track that was released when downloading was still in its infancy and the singles market was at its lowest ebb, those million sales are remarkable and represent almost three per cent of the total singles sold during 2004.

To date, Band Aid 20 has sold 1.1 million CDs and just over 50,000 downloads – potentially adding up to almost £3.5 million for the Band Aid charity. But its impact went much further.

Even as 'Do They Know It's Christmas?' was achieving its third Christmas number one, Bob Geldof talked of the "real political impact" its message could have, with Britain due to hold the EU presidency and host the G8 summit the following year. This connection ultimately led to the launch of 10 Live 8 shows on July 2, 2005, which took place in London, Paris, Berlin, Rome, Philadelphia, Johannesburg, Moscow, the Eden Project (UK), Barrie (Canada) and Chiba (Japan). Four days later the final event was held in Edinburgh, the closest of the 11 concerts to the G8 summit's location.

Band Aid 20 helped cap a remarkable chart performance for 'Do They Know It's Christmas?'. Released three times in the UK, it can (to date) claim a mammoth 12 weeks as official number one, 57 weeks on the Official Singles Top 75 and more than 5.3 million singles sales.

TONY CHRISTIE FEAT. PETER KAY 2005
(IS THIS THE WAY TO) AMARILLO

WRITERS: Neil Sedaka, Howard Greenfield

PRODUCERS: Mitch Murray, Peter Callander

ALBUM: N/A

PEAK POSITION: Number 1 (7 weeks)

WEEKS ON CHART: 41 (1971, 13; 2005, 28)

SALES: 1.31m

Tony Christie had the longest wait of any act in history for an Official Singles Chart number one with the track that itself holds the record for the slowest climb to the top – 33 years and 126 days after its chart debut.

All Christie had to do to claim both of these records was share top billing with a comedian from Bolton who does not feature on the track at all.

The song enquiring about directions to a city in Texas had been a million seller on its first release if total global sales are combined. It topped both the German and Belgian charts and made the Top 10 in the Netherlands and Australia, with around 50,000 sales coming from the UK, where it peaked at number 18 in January 1972 during a 13-week chart run. 'Amarillo' also bubbled under the American chart in 1972, with its highest placing being number 121, although one of its composers, Neil Sedaka, subsequently had a number 44 US hit with it in 1977.

Christie (real name Anthony Fitzgerald) was 55 years old and had been in the chart wilderness for more than 20 years when UK trio The All Seeing I featured him on their 1999 Top 10 hit 'Walk Like A Panther'. However, the real turnaround began when characters Max and Paddy (played by Peter Kay and Paddy McGuinness) sang along to 'Amarillo' as it played on the radio in their minibus during a 2002 episode of the TV sitcom *Peter Kay's Phoenix Nights*.

Kay's association with the song continued through live performances and TV appearances, culminating in his contribution to the Comic Relief 2005 telethon, for which he created a video which showed him miming to Christie's original recording accompanied by a series of celebrities, characters from *Phoenix Nights* and Christie himself. The video premiered during the Red Nose Day charity telethon on Friday March 11, 2005 and was released for sale the following Monday.

The DVD sold 74,305 in its first week on release and the CD single (which also included a version of the video accessible on a computer) had first-week sales of 266,844 – ironically, higher than the population of the entire Amarillo metropolitan area of Texas – replacing that year's official Comic Relief single, McFly's 'All About You'/'You've Got A Friend', at number one.

Although credited to both Christie and Kay, the track was a straight reissue of the 1971 hit recording and finally gave Christie his first week at the top of the Official Singles Chart, 34 years and 76 days after his chart debut in January 1971 with 'Las Vegas' – smashing the previous record of 29 years set when Jackie Wilson topped the chart posthumously with 'Reet Petite' at Christmas 1986.

'Amarillo' held the top spot for seven weeks from the end of March 2005, during a period when collectors' editions of all 18 UK number ones by Elvis Presley were being issued in chronological order on a week-by-week basis, which had already resulted in the fastest hat-trick of chart-toppers in UK chart history (completed in just four weeks, including the UK's 1,000th number one 'One Night'/'I Got Stung'), but the combination of Christie and Kay prevented Presley from adding three more to his total.

The track became the UK's best-selling single of the year and held the top spot on the historic Official Singles Chart dated week ending April 23, 2005, when download sales were added to the tallies of corresponding physical releases for the first time. During the single's run at the top, Christie – who had never had a UK Top 10 album before – spent two weeks topping the Official Albums Chart with his *Definitive Collection*.

Christie's only subsequent visit to the Top 10 of the Singles Chart was in June 2006 with a football-themed rewrite of 'Amarillo' in support of England's campaign at the FIFA World Cup in Germany.

SHAYNE WARD 2005

THAT'S MY GOAL

WRITERS: Jörgen Elofsson, Jem Godfrey, Bill Padley

PRODUCERS: Per Magnusson, David Kreuger

ALBUM: Shayne Ward

PEAK POSITION: Number 1 (4 weeks)

WEEKS ON CHART: 21

SALES: 1.1m

With *The X-Factor*'s first winner Steve Brookstein a fading memory in the autumn of 2005, the next contender to roll off the reality TV conveyor belt was Shayne Ward, a charming 21-year-old from Clayton, Greater Manchester, who, in spectacular fashion, shifted 742,180 copies of 'That's My Goal' in just four days to claim the coveted Christmas number one spot on the Official Singles Chart.

The single, which had absolutely nothing to do with football, first came to light on the night of the Series 2 *X-Factor* final, December 17, 2005, when it was performed by both winner Ward and runner-up Andy Abraham – a bin man from London. In the closest-fought final of the eight series to date, Ward claimed 50.6 per cent of the vote and it was his version of 'That's My Goal' that was rush-released on December 21, 2005.

To aid its success at retail, the additional tracks on the CD single were culled from Ward's first two *X-Factor* live show performances: renditions of Daniel Bedingfield's 'If You're Not The One' (reprised in the final) and Richard Marx's 'Right Here Waiting'. *X-Factor* followers may also recall Louis Walsh's charge tackling 'Summer Of '69', 'Cry Me A River', 'A Million Love Songs' and 'I Believe In A Thing Called Love' during the live shows.

Ward had won the competition just three years after reaching the latter stages of *Popstars: The Rivals* in 2002 – the show that gave us Girls Aloud.

'Goal' was the work of an experienced musical team: writing/ production duo Jem Godfrey and Bill Padley, who composed Atomic Kitten's 'Whole Again' and Holly Valance's 'Kiss Kiss' (both official UK number ones) plus Swedish songwriter Jörgen Elofsson, whose credits include hits for Britney Spears, Westlife, Steps, The Saturdays and two other singers who are no strangers to reality TV success – Kelly Clarkson and Gareth Gates.

Elofsson also co-wrote Westlife's 'Evergreen' hit, later covered by Pop Idol's Will Young as a double A-side with 'Anything Is Possible', one of only two singles (the other being Elton John's 'Candle In The Wind 1997' – 658,000 to Young's 403,000) to sell more copies than 'That's My Goal' (313,000) in their first two days on sale.

Ward fought off Nizlopi's novelty hit 'JCB Song' and a resurgent, reissued 'Fairytale Of New York' by The Pogues to debut at number one on the chart dated December 31, 2005, and it remained in pole position for four weeks before being edged out by a quartet of new entries, headed by Arctic Monkeys' 'When The Sun Goes Down'.

Given Brookstein's rapid demise, many thought the sun might go down on Ward's promising career after 'That's My Goal', but his eponymously titled debut album strode to number one in April 1996 and spawned a number two hit in 'No Promises', while a second album, *Breathless*, peaked at number two in December 2007 (only kept off the top by another *X-Factor* winner, Leona Lewis) and delivered another couple of Top 10 hits.

Ward was dropped by Simon Cowell's Syco Music label after the poor chart performance of *Obsession*, his third album from 2010. He was most recently seen in the West End production of the musical *Rock Of Ages*, playing Stacee Jaxx. "One door closed, a thousand more will open," as the man himself tweeted after finding himself without a recording contract.

GNARLS BARKLEY 2006

CRAZY

WRITERS: Brian Burton, Thomas Callaway, Gian Franco Reverberi, Gian Piero Reverberi	
PRODUCER: Danger Mouse (Brian Burton)	
ALBUM: St. Elsewhere	
PEAK POSITION: Number 1 (9 weeks)	
WEEKS ON CHART: 18	
SALES: 1.04m	

This American duo's hugely successful worldwide hit was the first track to top the Official Singles Chart based purely on download sales.

Gnarls Barkley comprised producer Danger Mouse (born Brian Burton) and singer and rapper Cee Lo Green. New Yorker Burton first came to prominence when he produced a notorious mash-up hybrid of material from The Beatles' 1968 self-titled album (aka 'The White Album') and rapper Jay-Z's landmark set *The Black Album*. With impeccable logic, he named it *The Grey Album*. His other production credits have included albums for Gorillaz and Beck.

Cee Lo Green was born Thomas Callaway in Atlanta, Georgia, in 1974. After a spell as a member of hip-hop group Goodie Mob in the late 1990s, he sang as a guest vocalist on Santana's *Supernatural* album in 1999. He had already briefly met Burton, but their working relationship began in earnest in 2005 after they both worked on the album *Ghetto Pop Life* by rapper Jemini.

Danger Mouse and Cee Lo named themselves Gnarls Barkley in tribute to maverick basketball player Charles Barkley. The lyrical content of their international breakthrough hit was based on an irreverent conversation they held about how people often refuse to take an artist seriously unless or until their sanity is called into question.

'Crazy''s music content, meanwhile, was heavily based on a song called 'Last Man Standing', composed by Italian brothers Gian Franco and Gian Piero Reverberi for a 1968 spaghetti western movie called *Viva! Django*.

The release and immediate popularity of 'Crazy' in the UK in spring 2006 came as UK chart rules were being changed to reflect the exploding popularity of digital downloading. Initially, the single was only accessible as a download. Previously, a single had been denied a chart placing if no CD or vinyl format was available to buy, but downloads now qualified, provided at least one physical format emerged within seven days. As a result, in April 2006, 30,000 downloads were sufficient to propel the song to number one. Its momentum at the top was maintained as a CD single was issued and two weeks later a 12-inch vinyl version.

In contrast to the US, where it spent seven weeks at number two on the *Billboard* Hot 100, 'Crazy' topped the UK Official Singles Chart for nine weeks. It was the longest run at the top since Wet Wet Wet's 15-week 'Love Is All Around' in 1994 and longer than any single ever issued on the Warner Bros. label (the previous record-holder being Cher's eight weeks with 'Believe' in 1998).

'Crazy''s lifespan on the chart would continue in an unorthodox fashion. It could probably have remained at number one for even longer, but with Gnarls Barkley and Warners keen to ensure music fans did not tire of the song's charms, the CD and vinyl formats were deleted.

In a further twist, because another chart rule specified that downloads only count for a further fortnight after the deletion of physical formats, the track would spend its last week on the chart (for now) at number five before disappearing completely. It did, however, return to the Official Singles Top 40 early in 2007 when the rules were relaxed and downloads without physical formats were permitted.

'Crazy' finally sold its one millionth copy in 2011. Without the aforementioned constraints, it would almost certainly have turned the trick five years earlier.

As it was, the single sold 820,000 copies in just two months and rounded off the year not only as sales champion but also as British radio's most played song of the year (with nearly 50,000 airings).

Cee Lo Green has gone on to become a vocal coach on the NBC talent show *The Voice*.

LEONA LEWIS 2007
BLEEDING LOVE

WRITERS: Ryan Tedder, Jesse McCartney

PRODUCER: Ryan Tedder

ALBUM: Spirit

PEAK POSITION: Number 1 (7 weeks)

WEEKS ON CHART: 28

SALES: 1.04m

The proliferation of TV talent show stars since the late Nineties has thrown focus on the ability of such competitions to create long-term, internationally viable talent. The arrival of Leona Lewis and 'Bleeding Love' allowed the advocates to make the case in favour.

By 2006, Simon Cowell was five years into his tenure as a reality TV show judge across both *Pop Idol* and his own *X-Factor* format. While he had discovered some impressive artists on US show *American Idol* (Carrie Underwood, Kelly Clarkson and Chris Daughtry to name a few), in his homeland Cowell had failed to unearth any British stars who could truly compete internationally.

While successful in the UK, neither *Pop Idol*'s Will Young nor *X-Factor*'s Shayne Ward looked likely to break the lucrative American market, and Steve Brookstein and Michelle McManus were both medium-term commercial failures. As every year passed, Cowell had become increasingly keen for his *X-Factor* winner to be someone not just special, but spectacular.

In 2006, 21-year-old Hackney resident Leona Lewis quite clearly had the potential to be that breakthrough talent. Young, beautiful and gifted with a truly remarkable voice, she also had what Cowell called 'the likability factor'; a real girl next door, if you will.

Lewis' *X-Factor* winner's song, 'A Moment Like This' – a hit Stateside for Kelly Clarkson following the inaugural series of *American Idol* – predictably went straight to the top of the Official Singles Chart upon its release on December 17, 2006. And not only did it take the coveted Christmas number one spot, it also became the fastest-selling single by a female artist in British chart history.

While Lewis basked in the spotlight, behind the scenes Cowell was busy preparing for re-launch. First, he persuaded Clive Davis, chairman of RCA Records, to personally sign Lewis to his J Records imprint for the US. Davis duly stoked the hype machine by telling *The Sun* that Lewis reminded him "of a young Whitney Houston", the iconic singer who he had himself discovered.

Next, Cowell tendered submissions from some of the world's best songwriters for Lewis' debut single proper, including Per Magnusson (Westlife), Novel (Alicia Keys) and Max Martin (Britney Spears). He eventually opted for 'Bleeding Love', a track penned by OneRepublic vocalist Ryan Tedder (who had just topped the US chart with his band's single, 'Apologize') and US singer/songwriter Jesse McCartney. The song had been scheduled for inclusion on McCartney's third studio album, *Departure*, but his label, Hollywood Records, didn't think it would be a hit. Cowell evidently knew otherwise.

Although the track had debuted on radio a few weeks beforehand, it was only when Lewis made her live return to *The X-Factor* on October 20, 2007 to perform 'Bleeding Love' that the full impact of her transformation to world-class pop star would be felt. As the camera panned to the stage, Lewis emerged out of the dry ice wearing a figure-hugging dress covered in Swarovski crystals. She delivered an emotive performance and conveyed the bittersweet pain of the track's lyrical content with a maturity beyond her years.

A week later, 'Bleeding Love' went straight in at number one on the Official Singles Chart, selling nearly 220,000 copies in its first week. Lewis had become the first *X-Factor* contestant to score two consecutive number one singles.

'Bleeding Love' continued to top the chart for a further six weeks and, by the end of 2007, had officially become the biggest-selling track of the year; the first by a British female artist to do so. Lewis had also become the first *X-Factor* winner to sell more copies of her second single than her first.

The song would go on to top charts in 17 different countries over the next year (including the US *Billboard* Hot 100). Simon Cowell could rest easy; Leona Lewis' future was assured, and he had (finally) discovered a genuine world-class star from the UK.

KINGS OF LEON 2008
SEX ON FIRE

WRITERS: Nathan Followill, Caleb Followill, Matthew Followill, Jared Followill

PRODUCERS: Angelo Petraglia, Jacquire King

ALBUM: Only By The Night

PEAK POSITION: Number 1 (3 weeks)

WEEKS ON CHART: 90 (2008/9, 87; 2012, 3)

SALES: 1.2m

One of the biggest-selling, most enduring singles of recent years, 2008's 'Sex On Fire' has, at the time of writing (April 2012), spent more time on the Official singles chart than any other number one single in history.

Although their 2007 album *Because Of The Times* peaked at number one in Britain, US rock family quartet Kings Of Leon had experienced more modest success on the singles chart. Prior to 'Sex On Fire', their peak was number 13 with 'Fans' in July 2007, while its follow-up, 'Charmer', failed even to make the Top 75.

But 2008 marked a sea-change in the group's fortunes as a singles act. Released on September 8, 'Sex On Fire' ended the five-week chart-topping run of Katy Perry's 'I Kissed A Girl'. It even trounced the efforts of Cliff Richard's 'Thank You For A Lifetime', which had been released to celebrate his 50 years as a hit solo artist but could peak no higher than number three.

'Sex On Fire' marked a substantial development in sound for Kings Of Leon, as an anthem for stadium shows and other large venues. Fittingly, it had already been performed to a rapturous reception as part of their headlining set at the Glastonbury Festival in June 2008, while a December tour of UK arenas was pronounced sold out before the single was released. Its parent album, *Only By The Night*, was also a number one, shifting 220,000 copies in its first week on sale.

According to one radio interview the band gave in Australia, 'Sex

On Fire' was first called 'Set Us On Fire', but an engineer misheard the lyrics as they were playing it in the studio and gave it the erroneous title. "It just kind of became a running joke," recalled drummer Nathan Followill, "and we stuck with it".

The other Followills making up Kings Of Leon are Nathan's brothers Caleb (lead vocals, rhythm guitar) and Jared (bass guitar), plus their cousin Matthew (lead guitar). Although they formed their group in Nashville, Tennessee in 1999, they were all born and raised in the state of Oklahoma, where their father was a preacher. The group was named after their grandfather Leon, who hailed from the Oklahoma town of Talihina. Initially writing songs with their producer Angelo Petraglia, they issued their debut EP in 2003, and within a few years were touring with the likes of Bob Dylan and Pearl Jam.

The foursome's first (and so far only) British number one, 'Sex On Fire' outsold all competition for three weeks and would spend 42 consecutive weeks in the Top 75, ending 2008 as the year's seventh best-selling single. But this was not the end of its chart career: it spent most of 2009 in the Top 75 as well.

In early September, the first anniversary of its original release, it zoomed back to number six, partly as a result of a televised Reading Festival appearance, but also because it was covered by *X-Factor* hopeful Jamie Archer for one of the TV show's auditions. The song's persistent presence throughout the year quietly made it number 18 in 2009's end-of-year sales chart.

'Sex On Fire''s weeks-on-chart tally has now exceeded those claimed by the likes of Frankie Goes To Hollywood's 'Relax', Judy Collins' 'Amazing Grace' and Bill Haley & His Comets' 'Rock Around The Clock'. The only singles to have spent longer on the chart are Frank Sinatra's 'My Way' (124 weeks) and Snow Patrol's 'Chasing Cars' (108 weeks), though those singles never got higher than number five and number six, respectively.

Given that 'Sex On Fire' had re-entered the Top 75 for the seventh time as of April 2012, Kings Of Leon may yet catch them all.

ALEXANDRA BURKE 2008

HALLELUJAH

WRITER: Leonard Cohen

PRODUCERS: Andreas Romdhane, Josef Larossi

ALBUM: Overcome

PEAK POSITION: Number 1 (3 weeks)

WEEKS ON CHART: 12 (2008, 11; 2009, 1)

SALES: 1.24m

The third million-selling winner from *The X-Factor*, Alexandra Burke's debut single 'Hallelujah' gave the first hint that the tide of public opinion might be turning against the talent show's Christmas stranglehold on the Official Singles Chart.

By 2008, public (and media) concern was growing that *The X-Factor* was beginning to dominate the Christmas chart (having contributed the previous three festive number ones – via Shayne Ward, Leona Lewis and Leon Jackson), not to mention autumn telly schedules and music in general, all via a TV format which was at risk of becoming tired. In addition, the majority of winners were showing little sign of developing long-term careers, aside from Leona Lewis.

When, in December 2008, Canadian singer/songwriter Leonard Cohen's track 'Hallelujah' was selected as *The X-Factor* winner's single, internet campaigns were launched to get an alternative recording to the top of the Christmas chart instead – with Cohen's original and US singer Jeff Buckley's 1994 cover the public favourites.

As it happened, while the media attention helped stir things up, the final result remained unchanged. Alexandra Burke's heartfelt performance of 'Hallelujah' in the grand finale not only secured the winning spot, but she also became the 2008 Christmas number one, had the biggest-selling track of the year and gained the title of fastest-selling female artist in Official Singles Chart history.

The daughter of Grammy Award-winning Soul II Soul singer

Melissa Bell, Burke was encouraged to become a performer from an early age. She entered her first reality TV singing contest, 2000's *Star For A Night,* aged 12, coming second behind Joss Stone. She also auditioned for the second series of *The X-Factor* (eventually won by Shayne Ward) in 2005 – then 17, she got as far as the final 21 contestants, but was dismissed by Louis Walsh during the judges' houses stage of the competition because he felt she was too young.

Burke regained her confidence by spending weekends singing in bars and clubs up and down the country, plus touring with charity choir Young Voices. Three years later, she returned to *The X-Factor.*

Mentored by Cheryl Cole (herself a former reality TV show contestant with Girls Aloud), Burke was ultimately selected in Cole's final three. Voting numbers revealed after the series end placed her regularly in the middle ground for the majority of the live shows, but Burke found herself in the competition's semi-final alongside Irish singer Eoghan Quigg and boy band JLS. Quigg was the bookies' favourite to win, but was eliminated in the penultimate show.

Driven on by her mother (who was battling kidney failure), Burke's emotionally charged delivery swung the odds in her favour and she took the lion's share of the eight million votes cast, putting her into the Christmas chart race. Her version of 'Hallelujah' was released immediately.

Selling more than 105,000 copies during its first day, it was clear from the beginning of the week that no one was going to catch her, despite the talk of alternative challengers over previous days. With end-of-week sales of 576,000, Burke had left the alternative 'Hallelujah''s in her slipstream, with Jeff Buckley's version at number two and Leonard Cohen's original at 36 in the Official Singles Chart.

Burke and Buckley had helped set an historic new record, making 'Hallelujah' the first song for 51 years to be placed at numbers one and two in the Official Singles Chart – the previous occasion had seen Tommy Steele and Guy Mitchell achieve the same landmark with their recordings of Melvin Endsley's song 'Singin' The Blues'. In addition, of course, the online campaign had sewn seeds of potential which ultimately would be harvested by the Facebook campaigners (husband and wife team Jon and Tracy Morter) who drove Rage Against The Machine's 'Killing In The Name' to beat 2009 *The X-Factor* winner Joe McElderry's 'The Climb' to the Christmas number one spot a year later, by 502,000 sales to 450,000.

LADY GAGA 2009
POKER FACE

WRITERS: Stefani Germanotta, Nadir Khayat

PRODUCER: RedOne (Nadir Khayat)

ALBUM: The Fame

PEAK POSITION: Number 1 (3 weeks)

WEEKS ON CHART: 66

SALES: 1.11m

Firmly established today as a Madonna for the new millennium, 'Poker Face' was the monster single which cemented that position for Lady Gaga.

Fame did not come quickly for the singer. In 2005, the then-19-year-old Stefani Germanotta had dropped out of New York's prestigious Tisch School of the Arts to focus on her musical career. After a short-lived deal with Def Jam Recordings (she was dropped after just three months), Gaga became a regular fixture on New York's underground club scene. Her show, Lady Gaga And The Starlight Revue, which saw Gaga and friend Colleen Martin (aka Lady Starlight) performing electro-pop reworkings of Seventies and Eighties glam rock songs, won much critical acclaim, but that elusive recording contract still seemed out of her grasp.

Two years later, following an internship with Famous Music Publishing, Gaga was offered a deal of sorts; a publishing deal to write songs for other people. After penning tracks for Britney Spears, New Kids On The Block, Fergie and the Pussycat Dolls, Gaga's talent was finally recognised by R&B star Akon, who was impressed with her vocal range during a studio session for what would become his 2008 album, *Freedom*. Akon promptly signed the singer to his Kon Live imprint with heavyweight major Interscope.

Gaga first made an impact in her own right with 'Just Dance', which held at the top of the Official Singles Chart for three weeks in January 2009 – and was the first single from her first album, *The Fame*.

The track, recorded with producer de jour, RedOne (Michael Jackson, Shakira, Jennifer Lopez), featured an accompanying video helmed by fellow New Yorker Melina Matsoukas – the woman responsible for the lavish promo clip for Leona Lewis' debut proper, 'Bleeding Love', in 2007 – but contrasted dramatically with other promos of the time.

Defiantly lo-fi, the most direct comparison was with that of the other new pop kid on the block, Katy Perry, whose 'I Kissed A Girl' trailed 'Just Dance''s release in the US by two months. Perry's promo looked considerably more extravagant, despite similar premises and budgets.

The promo clip for Gaga's next single, 'Poker Face', however, provided a stark contrast. Filmed at a luxury villa dubbed 'Poker Island' which was owned by online gaming company Bwin, the opening 20 seconds of the promo sees Gaga emerge from a swimming pool dressed in a one-shoulder, black PVC catsuit, five-inch stiletto boots and a mirror-ball Venetian mask. Looking utterly otherworldly, it is hard to believe the singer on screen is the same woman from the 'Just Dance' video.

The video for 'Poker Face' premiered on MTV UK on February 17, 2009 – three weeks after Lily Allen's 'The Fear' knocked its predecessor off the top of the Official Singles Chart. Going into heavy rotation on other British music channels, it shot straight to the top of the UK airplay charts.

'Poker Face' made its Official Top 40 debut at number 30 a month later in mid-March, purely on digital sales and a week ahead of its official release date. The following week, it climbed to number one, giving Gaga her second consecutive official singles chart-topper.

It stayed in pole position for a further two weeks, selling over 150,000 copies, and by the end of 2009 'Poker Face' had become the biggest-selling track of the year, shifting over 800,000 units. It also took the accolade of being the UK's then biggest-selling digital track of all time. The Gaga legend had been launched.

THE BLACK EYED PEAS 2009

I GOTTA FEELING

WRITERS: The Black Eyed Peas, David Guetta, Frédéric Riesterer

PRODUCERS: David Guetta, Frédéric Riesterer

ALBUM: The E.N.D.

PEAK POSITION: Number 1 (3 weeks)

WEEKS ON CHART: 78 (2009/10, 76; 2012, 2)

SALES: 1.3m

Occasionally a track comes along with a premise so simple that it connects with people of all ages, races and genders on a global scale. It doesn't get any more straightforward than the message at the heart of The Black Eyed Peas' 2009 feel-good anthem, 'I Gotta Feeling'.

Comprising rappers will.i.am, apl.de.ap and Taboo, plus singer Stacy 'Fergie' Ferguson (who joined the band in 2002), The Black Eyed Peas had made several false starts since their inception in the mid-Nineties. But, by the time they were gearing up to release their fifth album, *The E.N.D.*, in March 2009, they had become quite a going concern. The group had amassed nine international Top 10 hits (including the album's lead single, 'Boom Boom Pow') and had sold over 20 million albums worldwide.

Main man will.i.am was also in demand as a songwriter and producer, clocking up collaborations with Mary J. Blige, the Pussycat Dolls, John Legend, U2 and Diddy, to name but a few. Yet it would be the group's next single that would forever secure them, and specifically will.i.am as the track's principal architect, a place in pop history.

According to will.i.am, the inspiration for the track was borne out of the global recession: "Times are really hard for a lot of people and you want to give them escape and you want to make them feel good about life, especially at these low points," he told *Marie Claire* magazine. "It's dedicated to all the party people out there in the world

I GOTTA FEELING 257

that want to go out and party."

To get the party vibe they were after, The Black Eyed Peas enlisted the help of dance producer de jour, David Guetta (who was also working on his debut major label album, *One Love*, at the time) and his long-time collaborator Frédéric Riesterer. In late 2008, the group travelled to Paris' Square Prod Studios for initial production, with the track being completed in London's Metropolis Studios a few weeks later following additional production from will.i.am. The accompanying video, directed by Mikey Mee, was equally partytastic.

Shot in and around Los Angeles' Hollywood Boulevard, it featured The Black Eyed Peas, along with cameos from Guetta, Kid Cudi, Katy Perry and US band Gossip, engaged in scenes of unbridled hedonism at what appears to be the greatest house party... ever! However, with the track also proving popular with pre-schoolers, an alternative video featuring vintage footage of Mickey Mouse was also produced.

In their homeland, 'I Gotta Feeling' made its debut on the US *Billboard* Hot 100 week ending June 27, 2009 at number two, one place behind previous single 'Boom Boom Pow'. It would climb up to pole position and stay there for a staggering 14 weeks and become one of the longest-running singles in American chart history. In Canada, it would replicate that record, spending 16 weeks at the top of the Canadian Hot 100. It would also hit the top of the charts in Australia, Austria, Belgium, the Czech Republic, Denmark, Greece, Ireland, Israel, Italy, the Netherlands, New Zealand, Romania, Slovakia and Switzerland.

In the UK, its ascent to the top would be less rapid, but just as significant. 'I Gotta Feeling' made its debut in the Official Singles Chart Top 40 in July 2009 at number 39. By the following week, it had shot up 29 places to number 10, before assuming the top spot by knocking JLS's 'Beat Again' off number one in its fifth week on sale.

By the end of the year it would become the first track in official charts history to sell over a million copies on downloads alone in the UK.

EMINEM FEAT. RIHANNA 2010

LOVE THE WAY YOU LIE

WRITERS: Marshall Mathers III (lyrics), Alexander Grant, Holly Hafermann

PRODUCERS: Alex da Kid, Makeba Riddick

ALBUM: Recovery

PEAK POSITION: Number 2 (4 weeks)

WEEKS ON CHART: 44

SALES: 1.05m

'Love The Way You Lie' was the first song in the 58-year history of the Official Singles Chart to top the annual bestsellers list without reaching number one. With 854,000 copies sold in 2010, four weeks at number two and 14 weeks in the Top 10, 'Lie' had enough staying power to deny *X-Factor* winner Matt Cardle's 'When We Collide' (815,000 copies sold) top spot on the year-end tally.

'Lie' was co-written by Eminem (aka Marshall Mathers III) and mirrored the rap-pop blueprint of 'Stan', the number one single from 2000 that largely introduced singer/songwriter Dido to listeners outside the UK. The recipe was simple: Eminem spitting out venomous verses and Rihanna (aka Robyn Rihanna Fenty) providing a melodic chorus. The single tackled the issue of domestic abuse – something both musicians had personal experience of, albeit, in Rihanna's words, at "different ends of the table".

It was inspired by a demo by American vocalist Skylar Grey (Holly Hafermann), produced by Alex da Kid (Alexander Grant), which spoke of Grey's 'abusive' relationship with the music industry.

A burning house featured prominently in the accompanying video, in which the rapper and vocalist starred alongside American actress Megan Fox and German-born English actor Dominic Monaghan, with the actors playing a dysfunctional couple. The video was an instant hit on YouTube, where it was viewed a record 6.6 million times in the 24 hours after it was first added on August 5, 2010.

'Lie' already had seven chart weeks under its belt – including the first of its four weeks at number two – before a CD single was issued in August 2010, helping to ease the track back to its peak position in the Official Singles Chart.

On the Official Albums Chart, Eminem's *Recovery*, which debuted at number one in the same week 'Lie' entered at number seven, equalled the single's 14 weeks in the Top 10, with half of those weeks at number one. On July 31, August 7 and September 4, 2010, with the concurrent success of 'Lie' and *Recovery*, Eminem stood tall at number one on the UK albums survey, the US *Billboard* Hot 100 Singles Chart and the US *Billboard* 200 Albums Chart – although 'Lie' sat, respectively, at numbers two, four and two in the UK during those weeks, missing the 'transatlantic quadruple' feat achieved by just six acts in UK and US chart history.

'We No Speak Americano' (Yolanda Be Cool vs. DCUP), 'Club Can't Handle Me' (Flo Rida feat. David Guetta), 'Green Light' (Roll Deep) and 'Dynamite' (Taio Cruz) were the four tracks that prevented a seventh UK number one for Eminem and a fourth for Rihanna in the four non-consecutive weeks 'Lie' was perched at number two, although the girl from Barbados wouldn't have to wait long for her fourth with 'Only Girl (In The World)' followed by her fifth ('What's My Name?') and sixth ('We Found Love') UK chart-toppers. As of April 2012, she was the only female artist with three UK million sellers on her hit-laden CV.

'Love The Way You Lie' sold 9.3 million copies worldwide in 2010 and attracted five Grammy nominations, but on this occasion Mathers, Grant and Hafermann left the ceremony empty-handed.

The single's success spawned a sequel, unsurprisingly titled 'Love The Way You Lie (Part II)', which appeared on Rihanna's album *Loud*, and in 2011 British rapper Professor Green (Stephen Manderson) and singer/songwriter Emeli Sandé teamed up to release 'Read All About It', which had more than a passing resemblance to Eminem and Rihanna's 'Lie', although, unlike 'Lie', 'Read' did manage to climb to the top rung of the UK chart.

BRUNO MARS 2010

JUST THE WAY YOU ARE (AMAZING)

WRITERS: The Smeezingtons (Peter Hernandez, Philip Lawrence, Ari Levine), Cassius D. Kalb (aka Khalil Walton), Khari Cain (aka Needlz)

PRODUCERS: The Smeezingtons, Khari Cain

ALBUM: Doo-Wops & Hooligans

PEAK POSITION: Number 1 (2 weeks)

WEEKS ON CHART: 46

SALES: 1.12m

This heart-warming love story was not the first 'Just The Way You Are' to attract seven-figure sales. In 1978, Billy Joel's Official Singles Chart debut was a million seller in the US.

Bruno Mars was born Peter Hernandez into a musical family in Honolulu, Hawaii, on October 8, 1985 and was something of a child prodigy – even appearing at the age of four as an Elvis Presley impersonator in the 1990 film documentary *Viva Elvis* and reprising that role in the 1992 movie *Honeymoon In Vegas*. After graduating from high school, he moved to Los Angeles in 2003 and signed to Motown Records in 2004, but after the move failed to work out, the label dropped him.

He then began a career as a member (with Philip Lawrence and Ari Levine) of production/songwriting team The Smeezingtons, whose credits include Cee Lo Green's 'Forget You', the Sugababes' 'Get Sexy' and K'naan's 'Wavin' Flag', plus two singles that propelled Mars into the UK chart as a featured artist: B.o.B's UK chart-topping 'Nothin' On You' and Travie McCoy's number three hit 'Billionaire'. With fellow Smeezington Lawrence, Mars was also one of no less than 11 co-writers credited on Flo Rida's worldwide 2009 smash 'Right Round'.

'Amazing' made a chart-topping UK debut in the Official Singles Chart in October 2010, but was outsold by Tinie Tempah's 'Written In The Stars' in its second week on the chart, then fell to number four as, ironically, Cee Lo Green's aforementioned 'Forget You' began a two-week run at the top. Four weeks after its debut, however, 'Amazing' returned to number one to become the first ever single to reclaim the top spot after dropping out of the Top Three.

By the year's end, 'Amazing' had amassed sales of 766,000 and was named the third biggest-selling single of 2010, trailing only Eminem and Rihanna's 'Love The Way You Lie' and 'When We Collide' by *X-Factor* champion Matt Cardle. The single has now sold more than 12.5 million copies worldwide.

"I wasn't thinking of anything deep or poetic," explained Mars in an interview with *Blues & Soul (B&S)* magazine, citing "simple songs" such as Eric Clapton's 'Wonderful Tonight' and Billy Preston's 'You Are So Beautiful' (a 1975 US top 10 hit for Joe Cocker) as influences. "There's no mind-boggling lyrics or twists in the story. I'm just telling a woman she looks beautiful the way she is and, let's be honest, what woman doesn't want to hear those lyrics?"

The woman Mars is telling looks beautiful (and seducing with some nifty cassette tape artwork) in the 'Just The Way You Are' video is Peruvian-born Australian actress Nathalie Kelley, best known for *The Fast And The Furious: Tokyo Drift*. The video had been viewed almost 240 million times on YouTube by April 2012.

Fans of the trilby-loving singer/songwriter wondering if there was life in Mars after 'Just The Way You Are' didn't have long to wait for an answer as 'Grenade' was lobbed on to the UK chart in January 2011, landing instantly at number one, a position it also attained in the US and most other territories throughout the world.

Following the chart-topping bow for his debut album *Doo-Wops & Hooligans* later that same month, Mars completed a hat-trick of number one singles in May 2011 with 'The Lazy Song', which, true to its title – and by Mars' own impeccably high standards – gently strolled to the top after four weeks on the chart.

By that time, a Grammy for Best Male Pop Vocal Performance (for 'Just The Way You Are') was sitting proudly on Mars' mantelpiece, although his six nominations for the 2012 ceremony went unrewarded when Adele cleaned up in all the categories for which he was nominated.

RIHANNA 2010

ONLY GIRL (IN THE WORLD)

WRITERS: Crystal Johnson, Stargate (Tor Erik Hermansen, Mikkel S. Eriksen), Sandy Vee (Sandy Wilhelm)

PRODUCERS: Stargate, Sandy Vee

ALBUM: Loud

PEAK POSITION: Number 1 (2 weeks)

WEEKS ON CHART: 41

SALES: 1.04m

Robyn Rihanna Fenty's fourth UK number one, and the second of her three million-selling singles to date, found the singer in a playful mood.

Frolicking on an LA hillside miles from civilisation while hugging giant pink roses and swaying back and forth on a swing descending from heaven may not be everyone's idea of 'keeping it real', but for the accompanying video's three minutes 55 seconds it was easy to believe Rihanna was the only girl in the world.

The man entrusted with reflecting the singer's positive vibe in the video was Anthony Mandler, who directed a host of Rihanna videos including 'Unfaithful', 'Shut Up And Drive', 'Take A Bow' and her collaboration with Jay-Z and Kanye West, 'Run This Town'. The result was a new, sprightly Rihanna, a singer distancing herself from the dark, brooding former persona and the fare served up on the 2009 album *Rated R*.

"Rihanna came to us before we started recording this record and said, 'I feel great about myself. I want to go back to having fun. I want to make happy and up-tempo records'," said co-producer Tor Erik Hermansen. Evidently, her wish was their command and this Eurodance number, complete with club-ready dance beats, was the first single to be taken from Rihanna's fifth studio album, *Loud*.

The song was co-written by Grammy-winning US songwriter Crystal Johnson, aka Cri$tyle, whose satisfied customers include Janet Jackson, Mariah Carey, Jennifer Lopez and Beyoncé, together with the Norwegian writing/production duo Stargate and Frenchman Sandy Vee.

In the UK, the fourth biggest-selling single of 2010 is perhaps best remembered for its TV premiere on series seven of *The X-Factor*, when the singer's backing dancers indulged in a food fight live on stage. There were obviously no hard feelings when it came to the studio cleaning bill, with her memorable appearance coming just weeks before she returned for the series final and a steamy duet on her own 'Unfaithful' with a hot-under-the-collar series winner Matt Cardle.

Whether planned or not, *The X-Factor* threw up an interesting anomaly on the night of Rihanna's 'Only Girl' performance, October 31, 2010. On the judging panel alongside Louis Walsh, Gary Barlow and Dannii Minogue was Cheryl Cole, who that very same evening had debuted at number one on the Official Singles Chart with 'Promise This'. The number two record, 31,000 copies shy of the 157,000 sold by 'Promise This', was also a new entry: 'Only Girl'.

When Cole surrendered the official number one spot seven days later, 'Only Girl' took over at the summit and remained there for two weeks. In another fascinating twist to the Rihanna vs. *X-Factor* judges saga, its second week at number one was at the expense of 'The Flood', by Gary Barlow's Take That. There was also a connection with the show for the single that knocked Rihanna off the top spot – *X-Factor* series five runners-up JLS' 'Love You More'.

Barlow and co. exacted revenge on Rihanna later in November when their *Progress* release debuted at number one on the Official Albums Chart, ahead of the Bajan beauty's *Loud*. In December, Rihanna had the consolation of three simultaneous singles in the Top 10, with the Grammy-winning (Best Dance Recording) 'Only Girl' joined by 'What's My Name?' and the David Guetta collaboration 'Who's That Chick?' – compelling evidence of the fast-paced nature of today's digital-dominated singles chart.

Rihanna, meanwhile, was named the Sexiest Woman Alive by *Esquire* magazine in 2011, and she has branched out into films and creating fragrances.

MATT CARDLE 2010

WHEN WE COLLIDE

WRITER: Simon Neil

PRODUCERS: Richard Stannard, Ash Howes

ALBUM: Letters

PEAK POSITION: Number 1 (3 weeks)

WEEKS ON CHART: 12

SALES: 1m

The 1,152nd number one single, the 59th Christmas number one and recorded by the seventh *X-Factor* winner, 'When We Collide' is the most recent single in this book to pass the million-sales mark.

Its performer, Matt Cardle, was far from a typical reality TV contest winner when he swept to victory on Sunday December 12, 2010. Hailing from the small market town of Halstead in north Essex, Cardle had been working as a painter and decorator while fronting a little-known rock band called Seven Summers, when he decided to audition for *The X-Factor* in spring 2010.

He was an outsider from the start; his alternative roots setting him aside from most other contestants and the usual winning formula. Stubbled, sporting a military-style cap and performing in what quickly became a trademark falsetto, he was embraced by the show. By the time the series reached the live rounds in early October, Cardle was quickly becoming the hot favourite to win, topping the votes week after week, while being mentored by Dannii Minogue.

The profile extended to helping his previous material. From summer onwards, Cardle's weekly prime-time exposure and tabloid coverage of the show added impetus to the music by Seven Summers. The band's self-titled album had been released at the beginning of the year, featuring the vocals of Cardle – and, while the *X-Factor* star studiously avoided mentioning his old band, their album continued to tick over, selling around 9,000 copies plus an additional

4,000 single track downloads.

By the time the show hit December, it was hard to see any other winner and Cardle eventually swept the final, with more than 44.61 per cent of the votes cast, pushing Rebecca Ferguson and boy band One Direction into second and third places, respectively.

In that final, Cardle had performed 'When We Collide', a song which was, in many ways, a perfect choice for his debut single. Originally titled 'Many Of Horror' (before being retitled for Cardle), the ballad had previously been recorded and released in January 2010 by Scottish rock band Biffy Clyro, on their fifth studio album *Only Revolutions* (and written by their singer/songwriter and guitarist Simon Neil).

Aside from publishing income from the new Cardle version, Biffy Clyro also benefitted directly themselves. Inspired by the previous year's success in getting Rage Against The Machine's 'Killing In The Name' to Christmas number one (versus *X-Factor* 2009 winner Joe McElderry's 'The Climb'), a Facebook campaign was launched – ultimately helping lift the Biffy Clyro original to a lifetime peak of number eight in the Christmas week chart (the band's third Top 10 hit after 'Mountains' and 'That Golden Rule') and impressively boosting its lifetime sales by more than 100,000 copies in just a couple of months. The song is played during the closing credits of Michael Bay's US science fiction thriller *Transformers: Dark Of The Moon,* released in 2011.

Cardle's version predictably swept to the 2010 Christmas number one spot, selling 439,000 copies in its first week (the biggest one-week total of the year), 263,000 in its second week and 113,000 in its third. Within its first six weeks, the single was at 907,000 sales – after six months it had sold 970,000 copies.

It was 10 months before Cardle's follow-up single, 'Run For Your Life', was released, with parent album *Letters* following a week later. A number six single and number two album was not quite what the doctor ordered, but the sales of 84,000 singles and 270,000 albums were pretty respectable.

However, seven months later and without another hit single to his name, Cardle announced via Twitter that he had split from Sony Music label Columbia to go his own way. Within weeks, 'When We Collide' tipped over the million mark and Cardle was in the studio working on a new album.

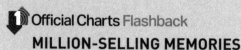

MILLION-SELLING MEMORIES
MATT CARDLE

Is it hard to believe that, in a relatively short amount of time, 'When We Collide' became one of the biggest-selling singles of all time?

I was amazed by the support I had for 'When We Collide', and the support Biffy Clyro had too was very overwhelming. I remember being told what the midweek sales were for the week of release and not knowing if it was good or bad. I had no idea about sales figures and so on, but was informed that it was an amazing figure – and it's mind-blowing to think it has gone on to sell over a million copies. I'm just so proud to have my voice on a track that has reached that status.

How did it feel to go from being an unknown musician to being the biggest pop star in the UK?

I have been a musician since I was nine years old, and had been trying my hardest to break into the industry ever since. It was really tough at times to keep faith, but *The X-Factor* gave me the break I desperately needed. I had such an amazing time on the show; I guess singing with Rihanna has to be one highlight.

Do you remember where you were and what you were doing when you found out 'When We Collide' had gone to number one?

I was in the tour van with my manager, tour manager, security guards, etc. when I heard. We were on our way to Radio 1 at the time to do the chart show with Reggie Yates… we had a huge celebration afterwards!

Reality TV shows have had a massive impact on the UK music scene – what do you think about this influence and how it has evolved?

Reality TV has had a huge impact on the industry, and not everyone will agree if it is a positive one or not, but you cannot deny the success of some of the artists that have come from it. I think if people are buying the music from these artists in such volume there is a place in the market for it.

Before *The X-Factor* you were in a band. How did you find the change in emphasis between being in a group and being a solo pop star? Which do you prefer?

I have spent most of my life in bands, as well as working on solo projects. I do love being in a band and getting to share the amazing experiences with friends, but I also like having complete control over what happens on stage, which I get as a solo artist.

With your new record, are you getting more control and, if so, what differences might we find when we get to hear it?

I have complete control over the songs and who I write with, the content and, this time around, the production, which is new to me but I'm very excited about it. I get to create this record exactly how I want it to be.

Do you remember following the charts as a child and teenager? What did it mean to you then?

I never really followed the charts as a child, it was never something that interested me; I was into bands like Rage Against The Machine, Nirvana and Pearl Jam and, as I was growing up, those guys were never really in the charts.

What was the first record you bought?

The first album I bought was *Bad* by Michael Jackson.

ADELE 2011
SOMEONE LIKE YOU

WRITERS: Adele Adkins, Dan Wilson

PRODUCERS: Adele Adkins, Dan Wilson

ALBUM: 21

PEAK POSITION: Number 1 (5 weeks)

WEEKS ON CHART: 64

SALES: 1.36m

'Someone Like You' had a seismic impact on music fans all around the world thanks to its simple, timeless quality – something that will endear it to many generations to come, and long after Adele's heartache is over.

Adele Laurie Blue Adkins was born to a single teenage mother in Tottenham on May 5, 1988. The Spice Girls and P!nk were major early influences, but it wasn't until a friend posted demos on Myspace that the BRIT School graduate courted the attention of XL Recordings.

In 2010, the singer/songwriter was left reeling after the break-up of an 18-month relationship. On learning that the man of her dreams had got engaged to another woman, she channelled her grief into writing a song about the experience. In 2011, her private despair became public knowledge – and then some.

The writing process was a cathartic experience for Adele. "After I wrote it, I felt more at peace," she told Q magazine in July 2011. "It set me free." 'Someone' was co-written with Dan Wilson, who first attracted attention as lead singer of US alternative rock act Semisonic (who scored four UK Top 40 hits between 1998 and 2001). The pair shared production duties on 'Someone', the second single to come from the record-shattering album *21*.

The up-tempo 'Rolling In The Deep' was the lead single from *21*, but following a spine-tingling, teary-eyed televised performance of 'Someone Like You' at the BRIT Awards on February 15, 2011, the piano ballad climbed an incredible 46 places to number one on the Official Singles Chart a week later.

That rapid rise triggered a dizzying array of chart and sales records for Adele that continued into 2012 – the first being the only female artist (and only the second act after The Beatles in 1964) to have two singles and two albums simultaneously in the Official UK Top Fives, a record she achieved for three consecutive weeks from late February.

The first million seller of the 2010s, 'Someone Like You' sold 1.24 million copies in the UK in 2011 – plus 3.5 million copies in the US – as Adele became the first British artist to sell one million digital copies of a single in the UK, accomplishing the feat on July 5, 2011 – 162 days after its release. Thanks to Nicole Scherzinger's one-week intervention on March 26 with 'Don't Hold Your Breath', 'Someone' also became the only single by a British female to return to number one in the Official Singles Chart, completing its five-week run at the top on April 2.

By the end of May 2012, the song had accumulated 64 non-consecutive weeks on the chart – a tally bettered by just eight singles since the first chart was published in 1952 – and was on course to eclipse both Judy Collins' 'Amazing Grace' (67 weeks) and Lady Gaga's 'Poker Face' (66 weeks) to become the longest-running single by a female artist in UK chart history. That same month, *Time* magazine named her one of the most influential people in the world.

Although 'Someone Like You' lost out to One Direction's 'What Makes You Beautiful' in the publicly voted Best British Single category at the 2012 BRIT Awards, Adele's Best Female Solo Artist win recognised her life-changing year as the poster girl for UK music worldwide. "I'm never going to write a song like that again," she said about 'Someone Like You'. "I think that's the song I'll be known for."

JESSIE J FEAT. B.O.B 2011

PRICE TAG

WRITERS: Jessica Cornish, Lukasz Gottwald (Dr. Luke), Claude Kelly, Bobby Simmons, Jr. (B.o.B)

PRODUCER: Dr. Luke

ALBUM: Who You Are

PEAK POSITION: Number 1 (2 weeks)

WEEKS ON CHART: 53

SALES: 1.07m

In the space of little more than 12 months, Jessie J has risen from promising young pretender to bona fide new star – with a million seller to her name.

Born Jessica Cornish in Chadwell Heath, Essex on March 27, 1988, 10-year-old Jessie failed an audition for a stage production of the musical *Annie* for being "too loud". But a year later, while a student at Colin's Performing Arts School, she won a spot in Andrew Lloyd Webber and Jim Steinman's West End musical *Whistle Down The Wind*.

At 16 she began studying musical theatre at the BRIT School, graduating in 2006 (the same year she began recording her debut album *Who You Are*) alongside Adele and Leona Lewis before hooking up with a short-lived girl group at 17 and bagging a contract with London-based Gut Records.

That could have been it. Doctors feared she would never walk again – let alone sing – after suffering a stroke at the age of 18, and when Gut folded before her music could be released, she was staring at an existence as plain old Jessica Cornish. Citing her health issues, she later said: "It's one of those things that makes you think, 'OK, life isn't guaranteed for anybody, so it's time for me to turn this on and really do it justice'."

Initially, Cornish threw herself into songwriting, notably for Justin Timberlake, Christina Aguilera and Miley Cyrus, who took the Cornish/Gottwald/Kelly composition 'Party In The USA' to number two in the USA in August 2009. But a couple of showcase gigs as Jessie J in America attracted Universal Republic, who offered her a recording contract despite her still scratching around for a deal in her homeland.

2011 was her breakthrough year. Jessie J was named winner of the BBC's Sound of 2011 poll in January, which sent her debut single, 'Do It Like A Dude' (a song she offered to Rihanna, only for the singer to insist that Jessie record it herself), into the Top 10 of the Official Singles Chart.

In February, nine days before picking up the Critics' Choice Award at the BRITs, 'Price Tag' debuted at number one with first-week sales of 84,000. It held on to the top spot the following week, before falling to Adele's 'Someone Like You'.

Co-written by Jessie J, a hint to her collaborators is provided in the opening words: "OK. Coconut Man. Moonheads. And Pea." While 'Pea' is Jessie J herself, 'Coconut Man' and 'Moonheads' were references to 'Price Tag''s US co-writers, respectively producer/ songwriter Lukasz 'Dr Luke' Gottwald and songwriter Claude Kelly. Fourth collaborator, B.o.B. (aka Bobby Simmons, Jr.) – already a UK number one artist courtesy of the 2010 cuts 'Nothin' On You' and 'Airplanes' – retained his dignity by avoiding a nickname.

The release of the long-gestating Jessie J album *Who You Are* was brought forward a month due to popular demand, but Adele's record-breaking 11-week run at number one with *21* put paid to her chances of a chart-topping debut album. In the weeks and months since, *Who You Are* has enjoyed six separate visits to the Top 10 during its 62 weeks on the Official Albums Chart

Described by one critic as a "sun-dappled, hip-hop-inflected mid-tempo head-nodder", this million seller simply urges listeners to dance and forget about today's money-obsessed society. "I think that's why my music uplifts people so much," said the singer, "because they can see that I'm a normal chick who just wants to bring some goodness to the world."

A new chapter for Jessie J began in March 2012 when she appeared as a coach on the BBC talent show *The Voice UK*. The series winner would pocket £100,000 and – like Jessie – a recording contract with Universal Republic. Her highest profile appearance, however, occured at the closing ceremony of the 2012 London Olympic Games when she duetted with Tinie, Taio Cruz and Queen.

PARTY ROCK ANTHEM

WRITERS: LMFAO (Stefan 'Redfoo' Gordy, Skyler 'SkyBlu' Gordy), Jamahl Listenbee (GoonRock), Peter Schroeder

PRODUCERS: Stefan Gordy, Jamahl Listenbee

ALBUM: Sorry For Party Rocking

PEAK POSITION: Number 1 (4 weeks)

WEEKS ON CHART: 59

SALES: 1.12m

If Stefan 'Redfoo' Gordy (the son of Motown Records founder Berry Gordy) and his nephew Skyler 'SkyBlu' Gordy ever had any pretensions to be viewed as 'serious' musicians, they were probably torpedoed by the massive success of their 'Party Rock Anthem', a slab of floor-filling nonsense with one simple ambition – to get the nation up on their feet and dancing like lunatics, with a lyrical nod to the 2006 Rick Ross track 'Hustlin''.

It found the multi-talented Redfoo and SkyBlu – DJs, rappers, singer/songwriters, dancers and producers – powerless to resist the charms of the Melbourne Shuffle, a fast-paced heel-to-toe dance which had its origins Down Under in Melbourne's late 1980s underground rave scene.

Fused with funky hip-hop moves, the Melbourne Shuffle – otherwise known as Rocking – was transformed into arguably the most boisterous dance routine since Holly Valance and Jason Donovan bust some moves on the 2011 series of *Strictly Come Dancing*, and it became the biggest dance craze immortalised on disc since DJ Casper's 2004 number one 'Cha Cha Slide'.

LMFAO formed in Los Angeles in 2006. Their first major international exposure came in summer 2010, when they were featured (along with Black Eyed Peas vocalist Fergie) on 'Gettin' Over You' by French DJ David Guetta and US urban vocalist Chris Willis. The song was a major hit in Europe, reaching number one on the Official Singles Chart.

According to the duo, their name is an acronym for Loving My Friends And Others, not the considerably more common meaning that crops up in text messages and on social networking sites. Nevertheless, the 'Party Rock Anthem' single and accompanying video proved a massive hit with trend-setting, Tweeting, Facebook-loving youngsters.

Amid the throng of street shufflers in the video are the single's featured artists, GoonRock (US producer/musician Jamahl Listenbee) and Lauren Bennett, a blonde bombshell from Kent and former *X-Factor* auditionee who replaced lead singer Nicole Scherzinger in early 2012 in the new line-up of the multi-platinum US pop act Pussycat Dolls.

The shuffling vibe recurred in subsequent LMFAO releases, including 'Sexy And I Know It' and the title track of the act's second album, 'Sorry For Party Rocking', but the worldwide smash 'Party Rock Anthem' served up the most impressive sales figures. It shifted an impressive 9.7 million copies worldwide in 2011 and, in the US, the track became the fastest to amass sales of six million, doing so in 48 weeks (six weeks sooner than America's biggest seller of 2011, Adele's 'Rolling In The Deep').

By mid-May 2012, 'Party Rock Anthem' had spent 57 weeks in the Top 75 of the Official Singles Chart, equalling the chart run of Bill Haley's 'Rock Around The Clock', the UK's first ever million-selling single.

Any listeners so inclined could seek out no fewer than 18 official remixes of the track which were circulated – from Benny Benassi to the Wideboys – and enjoy their own personal 'Anthem-athon', or, perhaps, stick to the album version and "just have a good time" for a lunatic four minutes 23 seconds.

MAROON 5 FEAT. CHRISTINA AGUILERA 2011
MOVES LIKE JAGGER

WRITERS: Adam Levine, Benny Blanco (Benjamin Levin), Ammar Malik, Shellback (Karl Schuster)

PRODUCERS: Shellback, Benny Blanco

ALBUM: Hands All Over

PEAK POSITION: Number 2 (7 weeks)

WEEKS ON CHART: 42

SALES: 1.27m

You know you're a musical legend when your name appears in two hit singles – released two weeks apart – despite not having offered up any chart-bothering records of your own for the previous three years.

Of course, Sir Mick Jagger and The Rolling Stones had attained legendary status long before this duet and Cher Lloyd's 'Swagger Jagger' came to pass – and it emerged that Lloyd's single was actually a reference to a street slang term "swagger jacker", meaning someone who has stolen another's style, rather than a direct reference to the Stones man.

However, both singles offered up compelling evidence that today's bunch of knowledgeable hit-makers are well aware of Jagger's name, image and moves, and the references surely helped raise the veteran's profile ahead of his collaboration with will.i.am and Jennifer Lopez, 'T.H.E. (The Hardest Ever)', which returned him to the Official Singles Chart in February 2012.

'Moves Like Jagger' never made the move to number one that Jagger achieved no less than eight times during his career with the Stones, but it had a record-equalling seven consecutive weeks at number two on the UK chart, following in the footsteps of All-4-One's 'I Swear', which was held off by Wet Wet Wet's 'Love Is All Around' in the summer of 1994.

The Maroon 5 single could claim to be the unluckiest number two of all time; debuting in the Official Singles Chart at number three in August 2011, it retained that position the following week as two more new entries breezed in above it. But then, rather than being stalled behind one huge seller, its number two status over the next seven weeks was, remarkably, preserved by six different acts, all of them new entries: Example, Pixie Lott, One Direction, Dappy, Sak Noel and, finally, for two weeks, the Rihanna/Calvin Harris collaboration 'We Found Love'. In its first eight weeks, 'Moves Like Jagger' had been no lower than number three but had been outsold by 10 singles!

In truth, 'Moves Like Jagger' was a welcome return to form – and the Official Top 10 – for both Maroon 5 and Christina Aguilera after some lean years.

California dreamers Maroon 5, who blossomed almost a decade after forming as garage band Kara's Flowers in 1994, consisted of Jesse Carmichael (now on hiatus from the band to study music and spiritual healing), Mickey Madden, James Valentine, Matt Flynn and PJ Morton in addition to lead vocalist Adam Levine, and had scored four minor UK singles since hitting number two with 'Makes Me Wonder' in 2007.

Meanwhile Aguilera, the woman who once discovered a 'Genie In A Bottle', had last troubled the Top 10 with 'Ain't No Other Man' in 2006, although she had made the Top 20 with all four subsequent releases, the last being 'Not Myself Tonight' in 2010.

The single's lyrics could have been ripped straight from the Sir Mick guide to seduction (undoubtedly a weighty tome) and perhaps a string of beauties – from Bianca de Macias to Jerry Hall or Luciana Gimenez – are the only ones who could fully appreciate lines like "Kiss me 'til you're drunk and I'll show you all the moves like Jagger."

The funky 'Jagger' was culled from Maroon 5's third studio album, *Hands All Over*, and topped charts in 18 countries around the world.

In the US, where it rose to number one on September 10, 2011, it has sold 4.9 million digital copies and given former Mickey Mouse Club presenter Aguilera (born in Staten Island, New York, on December 18, 1980) chart-toppers in three successive decades.

RIHANNA FEAT. CALVIN HARRIS 2011
WE FOUND LOVE

WRITER: Calvin Harris

PRODUCER: Calvin Harris

ALBUM: Talk That Talk

PEAK POSITION: Number 1 (6 weeks)

WEEKS ON CHART: 35

SALES: 1.13m

Bajan beauty Rihanna became the only girl in the world to receive a credit on three UK million-selling singles when the infectious 'We Found Love' passed that mark in February 2012.

The late Whitney Houston, Cher, Britney, Kylie and Adele have all achieved a UK million seller, but, before Rihanna blitzed the bestsellers list, Celine Dion was the only solo female with two million-selling singles, let alone three.

Written and produced by Scottish DJ/vocalist/producer Calvin Harris, who also bagged a featured artist credit, 'We Found Love', from Rihanna's sixth studio album *Talk That Talk*, was released on the Def Jam Records label and debuted at number one on the Official Singles Chart dated October 15, 2011, keeping 'Moves Like Jagger' by Maroon 5 and Christina Aguilera at number two for a sixth consecutive week.

In total, Rihanna's sixth official UK number one spent six non-consecutive weeks in pole position – she kindly allowed Professor Green and Emeli Sandé to keep her number one perch warm for a couple of weeks with 'Read All About It'

With the success of the single and its parent album, Rihanna became the first solo female to have two number one singles ('What's My Name?', 'We Found Love') and two number one albums (*Loud*, *Talk That Talk*) in the UK in the same calendar year, and both singles were among the 17 tracks that contributed to another record, for the most cumulative weeks on the UK Singles Chart in a calendar year (female, male or group) – a staggering 224 weeks in 2011.

Mind-boggling stats aside, the controversial video for 'We Found Love' was partly shot in a barley field in Bangor, Northern Ireland, and made national headlines when the farmer who owned the field confronted a scantily clad Rihanna, asking her to cover up, "find a greater God" and, ultimately, "Get orf me land"! Rihanna and video co-star Dudley O'Shaughnessy's amorous antics in the field were, appropriately, a case of finding love in a "hopeless place".

Other themes explored in the rebellious, fast-paced video are thought to be based on Rihanna's ill-fated relationship with Chris Brown. Rihanna's subsequent collaboration with Brown on *Talk That Talk* cut 'Birthday Cake' suggested, however, that the X-rated tune had rekindled the flames of passion between the two.

The singer's raunchy image is a far cry from the girl who grew up in Bridgetown, Barbados listening to reggae music. Born Robyn Rihanna Fenty in Saint Michael, Barbados on February 20, 1988, she was first heard singing – using a hairbrush as a microphone – at the age of three and had perfected the Disney classic 'A Whole New World' as a seven-year-old, but her dreams were put on hold to follow in her drug addict father's footsteps, flogging clothes from a street stall in Bridgetown to make ends meet.

At the age of 15, however, her life changed forever when she won a school talent contest and was immediately introduced to songwriter/producer Evan Rogers, who landed her an audition with Def Jam's Jay-Z and Antonio 'L.A.' Reid (now a judge on the US version of *The X-Factor*). Rihanna secured a recording contract within hours of the audition and is estimated to have sold more than 60 million singles and 25 million albums worldwide since releasing the single 'Pon De Replay' and the album *Music Of The Sun* in 2005.

'We Found Love', which topped charts in 19 countries across the planet, is yet another example of Rihanna's world-conquering adaptability – and Calvin Harris' ear for a floor-filling tune.

GOTYE FEAT. KIMBRA 2012

SOMEBODY THAT I USED TO KNOW

WRITERS: Wally de Backer, Luiz Bonfá

PRODUCER: Wally de Backer

ALBUM: Making Mirrors

PEAK POSITION: Number 1 (5 weeks)

WEEKS ON CHART: 21

SALES: 1.06m

The biggest worldwide hit in the first half of 2012, with more than seven million units sold up to that point, came from Australia. The UK accounted for a million of those sales, the USA for four million (where it topped the *Billboard* Hot 100 for four weeks), while it broke sales records in many parts of the world – it has, for instance, become the Netherlands' biggest-selling single of all time.

'Somebody That I Used to Know' not only represented Gotye's spectacular breakthrough as an internationally acclaimed recording act, it was also his first Top 40 hit in Australia, the country he had moved to as an infant. Born Wouter de Backer in 1980, in the Belgian city of Bruges, Gotye emigrated with his family when he was two. Evidence of his roots among the French-speaking (or Walloon) population of Bruges is in his stagename – 'Gotye' derives from 'Gauthier', the French equivalent of Wouter (or Walter, or Wally, for short).

Compared by some to Beck in his early years as a musician, Gotye cites an elderly neighbour who gave him a collection of more than 400 vinyl records as the inspiration behind his fascination with sampling. His subsequent music was, as a result, both sample-ridden and eclectic in its musical themes – right back to his early days as a member of the duo The Basics.

His Australian breakthrough followed in 2006, his *Like Drawing Blood* album receiving commercial and critical acclaim, leading to an Australian Recording Industry Association (ARIA) award (the Australian equivalent of the BRIT Awards) for Best Male Artist. However, an international impact eluded him until 'Somebody That I Used To Know'.

Early in 2011, Gotye started recording his third album, *Making Mirrors*, from a new studio set up in a barn at his parents' house in the Australian state of Victoria. As 'Somebody' emerged from these sessions, Gotye was not immediately sold on the song.

Having written the first verse and chorus, underpinned by the distinctive guitar hook from the introduction of 'Seville' (a 1967 instrumental by the Brazilian guitarist Luiz Bonfá), Gotye nearly abandoned it. Telling the story of the chaotic dissolution of a relationship, he later recalled, "I thought, 'There's no interesting way to add to this guy's story.' It felt weak."

Realising that the song needed a female voice for the second half, he first turned to his own partner Tash Parker as a guest vocalist, before opting to join forces with 21-year-old New Zealand singer Kimbra Lee Johnson, when the two were separately shortlisted for a songwriting competition. Kimbra was about to issue her own debut solo album, *Vows*.

On its Australian release in July 2011, it quickly became clear that 'Somebody' would change the course of both their careers. By mid-August, it had begun an eight-week reign at the top of its singles chart while it was on its way to winning a raft of awards, including ARIA's Single of the Year. Its appeal would rapidly spread abroad – it spent 12 weeks at the top of the chart in Gotye's native Belgium, and by the end of the year had enjoyed a chart-topping spell in Germany.

In the UK, Gotye had to wait until 2012. Released in the first week of January, and backed relentlessly by BBC Radio 2, the single swiftly climbed towards the top of the Official Singles Chart, beginning a total of five non-consecutive weeks at number one from February 12, and in May becoming the first single of the year to sell a million. The success also propelled Gotye's album *Making Mirrors* into the Top Five.

By summer, the song continued to hold a place in the British Top 20 and was firmly established as the biggest-selling single of 2012, 300,000 sales ahead of the next biggest, 'Call Me Maybe' by Carly Rae Jepsen.

ALMOST
A MILLION

In this era of on-demand digital music, a wider range of songs and albums are available to buy than at any time in the history of British music. The biggest digital record stores claim to offer their customers access to more than 25 million tracks, many of which had stopped selling many years ago when vinyl, cassette and CDs ruled the world.

This new digital availability has transformed the fortunes of many classic singles – Dexys Midnight Runners' 'Come On Eileen', for instance, stopped selling in the early Eighties but has sold an additional 100,000-plus copies in the eight years since downloads first became legitimate in 2004.

In addition, digital music has meant that sales never stop. Once restricted by the opening hours of the nation's record retailers and the amount of stock they could hold on site, sales of music now continue 24 hours a day, seven days a week, 52 weeks a year – via computers, laptops, digital tablets and smartphones.

So, while this book is built around the latest updated list of UK million sellers, nothing stands still – and a wide range of tracks are bearing down on that historic landmark, even as you read.

In total, when the deadline for compiling this latest list arrived at the end of May this year, there were 13 singles within 50,000 sales of a million, eight of which were 20,000 sales or less away. The most recent single to pass the million marker was Matt Cardle's 'When We Collide', but closest behind it were two duets and a debut single from another reality TV music competition winner – all three currently resting 10,000 sales short of the million mark.

The first, Elton John and Kiki Dee's 'Don't Go Breaking My Heart', was originally released in 1976 and was both artists' first number one, holding the top spot for six weeks. While Kiki has never had as big a hit since, Elton has been involved in a further six chart-toppers, of course, but only three on his own – including the UK's biggest-selling single of all time, 'Something About The Way You Look Tonight'/'Candle In the Wind 1997'.

For Kylie Minogue and Jason Donovan, 'Especially For You' reached the top at the height of their success. For Kylie, the single followed one number one and three number twos; for Jason it followed a number five and set in train a run of three successive number ones. Between them, the former Aussie soap stars (Kylie left *Neighbours* in 1988, Jason the following year) have scored 10 official number ones to date.

Released in 2008, 'Fight For This Love' was Cheryl Cole's debut single, taken from her debut solo album *3 Words*, selling 292,000 copies in its first week and holding on at number one for two weeks.

Sitting 20,000 sales short of the million mark are five singles, led by the Joe Meek-written and produced instrumental 'Telstar' by The Tornados. Named after a communications satellite, the single hit number one in the UK Singles Chart and held on for five weeks in October and November 1962. It also hit number one in the US, only the second single by a British act to do so. The first, earlier the same year, was Acker Bilk's 'Stranger On The Shore'. Another instrumental is not far behind, in the form of The Royal Pipes & Drums & Military Band Of The Royal Scots Dragoon Guards' recording of 'Amazing Grace'. Another five-week resident at number one, the recording was a hit internationally in 1972. While it wasn't the band's only hit (they scored two further Top 40 hits in 1972 and won a Classical Brit Award in 2009), they never hit the top spot again.

In turn, Atomic Kitten's 'Whole Again' was an Official Singles Chart number one for four weeks in 2001, the first of three chart-toppers for the trio. A band who went through a range of line-ups during their history (comprising Liz McClarnon, Natasha Hamilton and either Jenny Frost or Kerry Katona at the time of this hit), Katona left the band just days before the track hit number one, and it was later re-recorded for its parent album with Frost replacing the founder member.

'Mysterious Girl' by Peter Andre featuring Bubbler Ranx is also within 20,000 sales of a million – although it only peaked at two in the Official Singles Chart in 1995. The track, by the Brent-born, Australian-raised singer, maintained a place in the Top Five for 10 weeks solid, kept from the summit by the battle between three million sellers, 'Three Lions' by Baddiel & Skinner & Lightning Seeds, the Fugees' 'Killing Me Softly' and the Spice Girls' 'Wannabe'.

Also knocking on the million door is Cliff Richard & The Shadows' double A-side 'The Next Time'/'Bachelor Boy'. Sir Cliff & The Shadows have one million seller, of course, in the form of

'The Young Ones'. But this single, released later the same year and taken from the Cliff movie *Summer Holiday*, held number one for three weeks in January 1963 (becoming the first hit of the New Year) before being toppled by The Shadows' own tune 'Dance On!'

Some 25,000 sales short of a million, 'Bad Romance' was Lady Gaga's third (out of four) Official Singles Chart number one, holding the top spot for two weeks.

Two singles are 40,000 sales short of a million – UB40's cover of the Neil Diamond song (and Tony Tribe hit) 'Red Red Wine', which was the official number one for three weeks in 1983; and 'Mississippi', a four-week number one for Dutch act Pussycat in 1976.

Falling 50,000 sales short of the million marker are two singles, the first from another European act and the second from the biggest singles act of all time in the UK. Recasting a 1940s instrumental by Perez Prado, 'Mambo No. 5 (A Little Bit Of...)' was a two-week number one for German pop star Lou Bega in 1999 and used as the theme for Channel 4's cricket coverage (as well as being a smash in 10 European countries and the US). And, in turn, 'Help!' was only the seventh biggest single of The Beatles' eight-year pop reign, but was their eighth number one (out of 17), holding on for three weeks.

On top of those singles which are now within easy reach of the million mark, there will always be brand new material which comes from nowhere. It could be the latest release from established acts, perhaps an unforeseeable charity project or even a brand new hit by an unknown artist.

And, at the time of writing, there are already a few 2012 contenders who might well join the exclusive million sellers club, including 'Call Me Maybe' by Canadian singer-songwriter Carly Rae Jepsen and 'We Are Young' by New York alternative rock band Fun featuring Janelle Monae. Plus French DJ David Guetta is also closing in on the million mark with his single 'Titanium', featuring Sia.

The fact that this is an ever-changing, constantly evolving list is part of its beauty. Further million sellers will certainly emerge over the coming years – and will continue to do so for as long as music fans love music and want to collect pop hits.

Viva The Million Sellers!

THE FACTS
AND FIGURES

	TITLE	ARTIST	YEAR	FIRST WEEK ON CHART	SALES	DATE OF HIGHEST POSITION
1	Something About The Way You Look Tonight/Candle In The Wind 97	Elton John	1997	20/09/1997	4.9m	20/09/1997
2	Do They Know It's Christmas?	Band Aid	1984	15/12/1984	3.69m	15/12/1984
3	Bohemian Rhapsody	Queen	1975	08/11/1975	2.36m	21/12/1991
4	Mull Of Kintyre/Girls' School	Wings	1977	19/11/1977	2m	03/12/1977
5	You're The One That I Want	John Travolta & Olivia Newton-John	1978	20/05/1978	2m	17/06/1978
6	Rivers Of Babylon/Brown Girl In The Ring	Boney M	1978	29/04/1978	2m	13/05/1978
7	Relax	Frankie Goes To Hollywood	1983	26/11/1983	2m	28/01/1984
8	She Loves You	The Beatles	1963	29/08/1963	1.9m	12/09/1963
9	Unchained Melody/(There'll Be Bluebirds Over) The White Cliffs Of Dover	Robson Green & Jerome Flynn	1995	20/05/1995	1.86m	20/05/1995
10	Love Is All Around	Wet Wet Wet	1994	21/05/1994	1.85m	04/06/1994
11	Mary's Boy Child/Oh My Lord	Boney M	1978	02/12/1978	1.85m	09/12/1978
12	I Just Called To Say I Love You	Stevie Wonder	1984	25/08/1984	1.83m	08/09/1984
13	Barbie Girl	Aqua	1997	25/10/1997	1.79m	01/11/1997
14	Anything Is Possible/ Evergreen	Will Young	2002	09/03/2002	1.79m	09/03/2002
15	I Want To Hold Your Hand	The Beatles	1963	05/12/1963	1.77m	12/12/1963
16	Believe	Cher	1998	31/10/1998	1.74m	31/10/1998
17	(Everything I Do) I Do It For You	Bryan Adams	1991	29/06/1991	1.72m	13/07/1991
18	Last Christmas/Everything She Wants	Wham!	1984	15/12/1984	1.6m	15/12/1984
19	Imagine	John Lennon	1975	01/11/1975	1.6m	10/01/1981

20	Summer Nights	John Travolta & Olivia Newton-John	1978	16/09/1978	1.59m	30/09/1978
21	Two Tribes	Frankie Goes To Hollywood	1984	16/06/1984	1.58m	16/06/1984
22	I'll Be Missing You	Puff Daddy & Faith Evans	1997	28/06/1997	1.56m	28/06/1997
23	Perfect Day	Various Artists	1997	29/11/1997	1.55m	29/11/1997
24	Don't You Want Me?	The Human League	1981	05/12/1981	1.54m	12/12/1981
25	Can't Buy Me Love	The Beatles	1964	26/03/1964	1.53m	02/04/1964
26	I Will Always Love You	Whitney Houston	1992	14/11/1992	1.53m	05/12/1992
27	Three Lions	Baddiel & Skinner & Lightning Seeds	1996	01/06/1996	1.53m	01/06/1996
28	Tears	Ken Dodd	1965	02/09/1965	1.52m	30/09/1965
29	...Baby One More Time	Britney Spears	1999	27/02/1999	1.51m	27/02/1999
30	My Heart Will Go On	Celine Dion	1998	21/02/1998	1.48m	21/02/1998
31	Karma Chameleon	Culture Club	1983	17/09/1983	1.47m	24/09/1983
32	Ymca	Village People	1978	25/11/1978	1.46m	06/01/1979
33	Careless Whisper	George Michael	1984	04/08/1984	1.45m	18/08/1984
34	Rock Around The Clock	Bill Haley & His Comets	1955	07/01/1955	1.42m	25/11/1955
35	I Feel Fine	The Beatles	1964	03/12/1964	1.41m	10/12/1964
36	The Carnival Is Over	The Seekers	1965	28/10/1965	1.41m	25/11/1965
37	Gangsta's Paradise	Coolio Featuring L.V.	1995	28/10/1995	1.41m	28/10/1995
38	Eye Of The Tiger	Survivor	1982	31/07/1982	1.41m	04/09/1982
39	The Power Of Love	Jennifer Rush	1985	29/06/1985	1.39m	12/10/1985
40	We Can Work It Out/Day Tripper	The Beatles	1964	09/12/1965	1.39m	16/12/1965
41	Release Me	Engelbert Humperdinck	1967	26/01/1967	1.38m	02/03/1967
42	Someone Like You	Adele	2011	29/01/2011	1.36m	19/02/2011
43	Killing Me Softly	Fugees	1996	08/06/1996	1.36m	08/06/1996
44	Unchained Melody	Gareth Gates	2002	30/03/2002	1.34m	30/03/2002
45	Wannabe	Spice Girls	1996	20/07/1996	1.32m	27/07/1996
46	(Is This The Way To) Amarillo	Tony Christie Ft Peter Kay	2005	19/03/2005	1.31m	26/03/2005
47	Never Ever	All Saints	1997	22/11/1997	1.31m	17/01/1998
48	Come On Eileen	Dexy's Midnight Runners	1982	03/07/1982	1.31m	07/08/1982

49	Think Twice	Celine Dion	1994	22/10/1994	1.3m	04/02/1995
50	I Gotta Feeling	Black Eyed Peas	2009	18/07/2009	1.3m	01/08/2009
51	It Wasn't Me	Shaggy F tRikrok	2001	10/03/2001	1.28m	10/03/2001
52	Tainted Love	Soft Cell	1981	01/08/1981	1.27m	05/09/1981
53	Heart Of Glass	Blondie	1979	27/01/1979	1.27m	03/02/1979
54	Moves Like Jagger	Maroon 5 Ft Christina Aguilera	2011	20/08/2011	1.27m	03/09/2011
55	Wonderwall	Oasis	1995	11/03/1995	1.26m	18/11/1995
56	It's Now Or Never	Elvis Presley	1960	03/11/1960	1.26m	03/11/1960
57	Diana	Paul Anka	1957	30/08/1957	1.25m	30/08/1957
58	It's Like That	Run-D.M.C.Vs Jason Nevins	1997	21/03/1998	1.25m	21/03/1998
59	Hallelujah	Alexandra Burke	2008	20/12/2008	1.24m	27/12/2008
60	Green, Green Grass Of Home	Tom Jones	1966	10/11/1966	1.23m	01/12/1966
61	Sex On Fire	Kings Of Leon	2008	13/09/2008	1.2m	20/09/2008
62	Bright Eyes	Art Garfunkel	1979	03/03/1979	1.2m	14/04/1979
63	Merry Xmas Everybody	Slade	1973	15/12/1973	1.19m	15/12/1973
64	Heartbeat/Tragedy	Steps	1998	21/11/1998	1.18m	09/01/1999
65	Mary's Boy Child	Harry Belafonte	1957	01/11/1957	1.18m	22/11/1957
66	The Last Waltz	Engelbert Humperdinck	1967	23/08/1967	1.17m	06/09/1967
67	Earth Song	Michael Jackson	1995	09/12/1995	1.16m	09/12/1995
68	Do They Know It's Christmas?	Band Aid 20	2004	11/12/2004	1.16m	11/12/2004
69	Blue Monday	New Order	1983	19/03/1983	1.16m	15/10/1983
70	Stranger On The Shore	Mr Acker Bilk & His Paramount Jazz Band	1961	30/11/1961	1.16m	11/01/1962
71	Don't Give Up On Us	David Soul	1976	18/12/1976	1.16m	15/01/1977
72	Can't Get You Out Of My Head	Kylie Minogue	2001	29/09/2001	1.15m	29/01/2001
73	I Love You Love Me Love	Gary Glitter	1973	17/11/1973	1.14m	17/11/1973
74	Spaceman	Babylon Zoo	1996	27/01/1996	1.14m	27/01/1996
75	Saturday Night	Whigfield	1994	17/09/1994	1.14m	17/09/1994
76	We Found Love	Rihanna Ft Calvin Harris	2011	08/10/2011	1.13m	08/10/2011
77	No Matter What	Boyzone	1998	15/08/1998	1.13m	15/08/1998

78	Just The Way You Are (Amazing)	Bruno Mars	2010	25/09/2010	1.12m	25/09/2010
79	Party Rock Anthem	Lmfao Ft Lauren Bennett & Goonrock	2011	26/03/2011	1.12m	16/04/2011
80	I Believe/Up On The Roof	Robson & Jerome	1995	11/11/1995	1.11m	11/11/1995
81	Angels	Robbie Williams	1997	13/12/1997	1.11m	21/02/1998
82	Hit Me With Your Rhythm Stick	Ian Dury And The Blockheads	1978	09/12/1978	1.11m	27/01/1979
83	Teletubbies Say "Eh-Oh!"	Teletubbies	1997	13/12/1997	1.11m	13/12/1997
84	2 Become 1	Spice Girls	1996	28/12/1996	1.11m	28/12/1996
85	Torn	Natalie Imbruglia	1997	08/11/1997	1.11m	08/11/1997
86	Poker Face	Lady Gaga	2009	18/04/2009	1.11m	21/03/2009
87	I Remember You	Frank Ifield	1962	05/07/1962	1.1m	26/07/1962
88	That's My Goal	Shayne Ward	2005	24/12/2005	1.1m	31/12/2005
89	Ghostbusters	Ray Parker Jr.	1984	25/08/1984	1.09m	22/09/1984
90	Pure And Simple	Hear'say	2001	24/03/2001	1.09m	24/03/2001
91	Another Brick In The Wall (Part 2)	Pink Floyd	1979	01/12/1979	1.08m	15/12/1979
92	Back For Good	Take That	1995	08/04/1995	1.07m	08/04/1995
93	Blue (Da Ba Dee)	Eiffel 65	1999	21/08/1999	1.07m	25/09/1999
94	Price Tag	Jessie J Ft B.O.B	2011	05/02/2011	1.07m	05/02/2011
95	Hey Jude	The Beatles	1968	04/09/1968	1.06m	11/09/1968
96	The Young Ones	Cliff Richard & The Shadows	1962	11/01/1962	1.06m	11/01/1962
97	Somebody That I Used To Know	Gotye Ft Kimbra	2011	14/01/2012	1.06m	11/02/2012
98	Dancing Queen	ABBA	1976	21/08/1976	1.06m	04/09/1976
99	I Feel Love	Donna Summer	1977	09/07/1977	1.05m	23/07/1977
100	Love The Way You Lie	Eminem Ft Rihanna	2010	26/06/2010	1.05m	24/07/2010
101	Fame	Irene Cara	1982	03/07/1982	1.05m	17/07/1982
102	Ride On Time	Black Box	1989	12/08/1989	1.05m	09/09/1989
103	Only Girl (In The World)	Rihanna	2010	30/10/2010	1.04m	06/11/2010
104	Unchained Melody	The Righteous Brothers	1965	12/08/1965	1.04m	03/11/1990
105	Bleeding Love	Leona Lewis	2007	27/10/2007	1.04m	03/11/2007
106	Crazy	Gnarls Barkley	2006	01/04/2006	1.04m	08/04/2006
107	Stand & Deliver	Adam And The Ants	1981	09/05/1981	1.03m	09/05/1981

108	I Don't Want To Miss A Thing	Aerosmith	1998	12/09/1998	1.03m	10/10/1998
109	Can We Fix It?	Bob The Builder	2000	16/12/2000	1.02m	23/12/2000
110	Uptown Girl	Billy Joel	1983	15/10/1983	1.02m	05/11/1983
111	I Will Survive	Gloria Gaynor	1979	03/02/1979	1.02m	17/03/1979
112	Sailing	Rod Stewart	1975	16/08/1975	1.02m	06/09/1975
113	Sugar Sugar	The Archies	1969	11/10/1969	1.02m	25/10/1969
114	Save Your Kisses For Me	Brotherhood Of Man	1976	13/03/1976	1.01m	27/03/1976
115	I'd Like To Teach The World To Sing	The New Seekers	1971	18/12/1971	1.01m	08/01/1972
116	White Christmas	Bing Crosby, with The Ken Darby Singers And John Scott Trotter Orchestra	1942	03/11/1977	1.01m	24/12/1977
117	Don't Cry For Me Argentina	Julie Covington	1976	25/12/1976	1.01m	12/02/1977
118	The Lion Sleeps Tonight	Tight Fit	1982	23/01/1982	1.01m	06/03/1982
119	Eye Level	The Simon Park Orchestra	1972	25/11/1972	1.01m	29/09/1973
120	Long Haired Lover From Liverpool	Little Jimmy Osmond	1972	25/11/1972	1m	23/12/1972
121	Under The Moon Of Love	Showaddywaddy	1976	06/11/1976	1m	04/12/1976
122	Tie A Yellow Ribbon Round The Ole Oak Tree	Dawn FtTony Orlando	1973	10/03/1973	1m	21/04/1973
123	When We Collide	Matt Cardle	2010	18/12/2010	1m	18/12/2010